Contemporary Irish Writers

Contemporary Irish Writers and Filmmakers

General Series Editor:
Eugene O'Brien, Head of English Department,
Mary Immaculate College, University of Limerick.

Titles in the series:
Seamus Heaney: Creating Irelands of the Mind
by Eugene O'Brien (Mary Immaculate College, Limerick)

Brian Friel: Decoding the Language of the Tribe
by Tony Corbett

Jim Sheridan: Framing the Nation by Ruth Barton
(University College Dublin)

John Banville: Exploring Fictions by Derek Hand
(St. Patrick's College, Drumcondra, Dublin)

Neil Jordan: Exploring Boundaries by Emer Rockett and
Kevin Rockett (Trinity College Dublin)

Roddy Doyle: Raining on the Parade by Dermot McCarthy
(Huron University College, University of Western Ontario)

William Trevor: Re-imagining Ireland by Mary Fitzgerald-Hoyt
(Siena College, New York)

Conor McPherson: Imagining Mischief by Gerald Wood
(Carson-Newman College, Tennessee)

Forthcoming:
Jennifer Johnston by Shawn O'Hare

Brian Moore by Philip O'Neill

John McGahern by Eamonn Maher

Brendan Kennelly by John McDonagh

Contemporary Irish Writers

Roddy Doyle
Raining on the Parade

Dermot McCarthy

The Liffey Press

Published by The Liffey Press
Ashbrook House, 10 Main Street,
Raheny, Dublin 5, Ireland.
www.theliffeypress.com

A catalogue record of this book is
available from the British Library.

ISBN 1-904148-25-5

*This book has been published with the assistance of grant-aid
from An Chomhairle Ealaíon, The Arts Council of Ireland*

Printed in the Republic of Ireland by ColourBooks Ltd.

Contents

Chapter Five
What went wrong with Daddy?": *Family* and

Chapter Six
A Shocking Substitute: *A Star Called Henry* and Satire as

Conclusion
"We are on our own, but we are together.

About the Author

Dermot McCarthy is a Professor of English Literature at Huron University College, London, Ontario, Canada, where he has taught since 1977. He is the author of *A Poetics of Place: The Poetry of Ralph Gustafson* (1991), numerous articles on Canadian, British and Irish poetry and fiction, and five volumes of poetry — most recently, *A Rumour of Music* (1999). The present book on Doyle grew out of a study of contemporary Irish fiction which he is currently completing. He is also at work on a comparative study of Canadian and Irish writing from the eighteenth to twentieth centuries.

Series Introduction

Given the amount of study that the topic of Irish writing, and increasingly Irish film, has generated, perhaps the first task of a series entitled *Contemporary Irish Writers and Filmmakers* is to justify its existence in a time of diminishing rainforests. As Declan Kiberd's *Irish Classics* has shown, Ireland has produced a great variety of writers who have influenced indigenous, and indeed, world culture, and there are innumerable books devoted to the study of the works of Yeats, Joyce and Beckett. These writers spoke out of a particular Irish culture, and also transcended that culture to speak to the Anglophone world, and beyond.

However, Ireland is now a very different place from that which figures in the works of Yeats, Joyce and Beckett, and it seems timely that the representations of this more secular, more European, and more cosmopolitan Ireland should be investigated and it is with this in mind that *Contemporary Irish Writers and Filmmakers* has been launched.

This series will examine the work of writers and filmmakers who have engaged with the contemporary cultural issues that are important in Ireland today. Irish literature and film has often been viewed as obsessed with the past, but contemporary writers and filmmakers seem to be involved in a process of negotiation between the Ireland of the past and the Ireland of the coming times. It is on this process of negotiation that much of our current imaginative literature and film is focused, and this series hopes to investigate this process through the chosen *auteurs*.

Indeed, it is a sign of the maturity of these *auteurs* that many of them base their narratives not only in the setting of this "new Ireland", but often beyond these shores. Writers and filmmakers such as Seamus Heaney, John Banville, William Trevor and Neil Jordan have the confidence to write and work as *artists* without the necessary addendum of the qualifying "Irish". Their concerns, themes and settings take them outside Ireland to a global stage. Yet, as this series attests, their "Irishness", however that is defined, remains intact and is often imprinted even in their most "international" works.

Politically and culturally, contemporary Ireland is in something of a values deficit as the previous hegemonic certainties of party political and religious allegiance have been lost in a plethora of scandals involving church and state. The role of art and culture in redefining the value-ethic for our culture has never been more important, and these studies will focus on the notions of Irishness and identity that prevail in the late twentieth and early twenty-first centuries.

The role of the aesthetic in the shaping of attitudes and opinions cannot be understated and these books will attempt to understand the transformative potential of the work of the artist in the context of the ongoing redefinition of society and culture. The current proliferation of writers and filmmakers of the highest quality can be taken as an index of the growing confidence of this society, and of the desire to enunciate that confidence. However, as Luke Gibbons has put it: "a people has not found its voice until it has expressed itself, not only in a body of creative works, but also in a body of critical works", and *Contemporary Irish Writers and Filmmakers* is part of such an attempt to find that voice.

Aimed at the student and general reader alike, it is hoped that the series will play its part in enabling our continuing participation in the great humanistic project of understanding ourselves and others.

Eugene O'Brien
Department of English
Mary Immaculate College
University of Limerick

Acknowledgements

I am grateful to Eugene O'Brien, the Series Editor for The Liffey Press's Contemporary Irish Writers and Filmmakers series, for welcoming my proposal to contribute to the series and encouraging my approach to Doyle's work. I owe Brian Langan, the Senior Editor at The Liffey Press, a great debt of gratitude for his professional attention to detail, his consistently close reading of the manuscript, and for sharing his enthusiasm and knowledge of Doyle's work with me through his many helpful and generous comments on the work-in-progress.

I first read Doyle in a draughty Victorian mansion in Monasterevin, County Kildare, in the fall of 1992. The nine months my family and I spent in Ireland through that autumn, winter and spring profoundly changed my life, personally and professionally, and I must thank my old friends and colleague, Gary Owens, and his wife, Micki, for being the instruments of what turned out to be as much a homecoming as a discovery.

Of course, my greatest and deepest debt of gratitude is acknowledged in the dedication.

*For Jacques, Meghan and Graham
and in memory of Sally*

Chronology

1958	Roddy Doyle born in Kilbarrack, North Dublin on 8 May; along with two sisters and a brother, Doyle grows up in Kilbarrack, which he eventually recreates as the "Barrytown" of his novels.
1964–76	Attends a National School in Raheny, then St Fintan's Christian Brothers School in Sutton, County Dublin.
1976–79	Attends University College, Dublin; contributes to *Student*, an undergrad newspaper; visits Poland; joins the Socialist Labour Party. Graduates with BA in English and Geography.
1979–80	Remains at UCD for a Higher Diploma in Education.
1980–93	Teaches English and Geography at Greendale Community School, Kilbarrack. Contributes "the odd satirical article" to *In Dublin*.
1981–85	Attempts his first novel, *Your Granny is a Hunger Striker*; spends summer months of 1982 in London and begins to write in a serious and disciplined way.

1986	Writes *The Commitments*, the first novel in the "Barry-town" trilogy, in six months (January–June). Doyle and John Sutton, a friend from his university days and a founder of The Passion Machine theatre company, form King Farouk Publishing in order to publish *The Commitments*. Paul Mercier and Sutton ask Doyle to write a play for The Passion Machine and he begins *Brownbread*. At the same time, he begins *The Snapper*, the second novel in the trilogy. He volunteers to work with the pro-divorce campaign during the divorce referendum.
1987	*The Commitments* is published in March. Doyle meets Belinda Moller. *Brownbread*, directed by Mercier, opens at the SFX Theatre in Dublin on 16 September and moves to the Olympia Theatre in November.
1988	*The Commitments* is published by Heinemann (London).
1989	*The Commitments* is published by Vintage in the US in July. Doyle's second play for The Passion Machine, *War*, premieres at the SFX Theatre in September, directed by Mercier, and moves to the Olympia in October; Passion Machine also publishes the play. In November, Doyle marries Belinda Moller and begins *The Van*, the final novel in the Barrytown trilogy.
1990	*The Snapper* is published by Secker & Warburg (London).
1991	Doyle's son, Rory, is born in February. *The Van* is published by Secker & Warburg and shortlisted for the Booker Prize. In July, the film version of *The Commitments*, directed by Alan Parker, premieres at the Cannes Film Festival. Doyle, Dick Clement and Ian La Frenais are credited with the screenplay, though Doyle has said he "wasn't involved in any of the decisions".

1992	The Snapper is published by Penguin and The Van by Viking Penguin in the US. The Barrytown Trilogy and Brownbread and War are published by Secker and Warburg in the UK. Doyle's second son, Jack, is born. Doyle shares BAFTA award for Best Adapted Screenplay for The Commitments with Dick Clement and Ian La Frenais.
1993	The Snapper, directed by Stephen Frears from Doyle's screenplay, premieres at Cannes and is broadcast on BBC TV. Doyle's fourth novel, Paddy Clarke Ha Ha Ha, is published by Secker & Warburg. In June, he resigns his teaching position at Greendale to write full-time and in October wins the Booker Prize for Paddy Clarke. The Van is published in the US and a shortened version of The Snapper goes into general theatrical release.
1994	Paddy Clarke Ha Ha Ha (Viking Penguin) and Brownbread and War (Penguin) are published in the US. Having been invited by the BBC to write "anything I wanted", Doyle's Family, a controversial four-part TV series about the Spencers, another "North Dublin" family, directed by Michael Winterbottom, is broadcast in May.
1995	The Snapper wins a Goya award for Best European Film and The Barrytown Trilogy is published in the US by Viking Penguin. In November, Doyle campaigns for the pro-divorce side in the second divorce referendum. Shares a Royal Television Society award for Best Drama Serial with Andrew Eaton and Michael Winterbottom for Family.
1996	The Woman Who Walked into Doors, a novel based on the TV series, Family, is published by Jonathan Cape in the UK and Viking Penguin in the US. The film version of The Van, directed by Stephen Frears from Doyle's screenplay, and produced by Doyle's own production company, Deadly Films, appears. Doyle begins work on a screenplay of Liam O'Flaherty's novel, Famine.

1998	Doyle's daughter, Kate, is born in the summer. In the fall, he wins the Best Screenplay award for *Hell for Leather*, an RTE drama, at the International Widescreen Festival in Amsterdam.
1999	*A Star Called Henry*, the first novel in a new trilogy called "The Last Roundup", is published by Jonathan Cape in the UK, Alfred A. Knopf in Canada, and Random House in the US; later nominated for the *Irish Times* International Fiction Prize. Doyle "donates" a novella, *Not Just for Christmas*, to the Open Door Series, a literacy project from New Island Books. Serves on the selection panel for the Irish Film Board/RTE's "Short Cuts" competition.
2000	Doyle publishes his first children's book, *The Giggler Treatment*, dedicated to "Kate, Jack and Rory", with Scholastic Children's Books. Abel Ugba and Chinedu Onyejelem, Nigerian journalist-refugees living in Dublin, start *Metro Éireann*, a multi-cultural newspaper; in May Doyle's first contribution, "Guess Who's Coming for the Dinner?", begins to appear in eight instalments.
2001	*When Brendan Met Trudy*, directed by Kieron Walsh from Doyle's screenplay, produced by Deadly Films, is released. Doyle is appointed to the Irish Film Board. "The Deportees", a story featuring Jimmy Rabbitte Jr, runs for 15 instalments in *Metro Éireann*, from March 2001 to May 2002. "Guess Who's Coming for the Dinner?" is published as "The Dinner" in *The New Yorker* in February, and a play, also titled *Guess Who's Coming for the Dinner?*, directed by Báirbe Ní Caoimh for Calypso Productions, premieres at Dublin's Andrews Lane Theatre in October. *Rover Saves Christmas*, Doyle's second children's book, is published by Scholastic.

2001 (cont'd)	The Ro Theatre Company of Rotterdam premieres an "opera for soprano, actress and video screen" based on *The Woman Who Walked into Doors*, libretto by Guy Cassiers and Kris Defoort, score by Kris Defoort, directed by Guy Cassiers. Doyle attends a performance and tells Defoort he was "very, very moved by it. . . . The use of 'high' art for such a 'low' story was compelling, fascinating and just so, so good".
2002	Calypso takes *Guess Who's Coming for the Dinner?* on a highly successful national tour. *Rory & Ita*, a memoir of Doyle's parents which he transcribes and edits, is published under his name by Jonathan Cape. Doyle's third short story on issues of race and ethnicity, "57% Irish", begins to appear in *Metro Éireann* in August. Becomes a patron and judge for *Metro Éireann's* annual Media and Multiculturalism Awards.
2003	With Joe O'Byrne, adapts *The Woman Who Walked into Doors* for the stage; the play, directed by O'Byrne, and with Hilda Fay playing Paula and Brian O'Byrne as Charlo, premieres at the Helix Theatre in May. A touring production of the Cassiers/Defoort opera based on *The Woman Who Walked into Doors*, performed by the Ro Theatre Company that premiered it, is announced for the Gaiety Theatre, Dublin, 9–11 October.

List of Abbreviations

Introduction

Raining on the Parade: Roddy Doyle, the 1990s, and the Myth of the "New Ireland"

It is as much a consequence as a paradox of its antiquity that Ireland has been "new" or about to become "new" so many times in its history. The most recent "new Ireland" emerged in the 1990s, when the country was found to be the lair of a "Celtic Tiger", a genetically modified economic-cultural mutant that quickly caught the world's attention as it boldly leapt into the centre ring of the postmodern global circus. Between 1990 and 1995, Ireland's was the only European economy to show steady improvement; *Fortune* magazine named Dublin the top business city in 1997 (Jeffers, 2002: 16). Wherever one looked, Ireland, Irishness and Irish artists were prominent: U2, The Cranberries, Enya; Sinead O'Connor on *Saturday Night Live* and *Riverdance* at Radio City Music Hall; *My Left Foot* and *The Crying Game* in world cinemas; *Angela's Ashes* and *How the Irish Saved Civilization* on bestseller lists.

But even before the "dotcom" meltdown in late 2000 and the post-"9/11" recession, economic analysts and social

commentators were noticing that, for all the vaunted economic success and cultural triumphs, the gap between the
rich and the poor was widening, not closing. In 1999, Ireland
continued to have "the second highest level of poverty in
the industrialized world for the second year in a row"
(Jeffers, 2002: 17). The Celtic Tiger was merely pawing at
the surface — or more precisely, scratching the backs of the
Irish professional class and the multinationals — and not
bringing about the deep structural changes to Irish economic
life that would secure a better future for everyone (see
O'Hearn, 1998; Allen, 2000; Clinch et al., 2002; Kirby,
2002a, 2002b). The American and other computer and
pharmaceutical companies that had located in Ireland because of the tax benefits and low labour costs sent their
profits out of the country and quickly pulled up stakes
whenever they found a better offer elsewhere. Three years
into the new century, the Celtic Tiger now seems more like
Alice's Cheshire Cat — now you see it, now you don't (see
Kelly, 2002: 77).

Dominic Head has observed that "novelists have often
caught the mood of great uncertainty in which a culture based
very much on its own internal systems of class differentiation
is rapidly overtaken by an international economy that renders
the national social explanation obsolete" (Head, 2002: 80). At
home and abroad Roddy Doyle is perhaps the contemporary
Irish writer most associated with the "new Ireland" of the
1990s (McCarthy, 2000: 138; White, 2001: 1–3). This is not
to deny the literary and cultural importance of other writers
and filmmakers who came to prominence during these years,
but Doyle "burst" upon the literary and cultural scene at the
beginning of the decade with the national and international
success of his first novel, *The Commitments* (1988) and its film
version (1991), and his personal fortune and the country's
seemed symbiotically connected throughout the decade.

In 1993, for example, as Ireland's economic fortunes began to peak, Doyle published his Booker Prize-winning fourth novel, *Paddy Clarke Ha Ha Ha*. Many Irish novelists have been shortlisted for this prestigious prize, but to date Doyle's novel has been the only one to win and remains "the most commercially successful Booker winner" (Foran, 196: 60). In 1996, Charles Foran described Doyle's first three novels — what came to be called *The Barrytown Trilogy* — as "an unstoppable promotion machine for Irish writing" and even suggested that "If there is a cultural renaissance under way in Ireland, it's because of the confidence-building success of people like [Roddy Doyle]" (Foran, 1996: 58, 60).

But while "confidence-building" or self-esteem form a central theme in all his writing, Doyle himself has always been ambivalent about his role in or relation to any such "cultural renaissance" (see Paschel, 1998: 149; Sbrockey, 1999) and his novels, for all their vibrant comic realist celebration of working-class *élan*, give increasing expression to the sense that, while "traditional Ireland" has been "overtaken by an international economy that renders the national social explanation obsolete" (Head, 2002: 80), what is uncertain — and perhaps even unwanted — is the formation of any new national master-narrative.

If "Realism is the form of totality and social stability" (McCarthy, 2000: 113–14), then the trajectory of Doyle's career — the gradually sharpening curve from the conventional, focalised third-person narrator and vernacular realism of the Barrytown trilogy to the self-conscious and unreliable first-person narrator-protagonist and what many critics saw as "magic realism" of *A Star Called Henry* (1999) — is particularly significant. In many respects, it is an accelerated re-enactment in a single decade and career of developments in English and international fiction over the past half-century (see Head, 2002: 4, 244). But in Doyle's case, it seems to express a growing tension in his work in the relationship between an increasingly insecure and problematic subjectivity and an increasingly unstable social order. It is Brian Donnelly's measured view of Doyle that "Few contemporary Irish writers serve better one of the most fundamental impulses of the novelist since the time of Defoe: to record and preserve the spirit of the times" (Donnelly, 2000: 23); however, "the spirit of the times" which Doyle's work captures is not the jingoistic "PR" of the Celtic Tiger but the mixed joy and ambivalence, hardship and uncertainty that living through such rapid and continuing economic, social and material changes brings to people.

For Foran and others, "Roddy Doyle" is integral to the "new Ireland" of the 1990s. But the significance of Doyle's texts in relation to the construction, commodification, consumption and export of "Ireland" and "Irishness" during the decade is as ambiguous as the process itself is complex. As well as being highly successful entertainments ranging from comic realism to historical farce, nostalgia to satire, Doyle's novels and films became increasingly more pointed interventions in the period. His recent play, *Guess Who's Coming for the Dinner?*, continues in the vein of *Family* (1994) and *The Woman Who Walked into Doors* (1996) by provoking a reticent public discourse to take up the issue of racism in Irish society in the same way the TV series and novel drew attention to the dirty public secret of spousal abuse. While Doyle himself, ingenuously at times, has tried to downplay the "Irishness" of his fiction, suggesting that the international success of his novels and films is evidence of his stories' "universal" appeal (see Paschel, 1998: 153), it is with their ambiguous relationship to the "new Ireland" of the 1990s and since that the following discussion is most concerned.

The "Myth of the New Ireland"

In the introduction to *Seamus Heaney: Creating Irelands of the Mind* (2002), Eugene O'Brien evokes an image of an "Ireland" that has finally *arrived*, that has been a long time catching up with the advanced western societies, but which is now incontestably and deservedly sitting at the table of modern nations, "not just . . . in economic terms, as evidenced by the much-lauded Celtic Tiger phenomenon", but "in cultural, social and intellectual terms, as we become more confident of our place in Europe, and of our position as a bridge between Europe and America" (O'Brien, 2002: 4–5). For O'Brien, Heaney's poetry not only reflects that long journey from institutional atavism to enlightened modernity, it has contributed to "the psychic growth" (O'Brien, 2002: 2) which has seen the Irish "become central figures in a developing European Union, while retaining our Anglophone connections with America, and becoming less restricted by the heritage of our past, as we look towards the future" (O'Brien, 2002: 4). This all seems a far cry from Roddy Doyle's opinion that "We're still the pot-bellied ugly bastards that we always were!" (Costello, 2001: 97) — and yet, presumably, Roddy Doyle is as much a part of the consciousness of contemporary Ireland as Seamus Heaney; indeed, as we've seen, for Brian Donnelly, Doyle seems hardwired into the *Zeitgeist*.

Any version of a "new Ireland" — or *Zeitgeist* — is a "myth" in Roland Barthes's sense of myth: a cultural construction that "makes us understand something" at the same time as "it imposes it on us" (Barthes, 1972: 117). Is there an essential, singular, coherent, collective Irish psyche? There is a sub-text of utopian quest in O'Brien's account of Ireland's psychic maturation which makes it a socio-psychoanalytic version of the emigrant narrative that has been important to Irish self-representation for the past two centuries. Ireland has now arrived on the shores of yet another new world, but one that is *internal*, temporal-spiritual rather temporal-spatial, the world of authentic modernity.

Ireland has finally become "contemporary", as if the Irish condition before now was characterised by a kind of historical lagging, an ontological limp that kept it always in modernity's shadow, always *about* to be modern. But at last, the patient pilgrim has finished the stations of history, having shuffled from the first, in which it was condemned to history, to the last, when history itself is laid in the tomb and a transcendent, post-nationalist Ireland arises out of its evolution from colonial to postcolonial, rural-agricultural through urban-industrial to post-industrial, Catholic and nationalist to secular and post-nationalist — the last being the transcendent apotheosis of "Ireland" itself. This "new Ireland" is populated by the "new Irish" — complex cosmopolitans, Irish-Europeans, citizen-consumers in a global marketplace. At long last, after centuries of having been relegated to the margins in their own story, they can now centre their own narrative in a de-centred age.

Doyle's relation to this new myth is ambiguous and his value as an artist to contemporary Irish culture lies precisely in this ambiguity and the resistance and scepticism it contains. The value of Doyle's fiction in this respect is that its effect has been counter-mythological, a cold caustic rain on the green parade of the 1990s. If Doyle's narrative imagination articulates anything of an abstract nature, it is that any ambition to be "central" to anything is suspect; that playing the nation-state game as that game has been played for the past three centuries is not worth the candle; that replacing the stereotypical "stage Irishman" role with another on the "world stage" is still "performing" or "acting" in a way that calls into question the authenticity of the agent concealed within the role.

O'Brien is undoubtedly correct in his observation that the "probing and questioning of the past, and of received ideas, is perhaps the most important intellectual activity that is taking place in contemporary Ireland" (O'Brien, 2002: 2); and without exception, each of Doyle's novels has been part of that activity. For all their comedy, *The Commitments*, *The Snapper* (1990) and *The Van* (1991) challenge the invidious middle-class myth that "The poor [are] . . . victims of their own making" (O'Hearn, 1998: x) as well as aspects of an equally repugnant myth of working-class masculinity. In the mid-1990s, as a growing prosperity seemed to sanction social complacency, Doyle produced a TV script and two novels addressing the theme of marital breakdown in ways that flagrantly went against the popular mood (see Rockwell, 1993: C11; Foran, 1996: 61). In *Paddy Clarke Ha Ha Ha*, he consciously set out to challenge the view that marital breakdown was a "modern" problem in Irish society: "I wanted to force the reality that it's always been a problem. I wanted to make a rosy period [the 1960s] in Irish history clash with what's considered to be a modern reality" (Sbrockey, 1999); the TV series, *Family* (1994), and Doyle's careful contextualisation of Paula Spencer's life in *The Woman Who Walked into Doors* (1996), are vivid images of how in Ireland since the 1960s "the process of change has led to increasing problems of social exclusion — rising poverty, inequality, and social marginalisation" (O'Hearn, 1998: xi).

By the end of the 1990s, Doyle recognised the changes that had occurred. He had begun the decade "writing a book [*The Van*] about a man in his forties who was an unemployed plasterer and the likelihood was that he would never work again, and now there's no such thing as an unemployed plasterer any more" (Costello, 2001: 96). But although he considered "the economic boom . . . fantastic", he also recognised that poverty was still a problem throughout the country; similarly, while he is certain that "As an atheist, I am happier living in Ireland in 2001 than I would be if I was 42 in 1981", he is less pleased with the "global commodification . . . of everything . . . the blandness of things and . . . [the] rule by press release" (Costello, 2001: 97). He could be celebratory and optimistic — "We are opening ourselves to different cultures. The possibilities are fantastic and I would like to think that these possibilities aren't just cultural but social too" (Costello, 2001: 98) — but at the same time, in the short story and play, "Guess Who's Coming for the Dinner?" (2001, 2002), the film, *When Brendan Met Trudy* (2002), and in his other recent stories written for *Metro Éireann*, his engagement with the issue of racism suggests that he recognises that Irish society has a long way to go before the "social possibilities" of an open and inclusive society become realities.

Some readers have noticed that from *The Commitments* (1988) to *A Star Called Henry* (1999), Doyle's novels "have darkened over the years, shifting from exuberant optimism to something bleaker and sadder and not so convinced of people's innate goodness" (Gerrard, 2001). As Ireland — and Doyle — were prospering, "It is as if [Doyle] created a dark looking-glass reflection of his own successful and self-avowedly contented life. Where he is happy, his characters suffer. They fail where he succeeds. They remind him of worlds he is lucky enough not to inhabit" (Gerrard, 2001).

The widespread and passionate outbursts of opprobrium following the screening of *Family* in May 1994 — "the denunciations came from all sorts of politicians, from priests, my old teachers' union, virtually everybody queued up to condemn it in some way" (Taylor, 1999) — affected Doyle deeply, and confirmed his sense of the necessity for Irish writers to speak the truth against hypocrisy. The virulence of the reaction may also have been fuelled in part by the public's sense that the author of the Barrytown trilogy was "misbehaving". After *The Van* — a novel "loving to a fault about the community it depicts" (Foran, 1996: 62) — and the comically effervesced film-version of *The Snapper* appeared in 1993, Doyle was in danger of becoming a hostage to his own image, a sort of Irish Billy Connolly in prose, often hilarious, often "rough", but hardly threatening.

Paddy Clarke Ha Ha Ha (1994) broke the pattern set by the trilogy, but the Barrytown setting, outrageous humour and over-the-top sibling violence showed enough of the old "Doyler" to offset the surprise of a first-person narrator, nostalgia and pathos. But with *Family*, Doyle broke completely with the image of "Roddy Doyle", the author of the Barrytown trilogy. The series was a slap in the face to the society that had accepted and rewarded him as its ribald entertainer. *Family* was not entertaining; it was painfully, shamefully embarrassing, and definitely not good for tourism — a serious "speed-bump" on "the bridge between Europe and America". Even so, the controversies which TV series occasion belong to the ephemera of postmodern video culture and have the half-life of decaying fruit. *The Woman Who Walked into Doors* (1996) reprised the theme of *Family* but produced a lasting portrait of an abused woman by delving into the psychological complexity of the character of Paula Spencer.

With the Rabbittes, the Clarkes and the Spencers, Doyle contributed "a new set of images for the Ireland of the late 20th century" (Gordan, 1996: 7), images that were simultaneously recognised, applauded, praised, denied, abhorred and excoriated. But with *Family* and *The Woman Who Walked into Doors*, Doyle made it clear that he was no class jester, and with *A Star Called Henry* (1999) he again surprised readers by producing a parody of a historical fiction about the founding of the modern Irish state.

The myth of the "new Ireland" cannot be separated from "that perennial Irish problem" (Jeffers, 2002: 1) and "perpetually fractious theme" (Harte, 1997: 17) — the issue of Irish identity. Of course, the question should be asked whether this "problem" and "theme" are indeed "perennial" and "fractious" for Irish people or merely an indestructible academic hobbyhorse which it has become *de rigueur* for anyone in Irish studies to put through its static paces (see Traynor, 2002). Although Doyle was prominently associated with the "new Ireland" of the 1990s, Irish identity and Irishness are simply non-issues in his fiction before *A Star Called Henry*. Nationalism, religion, politics, history and the Troubles in Northern Ireland are conspicuously absent from the first five novels; their fictive worlds are consistently local, circumscribed and familial. If the "new Irish" are "more confident of [their] place in Europe, and of [their] position as a bridge between Europe and America" (O'Brien, 2002: 5), Doyle's characters and narrator-protagonists are definitely "outsiders" within this "new Ireland", whose identities are defined by class, age, gender and urban region, not religion, history or nationalism. The novels do not look outward to Europe or America, or even to some sense of a larger Ireland; in fact, Ireland seems more a *city-state* called "Dublin" than a nation-state, and his characters struggle for self-confidence in large part because none has a secure grip on their place in the new Irish economic and social orders.

   A Star Called Henry marks an important change in this respect, for while the "tall tale" of Henry Smart is as entertaining as anything Doyle has written, the point of view it takes towards the historical events it recounts is very much based in Doyle's attitude to the Ireland that continues to emerge from that past, his own contemporary Ireland, the "new Ireland" of the 1990s. *A Star Called Henry* is the beginning of a second trilogy entitled "The Last Roundup" and what Doyle seems to want to "round up" is his version of twentieth-century Irish history. The second volume, to be set in America during the inter-war period, is to deal with the Irish immigrant experience, and the trilogy will conclude with Henry returning to "a different Ireland" (Riding, 1999: E2).

Different Irelands and the Generation of '66

"A different Ireland", in fact, is where Doyle began his career as a novelist; that is, a very different Ireland from the
1990s as well as from the Free State that Henry Smart helps
achieve in 1922. Doyle needs to be placed in the context of
the generation born in the late 1950s and early 1960s and
that generation needs to be understood in relation to the
era against which it reacted.

By the time Doyle was born, in 1958, Ireland had
changed from a rural-agricultural society with a subsistence
economy to an agricultural-industrial society with a market
economy, and by the time he reached his teens, to a post-
industrial society with a large service economy (White,
1997: 115). What Doyle records in *Paddy Clarke Ha Ha Ha* is
not just the effects of the massive population shift to the
cities and the growth of new suburbs that these economic
changes brought, but the fact that, like other postcolonial
countries in the post-war era, when Ireland opened itself to
economic modernisation, it was "simultaneously subjected
to a media and communications barrage" (Jeffers, 2002: 15)
which gradually opened serious moral, spiritual and ideological fissures in Irish society and culture because of the images
of social and cultural modernisation it brought from abroad.

Slow change allows a society to adapt by modifying traditional values and perspectives to accommodate the new circumstances. Between the 1960s and 1990s, the ways Irish
people thought and behaved changed as an "urban consum-
eristic mentality" and "more secular worldview" became
prominent (White, 1997: 115, 116; see also Brown, 1985:
185–204; and Shade, 1979: 26–46); but the rapidity of
change meant that the new behaviour and perspective were
not rooted in a new foundation of coherent cultural values.
The old bases of individual and collective identity, like a decaying sea-wall, were breaking up from the relentless pound-

ing of novelty and rising expectations, but what was replacing them originated outside Ireland, in New York and Los
Angeles, London, Paris and Brussels (White, 1997: 113-14).
Irish identity was coming to be determined by economic
factors, not political, as a consciousness of Ireland's position
in a postmodern Eurocommunity displaced its postcolonial
doldrums (Jeffers, 2002: 1).

Doyle entered adulthood and began his career as a
teacher at Greendale school in Kilbarrack just as Ireland entered the 1980s, as the boom ended and many of the chickens of modernisation came home to roost and the hangover
of self-doubt followed the binge-growth of the 1960s and
1970s. Unemployment rose to record levels and emigration
became a form of national service. A young, educated generation increasingly frustrated by the lack of employment
opportunities in their own country and tantalised by the images of material plenty elsewhere, tended to look at the
older generations — and the past in general — as the dead
hand that lay upon their future.

Desmond Fennell described the nation at the end of the
1970s as "dazed" and in need of self-esteem and a new self-
image to replace the defunct Gaelic, Catholic and republican
image of the past (in Brown, 1985: 329). Denis O'Hearn recalls that Ireland in the 1980s was "in a kind of funk"
(O'Hearn, 1998: 55) and Declan Kiberd that "a pervasive
sense of failure, too deep for words or open admission" in-
fected the country (Kiberd, 1996: 609). It wasn't too deep for
Fintan O'Toole, however, who wrote about his parents' generation, Ireland under de Valera, and the nationalist myth of
1916: "Our parents had been fed on failures — the failure to
provide work, the failure to provide freedom, the failure to
cherish the children of the nation" (O'Toole, 1988: 42).

This is the context within which Doyle wrote *The Commitments* in six months in the winter and spring of 1986.
Jimmy Rabbitte Jr's idea for a "Dublin soul" band — like his

father's and Bimbo's effort to make a go of a "chipper" in *The Van* — should be read against the background of the "deep inferiority complex of the 1970s and 1980s" (O'Hearn, 1998: *xi*). Thus, by the time economic recovery arrived in the mid-1990s, Doyle had finished the Barrytown trilogy. His perspective on contemporary Ireland was set *before* the Celtic Tiger was identified, just as his attitude to nationalist Ireland was fixed long before Henry Smart emerged from his imagination.

It would be interesting to compare the phenomenon of the "Angry Young Men" in post-war British writing and that of Mac Anna's "Dublin Renaissance" of the 1990s. If the former were expressing the disillusionment of youth in the brave new world of post-Beveridge Britain (Head, 2002: 14), writers such as Doyle, Dermot Bolger, Michael O'Loughlin, Joseph O'Connor, Paula Meehan and Sebastian Barry were reacting not only to the unfulfilled promise of post-revolutionary Ireland but also to the social consequences of the modernisation which the Whitaker Plans brought. Also, what many of these writers were reacting to was what they considered the "great lie" of official "state culture", namely, that essential Irish identity was rooted in Gaelic, Catholic, republican and rural Ireland.

Michael O'Loughlin, born the same year as Doyle, describes himself as belonging to "a generation of '66" — an ironic allusion to the fiftieth anniversary of the 1916 Rising — and claims that "People from that generation tend to share a number of characteristics": "An almost total alienation from the state, a cynicism with regard to the national institutions and political life . . . an unspoken assumption, that everything emanating from official sources is a total lie" (O'Loughlin, 1988: 43). Much of this cynicism seems to derive from the generation's experience of the state manipulation of "history" through the school system (see also, Bolger, 1988b: 7). For O'Loughlin, by the 1970s,

> The South's political lies were finally catching up with
> it. One of these was that 1916 was the culmination
> of the 700-year struggle for an "Irish Republic". This
> lie, comfortably shared by the Fianna Fáil [sic] and
> the Provos, eventually became too embarrassing. In
> an act of astonishing political opportunism, 1916 was
> revised. By 1976, and the 60th celebrations, a differ-
> ent tune was being played. For people of my genera-
> tion, who were and are, in an important sense,
> neither republican nor non-republican, this was a
> lesson they would never forget. To see history so
> swiftly rewritten was to realise that what was called
> history was in fact a façade behind which politicians
> manoeuvred for power. (O'Loughlin, 1988: 43)

Although the myth of de Valera's Ireland as "an anti-modern
Other against which contemporary Ireland could continue to
define itself" (Cleary, 2000: 114) has not figured significantly
in any explicit manner in Doyle's fiction, nothing explains better the attitude underlying Doyle's approach to "history", the
1916 Uprising, and the whole "heroic" period in *A Star Called
Henry* than these statements by his contemporaries; like
them, he "grew up in the 1960s in the almost iconoclastic
shadow of the leaders' images" (Bolger, 1988b: 8), and if
there is no line in the novel as iconoclastic as Fintan
O'Toole's "If Pearse is Christ, give us Barabbas" (O'Toole,
1988: 42), *A Star Called Henry* nevertheless puts paid to the
"history" Doyle was subjected to in school and at home.

Writing was only "a vague ambition" for Doyle throughout his adolescence and even during his undergraduate
years. But it is important to recognise that when he does
begin to write, he begins as a "reactionary" writer, contributing "satirical things" to a UCD student paper and *In Dublin*,
and then, when he decided to take writing seriously in the
summer of 1982, attempting a satirical novel about Dublin
supporters of the H-Block campaign in Belfast (White, 2001:

172). The focus on the individual in society in his first three novels may also be seen as a reaction against the inward-looking, psychological preoccupations of Irish poetry and fiction during the 1960s and 1970s (Brown, 1985: 318–19; Kiberd, 1996: 584). But what Doyle was reacting against most at the beginning of his career was the absence from the page and the stage of the kinds of people with whom he was most familiar.

His experience with the youth at Greendale obviously informs *The Commitments*, but what seems to have provided the real impetus behind his first novel was the example of his friend, Paul Mercier, the playwright-founder (along with John Sutton and John Dunne) of the Passion Machine theatre company in Dublin, whom Doyle first met at UCD and who eventually became a colleague at Greendale. When Doyle saw Mercier's *Wasters* (1985), he not only saw "characters I recognised . . . for the first time in my life" but characters who spoke "the language I heard every day" (Doyle, 1992: 1). Doyle has said that Mercier "more than anyone else . . . gave me the notion that I should try and do this. His example really gave me the push that I would need" (Sbrockey, 1999).

The "policy" of the Passion Machine company — "to present theatre that depicted contemporary everyday life and to attract a large audience to this work" (Sutton, 1989: i) — places Doyle's aims and achievement with his trilogy solidly within Passion Machine's orbit. Sutton's claim that "The plays have succeeded in giving us a sense of ourselves" (Sutton, 1989: i) can be heard in Jimmy Rabbitte Jr's rationale for forming the band in *The Commitments* (see C, 6). Mercier's and Sutton's "philosophy" and their productions "celebrating aspects of Irish life that had not been treated before in Irish Theatre" (Sutton, 1989: i) clearly inspired Doyle to do the same using the novel form and the plays he eventually wrote for the company, *Brownbread* (performed in 1987) and *War* (performed in 1989), are extensions of his

first Barrytown novels. (*War*, in particular, is closely connected to *The Snapper*.)

Doyle has acknowledged that when he started writing
"what I and people like me who grew up in Dublin were
fighting against all our lives" (Paschel, 1998: 148) was the
"lie" that "Rural Ireland was the real place, pure Irish music,
landscapes rather than people or even workers" (Paschel,
1998: 148). Joseph O'Connor recognises that Doyle's fiction
celebrates "another Ireland just as profoundly at odds with
its own mythology; an Ireland of the suburbs which has
really been absent from the pages of Irish fiction for too
long" (O'Connor, 1995: 140).

A problem, and profoundly so, concerning this rural-
urban dialectic in Irish discourse is that the binary distributes
characteristics between the two "worlds" only in terms of
absence and presence. The criticism that Smyth records,
that Doyle ironically cannot escape the tradition of Irish pastoral because his fiction implicitly juxtaposes a fallen urban
world with a pastoral ideal (Smyth, 1997: 68; see also
Kiberd, 1996: 609), illustrates how in much academic criticism, where binary thinking is as "natural" as it is rigid, the
fallout of de Valera's "Ireland" continues to glow in the dark.

One debilitating effect of this seemingly interminable
ideological hangover is the implicit belief that an analogue to
what Neil Corcoran describes as the "cartography of passionate natural piety" (Corcoran, 1997: 70) provided by the
poetry of Heaney, Mahon and Longley, for example, is not
accessible to urban fiction. The notion of a "passionate *urban
piety*" is apparently unthinkable and it may indeed seem far-
fetched (though not necessarily) if one only considers the
fictional representations of "the violent, drugs-infested,
working-class estates of the northside" (Corcoran, 1997:
123) in Bolger's fiction, for example, or even if one reads
Doyle sympathetically, but still patronisingly, as Corcoran
does when he describes Doyle's "apparently debased culture

and language as in fact the vehicle of great emotional range and depth" (Corcoran, 1997: 128).

The Barrytown trilogy, *Paddy Clarke Ha Ha Ha* and *A Star Called Henry* do indeed express a passionate urban piety, by which I mean a deep, intuitive understanding of, respect for, and faithfulness toward the truth of experience borne out of family, community and place, and an attitude towards the art of narrative that sees in its entertainments as well as its didacticism a fundamental responsibility to the careful observance of truth and humility before the joyful and sorrowful mysteries of life.

Even as dark and vicious a novel as *The Woman Who Walked into Doors* can be read as an expression of this sense of a serious duty and calling, representing as it does the voice of a character whose dignity and self-identity have been traduced to the point of erasure and who has decided to *write back*, to speak herself, and thereby speak her self into presence. It is correct that the first community to which any extrapolation of Paula's experience and triumph should be extended is that of abused women in general; however, Doyle's practice here is also a continuation of the more specific agenda of writing the poor urban Irish into presence, or visibility, which has characterised his career from the outset.

Reading Doyle Imagining Ireland

Once upon a time, the distinction between history and fiction was as "real" as historians were confident that history and myth occupied opposite extremes on the narrative spectrum: if history represented the Ireland of fact, myth produced an "Ireland" of the imagination. Today most would agree, however, that, while there is an Ireland populated by Irish people, as soon as you begin to *represent* either, you have taken a seat in the great scriptorium of "discourse" and no matter how "true" you believe your words to be, they are still images and metaphors and what they present to the reader can only ever be — to echo Eugene O'Brien's title — a version of some "Ireland" of the mind.

There is an Ireland, fortunately, that will always remain outside discourse, and Irish people — like people in any society — must struggle to maintain a constructive scepticism toward the complex of discourses that seek to define them to themselves and others — be these "official" or "revisionist" histories, nationalist, neo-nationalist, or post-nationalist myths of a "new Ireland", or contemporary fictions like the novels and films of Roddy Doyle.

A nation may be, in the phrase of the anthropologist Benedict Anderson, an "imagined community" (Anderson, 1991), as long as we grasp the paradox that the imagined community is not an *imaginary* community. Novelists, particularly those who write "social novels", make significant contributions to the "imagining of the nation" (Head, 2002: 121) and Doyle is no exception. Steven Connor argues that "the novel is central to modern societies" because "it dramatises the process of integrating self-formation that is important to them. The centrality of the novel principally concerns the powerfully cohering function of narrative" (Connor, 1996: 7).

Doyle's relation to the imagined community of contemporary Ireland is dialectical in that what his novels dramatise in the characters' experience is usually a process of "integrating self-formation" that occurs in the context of social pressures that *undermine* individuation, and that may also include stages of self-*de*formation as well as *re*-integrating self-formation. Doyle's novels also interrogate and challenge the coherence of the national narrative more than they bolster it by steadfastly refusing to look beyond the imagined community of north Dublin. Even Doyle's most national novel, *A Star Called Henry*, remains rooted in the world of Dublin.

Doyle has unequivocally denied that he thinks "the function of literature . . . is to mirror the ideological forces of social change and transformation at any given moment of historical transition" (Costello, 2001: 92), but the imagined community is only partly the reflection of authorial intention. What Steven Connor states about the English novel since 1950 also applies to the fiction of Doyle's generation in Ireland: it does not just reflect history but is "one of the ways in which history is made and remade" (Connor, 1996: 1). This is particularly so with novels like Doyle's "that strike a chord in the public consciousness by virtue of their engagement with the present" (Head, 2002: 3).

Doyle has his predecessors in modern Irish fiction, from George Moore to Joyce, O'Casey and Behan. If Behan "gave expression to the cultural dispossession of working-class Dubliners, who found themselves ostracised from the political visions of successive Free State governments, and dislocated in the slum clearances of the thirties" (Brannigan, 2002: 15), Doyle, in a later generation, celebrates the working-class Dublin culture that has arisen out of that and subsequent dislocation, dispossession, and ostracism (see Mahony, 1998: 245).

However, to focus on Doyle's representation of an under-represented working-class Dublin without recognising that the quality of that representation is more complex than celebratory is to limit the significance of Doyle's achievement by confining it within a narrow mimetic pigeonhole. Satire is more than a "subtext" (O'Toole, 1999: 39) in Doyle's fiction, but concentrating on the humour can make it so. The view of "Roddy Doyle" as comic entertainer, "the author of the Barrytown trilogy", is a construction of the Celtic Tiger and its commodification of Doyle for export. There is a continuity of serious moral concern in Doyle's fiction with children, adolescents, married women, the family and the community; with self-esteem and self-understanding, unemployment and poverty; with class divisions and social coherence and the failures or irrelevance of the institutions of the Catholic Church and religion, state education and nationalist politics; with individual identity, self-growth, and hope for the future.

All of these concerns manifest themselves in the continuous exploration in his fiction of the ambiguous nature of the relation between the individual and the collectivity. Whether the latter is a band of musicians and singers, the family, the lads down at the local, a child's gang of friends, or the Irish Republican Brotherhood, Doyle's novels study the ambivalent economies of need and belonging, independence and acceptance, the price of self-esteem and the value of self-identity. Beginning in *The Commitments* and increasingly in the novels that follow, Doyle's protagonists find themselves in situations of conflict between the need for social acceptance and the challenge to personal integrity that acceptance often poses, between a shame caused by the sense of having violated communal or group norms and a guilt that follows from considering those norms irrelevant to a new, emergent, but still unknown self.

Whether it is the growing shadow that falls over Doyle's representation of the Rabbittes in the Barrytown trilogy, the lost world of childhood in *Paddy Clarke Ha Ha Ha*, the domestic war zone and social wasteland of abuse and addiction in *The Woman Who Walked into Doors*, or the fraudulent nationalism of *A Star Called Henry*, Doyle's novels not only reflect a society going through rapid change but, as they circulate within the society, intervene in that change by throwing into relief or juxtaposition images of Ireland's past and present which pose questions about its future.

Chapter One

Gettin' Up: *The Commitments* and "Dublin Soul"

Roddy Doyle's importance as the pre-eminent novelist of the "new generation" of younger writers who emerged in Ireland during the 1990s derives from the paradoxically balanced combination in his work of raucous entertainment, specific outrage and subtle disquiet. He was recognised, praised and vilified for the first two qualities immediately; but it is the last, ironically, that may give his celebrated comic realism its "legs" and Doyle his ultimate place in the literary and cultural history of the period.

Social and cultural life in Ireland over the past twenty-five years have reflected a sharpening dialectic between tradition and modernity, a dialectic that has insinuated a variety of material and psychological tensions into collective and individual Irish life. A growing number of economic, moral, ethical, and spiritual challenges have widened the gaps between genders and generations, classes, regions and races. Doyle's disquieting take on the changes in Ireland during his lifetime seems to be that, while there is much to celebrate about the "new Ireland" that has emerged, modernity and modernisation have made individual authenticity based in the traditional forms of collective identity that once shaped the individual's sense of selfhood increasingly problematic. From *The Commitments* to *When Brendan Met Trudy* and *Guess Who's Coming for the Dinner?*, Doyle's novels, films and plays show individuals coming to discover and accept (or, on occasion, reject) the need to change within themselves in order to accommodate the changing circumstances and communities around them; but also, the more successful characters learn that any such accommodation must also recognise that, as Yeats put it, "The soul . . . is self-delighting, / Self-appeasing, self-affrighting" (Yeats, 1983: 189).

While it may celebrate the new individuality, Doyle's fiction does not ignore the perils of "going it alone". Doyle may reject the traditional signifiers of "Irishness" — nationality and nationalism, Catholicism and historical connection to land — and seem to put in their place class, generation and gender; to displace Ireland with the "city-state" of Dublin; and to show contemporary "Irishness" to be a postmodern, post-national, post-"Irishness", in fact. However, his texts also suggest that class, generation and gender can be just as confining as the shibboleths of de Valera's Ireland and that Ireland's growing consumption of global culture, like any diet, needs to be balanced. What put Doyle at the vanguard of the new Irish fiction of the 1990s was not so much his vivid urban realism — the sewer-mouthed dialogue and parking-lot sex, the binge-drinking and Technicolor puke — as "ground-breaking" and "envelope-pushing" as the reviewers claimed it to be. His real significance lay in the way he showed his characters having to *negotiate* individual identity in a culture that was becoming increasingly fluid and unstable, heterodox and hybrid, divided and divisive.

Voice and Identity: Dubbin' the Truth

Voice and identity are profoundly connected, and fiction, by its very nature as an art of verbal representation, draws at-

tention to the connection. In *The Snapper*, Doyle's second
novel, Jimmy Rabbitte Jr gets the opportunity to sub for a DJ
on Radio 2, Ireland's national pop station. He has no trouble
coming up with a stage-name, "Rockin' Rabbitte", but he is
insecure about his voice. He tells his sister, Sharon, "I sound
like a fuckin' harelip — I'm thinkin' o' gettin' elocution lessons" (*S*, 138). This leads to the comic motif of Jimmy trying
to lose his north Dublin accent and Sharon and his father,
Jimmy Sr, "slagging" him for his efforts. When he finally gets
in front of the microphone, however, Jimmy quickly abandons his attempt to sound like someone else. Sharon turns
on the radio just as a song ends and Jimmy comes on:
"–THOT WAS OLEXONDER O'NEAL WITH FAKE. THERE'S
NOTHIN' FAKE ABOUT THIS ONE. HERE'S THE GODFATHER OF
SOUL. — JAMES BROWN, YIS SIMPLEHEADS YIS" (*S*, 211). It is
ironic that Jimmy should jettison his fake voice as he introduces "THE GODFATHER OF SOUL", considering the central
role James Brown's music plays in Jimmy's "soul" project,
the much more elaborate attempt at self-invention at the
heart of Doyle's first novel.

This bit of comic business in *The Snapper* is, in a sense, a
minor reprise of that major theme in *The Commitments*, which
Doyle wrote between January and June of 1986 — he finished
it "at half-time in the World Cup game" (Costello, 2001: 88).
That autumn, Doyle and a friend, John Sutton, formed King
Farouk Publishing in order to publish it, and in March 1987,
1,000 copies of what turned out to be the first instalment in
the "Barrytown trilogy" appeared in Dublin. Named after the
fictionalised version of Kilbarrack that provides all three novels with their north Dublin setting, the trilogy could as well be
called the "Rabbitte trilogy", after the family whose experiences and relationships the novels describe.

Fittingly, and prophetically, for a series of novels that focus on a contemporary Irish working-class family, Doyle dedi-
cated *The Commitments* to his parents, also the subjects of the

recent memoir, *Rory & Ita* (2002). Beneath the dedication, a character in the novel, Joey the Lips Fagan, counsels the reader to "Honour thy parents . . . They were hip to the groove too once you know. Parents are soul." While family is not yet a theme for Doyle in *The Commitments*, the image, concept and metaphor of "soul" occupy the novel's thematic centre stage and triangulate much of the novel's irony, humour and satire. Ultimately, the play on "soul" not only provides the novel with its serio-comic depth, it identifies the element of deeper thematic continuity that binds all three novels in the trilogy: "soul" should be read as a metaphor for identity and Doyle's ironic play with the metaphor not only contributes to the comedy in the novel, it generates the ambiguity, uncertainty and ambivalence in regards to the issue of identity which makes the novel so significant in relation to its historical and cultural moment.

The *Commitments* tells the story of a group of north Dublin young people who form a band in order to get rich, famous, and the "odd ride now an' again" (*C,* 6). After some promise, not much comes off in any category in the end. The fun Doyle has with Jimmy, The Commitments, and their invention of "Dublin soul" thinly masks the novel's exploration of the issue of contemporary Irish identity. Introduced in the dedication, "soul" appears immediately afterwards in the novel's epigraph, which is taken from James Brown's "Superbad":

        —SOMETIMES I FEEL SO NICE—

        GOOD GOD————
        I JUMP BACK——

        I WANNA KISS MYSELF————!
        I GOT—
        SOU—OU—OUL—
        AN' I'M SUPERBAD————

Before the story even begins, the dedication and epigraph raise questions about language, identity and self-expression that are central to it. In the dedication, distinctly American idioms have been appropriated to express a traditional Irish value — respect for one's parents — but in the epigraph the same language expresses a self-esteem that is not only *internally* derived but derived through *opposition* to traditional Irish norms and expectations. The meanings and values of words like "God", "soul", "good" and "bad" have long and complex histories in Irish culture. What Doyle achieves through Brown's ironically echoic vocabulary is not only a merging of alien and native discourses, but in effect a challenging of traditional Irish-Catholic religious-spiritual meanings and values by the African-American secular meanings and values of the same words.

The concern with the self ("Sometimes I feel so nice") and pleasure — and to be precise, sexual pleasure ("feeling good" as opposed to *being* good), raises the traditional moral-religious conflict between sensuality and morality. Self-enjoyment and self-esteem come together in the ironic conflation of "I got / Soul / An' I'm superbad", where "soul" is and is not the religious signifier. African-American culture appropriated the word as part of its own racial-political project — the "Black is Beautiful" movement of the 1960s and 1970s. Doyle's appropriation brings it inside the context of Irish class divisions. The intention behind the use of American music in the novel may have been simply a "humorous effect" (see White, 2001: 166); but texts become more than their author's intentions. Even before the narrative begins, the appropriation of African-American idioms in the epigraph sets in play a set of contradictory relations between "feeling nice" and "feeling good", "being good" and "being bad", having a soul and "getting soul", and of being and feeling "good" by being "superbad" that ultimately have the potential to become revisionist ratios of a new *Irish* sense of self in the novel.

The reader may *hear* James Brown in the epigraph — it *is* a quotation from a recording — but the Irish reader would also hear an *Irish voice* "dubbing" or "speaking over" Brown's, and that effect *in the reader* is precisely what Doyle's story presents, literally, symbolically, and punningly, *in the characters'* experience. The characters, all "Dubs", form a band whose strategy for success is to "dub" classic American "soul" songs in the sense of not only performing them in their own voices but "Dublinising" them through the insertion of allusions to local landmarks and working-class experience.

In Doyle's hands, this story of a group of young people in Dublin at the end of the 1980s becomes a story of a generation in a society at a crossroads. *The Commitments* describes a group of people who go through a process of change. They emerge from the experience different in some ways and the same in others; but most importantly, they discover things about themselves they did not know before. The most important change any of them undergoes is in self-understanding.

What makes this all the more effective is the light-handed way the novel develops such serious themes. Comically and ironically, the novel shows its characters going through a process whose significance as a reflection of events and issues in the Ireland of the 1980s extends far beyond its obvious value as entertainment. Beneath the "situation-comedy" patter of Doyle's dialogue is the serious business of identity and self-esteem. *The Commitments*, for all its hip and lip, cannot escape the consequences of its own wit. But while, historically, *The Commitments* is the novel that put the whole issue of "Irishness" and Irish identity on the discursive agenda for the 1990s (Smyth, 1997: 66), Doyle's approach to identity explicitly turns away from a concern with *Irish* identity in any traditional sense. The north Dublin setting and use of American popular culture in his first novel continue throughout the trilogy and into *Paddy Clarke Ha Ha Ha* and *The Woman Who Walked into Doors* and they repre-

sent more than his scornful rejection of Bord Fáilte's Ireland.
They are expressions of Doyle's own ideological opposition
to the traditional "totems" of Irish identity — "Land, Nationality and Catholicism" (O'Toole, 1992: 1).

The voice and language of the epigraph also clash immediately with the distinctively "Dub" voices and language of
the opening sections of the novel. In 1987, as soon as you
read the first pages of The Commitments you knew you were
hearing something new in Irish fiction. While playwrights and
novelists from Shakespeare to Shaw, Edgeworth to Somer-
ville and Ross, inserted the forms of English spoken by the
Irish into their works, until Synge and Joyce it usually was for
the effect of contrast with the "standard English" that provided the work with its discursive — and ideological —
norms (see Welch, 1996: 244–5). Doyle, however, does not
use dialect in this manner; in the Barrytown trilogy, his characters' Dublin dialect is the norm and does not contrast significantly with the narrative voice because Doyle consciously
set out to use a narrative voice as close to the characters'
voices as possible (Paschel, 1997: 156). Doyle explained his
intentions: "I've always wanted to bring the books down
closer to the characters — to get myself, the narrator, out of
it as much as I can. And one of the ways to do this is to use
the language that the characters actually speak, to use the
vernacular, and not ignoring the grammar, the formality of it,
to bend it, to twist it, so you get a sense that you are hearing
it, not reading it. That you are listening to the characters. You
get in really close to the characters" (White, 2001: 181–2).

Although it might be argued that Doyle's language in The
Commitments itself risks becoming monologic because of the
homogeneity of the vocabulary, idioms, phrasings and accents
of the characters and narrator alike, reading Doyle one is
continuously aware of what the theorist of the novel, Mikhail
Bakhtin, calls the dialogics of the novel as discourse. Doyle's
version of a transcribed working-class, urban, Irish vernacular

and his use of a focalised narrator implicitly challenge the broader Irish community's assumptions regarding "standard" Anglo-Irish English and, questions of realism aside, Doyle's "Barrytownese" does seem intended to scandalise. The scatological, sexual, profane, and generally unrelentingly "vulgar" argot of Doyle's characters represents a new urban realism to be sure, but it is also quite traditional if seen as a contemporary expression of what Bakhtin calls the *carnivalesque* — the expression of a popular culture that sites itself in difference and opposition to the norms, conventions, and conformism of the "official" culture.

A recognisable form of late-twentieth-century "Hiberno-English", Doyle's language in the trilogy is nevertheless self-consciously oppositional to the literary traditions and traditional tastes of the predominantly middle-class world that reads such fiction. Like his choice of subject matter and setting, Doyle's decision to represent his characters the way he does is as ideological as it is literary. Beginning with *The Commitments*, all of Doyle's novels "attempt to articulate a part of late twentieth-century experience that had largely remained outside the horizons of Irish literature, ways of life hidden from the concerns of people who typically buy and read literary fiction in Ireland" (Donnelly, 2000: 27). Doyle's language and style in the Barrytown trilogy are central to what Fintan O'Toole describes as the "conflict between writing the nation and reading it [that] lies at the heart of Irish culture in the twentieth century" (O'Toole, 1997b: 82).

Doyle's text actually raises these issues, comically and obliquely, in its opening pages. Ray informs Derek and Outspan how he thinks the name of their band, "And And And," should be punctuated:

> –I think maybe we should have an exclamation mark, yeh know, after the second And in the name.
> –Wha'?

–It'd be And And exclamation mark, righ', And.
It'd look deadly on the posters.
Outspan said nothing while he imagined it.
–What's an explanation mark? said Derek. . . .
–Is it not supposed to go at the end?
–It should go up his arse, said Outspan . . . (C, 2–3)

When Derek and Outspan recount Ray's "deadly" idea to
Jimmy, his reaction — "Fuck, fuck, exclamation mark, me" —
sums up not only his scorn for what's "been done before" (C,
3–4) musically, but his creator's attitude to fiction that would
represent these characters in any other way. There is a sly
self-referential quality about this scene. Doyle's project in
this novel and the trilogy as a whole is to represent the
world he knows in a way that it can recognise itself. He has
no intention of "doin' bad versions of other people's poxy
songs" (C, 6) — that is, of constructing yet another image of
the working class to amuse middle-class readers.

If, ironically, that is precisely what his novels have done,
the amusement is not unalloyed and does not come without
a price. Jimmy's Hot Press advertisement discourages "Red-
necks and southsiders" (C, 11) from applying to join The
Commitments, but when writing his novel Doyle would have
known that the latter, at least, middle-class "southsiders",
would form the majority of his readers. And for them, what
the novel's heterodox idiolect expresses would be as disturbing as its unorthodox manner. If "Dublin soul" is to be
"The workin' man's rhythm. Sex an' factory" (C, 39), Doyle's
representation of his characters' upfront attitudes to "ridin'"
is as subversive as his representation of their attitude to
politics is iconoclastic. "Party politics, said Jimmy, –means
nothin' to the workin' people. Nothin'. — Fuck all" (C, 39).

Anti-romantic, unconventional, and disrespectful, Doyle's
characters compose a collective affront to traditional middle-
class attitudes. In the areas of sex and politics most obvi-

ously, his novels proclaim, a "new Ireland" has diverged from
the old to the extent that a younger generation is breaking
with an older. The institutions and discourses that traditionally dominated sexual and political behaviour, Catholicism
and the Catholic Church, and nationalism and the historical
parties, are irrelevant to the characters and generation Doyle
represents in the novel. One of the ironies of the title is obviously that these characters will *not* commit themselves to
the historical forms or norms of Church or State, but especially not to the old parties and party system. The sense one
takes from *The Commitments* is that these are irrelevant because they either do not speak to the people's needs — as in
the case of "Fianna fuckin' Fáil" (*C*, 8) — or, in the Church's
case, because its ideology and monumental hypocrisy are so
at odds with and offensive to the reality of young people's
everyday life that the institution does not just fail them; it
actually undermines their attempts at self-esteem. While it is
true that "Jimmy and The Commitments have no real political agenda at all" (Booker, 1997: 32), their outright rejection
of traditional party politics *is* a political act and expresses,
presumably, Doyle's sense in the late 1980s of the disconnection that had occurred between young people and traditional
party politics. Jimmy's remarks also express a fundamental
point Doyle makes throughout his writing; namely, that,
more than nationality or nationalism, class is the greater de-
terminant of individual identity in contemporary Ireland.

The politics of identity encountered in *The Commitments*
is the struggle for self-esteem and self-confidence by a
younger generation that is unemployed or under-employed
and with very little prospects for the future; a generation
that needs to *make* commitments to change those prospects
through its own initiative rather than relying on the patronising institutions of Church and State that have so miserably
failed it. Where Doyle shows meaningful change is at the
level of the individual. *How* he shows that change is in the

story of the band; but for all the hyper-realistic dialogue he uses in that story, Doyle's novel is more fable than social realism and the way he uses "soul" music makes this clear.

Caramine White has argued that the "central function" of the music in *The Commitments* is to construct "the parallel between the black American and Irish experiences" (White, 2001: 53); but first and foremost, the primary purpose of the music is mimetic: *The Commitments* is a novel about a band — the characters listen to, talk about, rehearse and perform music. That's why there are so many transcribed songs. Secondly, as Doyle himself admitted, he thought he could achieve humorous effects with the lyrics by counterpointing the American idiom and the Irish voice or a specific lyric and a scene. But the deeper thematic significance of the music in *The Commitments* needs to be understood in relation to the literal and symbolic acts of appropriation and performance which Doyle uses to structure the characters' struggle for self-esteem and self-identity. The numerous images and scenes of "rehearsal" in the novel are in this sense tropes for identity-formation.

The racial analogy that has been drawn between African-Americans and the working-class, urban Irish because of Doyle's use of soul music in the novel and what has been described as "the near-canonical status" (Cullingford, 2001: 158) of the passage in which Jimmy proclaims "The Irish are the niggers of Europe, lads" (*C*, 9), is profoundly inappropriate and not really warranted by the novel itself. On the most superficial level of plot, Doyle uses soul music simply as Jimmy's idea of something that will give the new band a competitive advantage in the Dublin music scene. But as he talks Derek and Outspan out of forming a band with Ray and forming one with him instead, Jimmy's rhetorical questions make clear that forming a band for him is going to be a way of addressing issues of identity, self-esteem, and self-affirmation: "Yis want to be different, isn't tha' it? Yis want

to do somethin' with yourselves, isn't tha' it?" (*C*, 6). Being
different and doing something with one's life, Doyle suggests,
are clearly related, especially for Irish youth in the mid-
1980s, when the economy seemed to make any form of the
latter a mark of difference.

The year before Doyle wrote the novel, unemployment
in Ireland reached a record 17 per cent of the workforce
and the country had the highest rate of people on welfare —
700,000 — in the European Community (Gray, 1996: 313).
This economic and social background is glimpsed when
Jimmy refers to "these tossers here" (*C*, 6), the unemployed
and under-employed regulars around them in the pub. The
boys are already surrounded by their future unless they can
think of something to avoid the rut their society has prepared for them. So when Jimmy stumbles upon his idea for
"Dublin soul", it is clear that the horizon of identity Doyle's
text has constructed is based on economic not racial markers. To suggest that Doyle means the reader to equate
north Dublin young people of the 1980s with young black
Americans during the 1960s and 1970s is to make him
grossly insensitive as well as embarrassingly ingenuous. The
characters Doyle creates and the segment of Irish society
they represent are not the victims of systemic racism. The
view that "Modern Dubliners have experienced similar economic oppression" to that experienced by African-
Americans, and that "the social oppression and lost feeling
of 1960s American blacks are likewise part of the consciousness of Dublin youth" (White, 2001: 45–6), is absurd.
Doyle does not practise such "shameless appropriation",
nor does he participate in "spurious ethnic chic" (Cullingford, 2001: *x*, 7). While it is true that the Irish and African-
Americans have diasporic histories, the differences between
emigration and slavery are so extreme that they make any
such categorical link a most spurious rhetorical distortion.

Moreover, as Elizabeth Butler Cullingford points out, Doyle's lads are far too "casually racist" — and insecure about the size of their "gooters" — to identify meaningfully with African-Americans: "Jimmy is not primarily interested in the symbolic relationship of the oppressed Irish with former slaves. . . . The Commitments are 'black' because they are proletarian, not just because they're Irish" (Cullingford, 2001: 158–9). Jimmy pushes identification with African-Americans because he sees the working-class urban Irish to be systemically *economically* disadvantaged in the same way that African-Americans are racially.

Doyle's use of soul music in *The Commitments* should be interpreted as well in relation to the high quotient of American popular culture that circulates in his fiction. A prominent feature of his work, from *The Commitments* to *The Woman Who Walked into Doors*, is the way it records the growing presence of American popular culture in late-twentieth-century Irish culture. What needs to be emphasised as well is that this motif in his fiction does not express an anti-American sentiment; Doyle seems to understand this cultural phenomenon as a characteristic of late twentieth-century capitalism, rather than as American cultural imperialism (Booker, 1996: 36–7).

Doyle's fiction expresses no animus against American cultural hegemony, no paranoia about globalisation, no regret about the marginalisation of traditional Irish cultural forms. When Jimmy tells the boys "Your music should be abou' where you're from an' the sort o' people yeh come from" (*C*, 8), he is not only connecting voice and identity in the image of performance in language that points to the novel's thematic core; he is affirming Doyle's credo as a novelist.

The metaphor of "Dublin soul" organises the book thematically in the same way that the character, Jimmy Rabbitte Jr, organises the fictive band. What happens when Deco inserts local references into "Night Train" is a kind of cultural currency exchange; by appropriating the American songs the way they do, the allusions empower the local by placing it *inside* the powerful form of the "classic" American song. However, while the references have "the effect of anchoring the novel in 1987 working-class Dublin", it is an essentialist illusion that they "[allow] the reader a glimpse into its collective consciousness" (White, 2001: 45). To begin with, it is debatable that there is a homogeneous, monolithic, socioeconomic entity called "working-class Dublin". Secondly, the allusions are neither substantial enough to represent a "collective consciousness" nor particular enough to differentiate this working class from any other. To suggest that "Jimmy is attempting to borrow a tradition [i.e. "soul" music] that he hopes will be successful once again in uniting a people" and argue that "Jimmy's mission accounts for the odd name of the band: he wants The Commitments to commit themselves to the transformation of their city" (White, 2001: 48), is to make him — and Doyle — into a crypto-nationalist, and Dublin into Ireland. *The Commitments* describes a group of wannabe musicians and singers, not Young Ireland Redivivus. Jimmy Rabbitte Jr is no Thomas Davis. Such ambitions are alien to the characters' and their creator's sensibilities.

The concept of "Dublin Soul" is conceived *extempore* at the climax of Jimmy's bravura speech to Derek and Outspan at the beginning of the novel. Later, when Jimmy repeats his ideas to the full group, Doyle inserts considerable comic counterpoint to deflate his intellectualising, but the point that the Irish — Dubliners in particular — need "soul" (*C*, 40) emerges unscathed, and when Joey adds that "soul" is also "dignity . . . pride . . . confidence . . . assertion" and "self-respect" (*C*, 41–2), the point is firmly established.

"Dublin soul" does not materialise, however, until Deco inserts the names of the Dublin train stations into the band's version of "Night Train" at their first public performance (*C*, 105). Premonitions occur in the rehearsals when he adds references to Clery's clock in "What Becomes of the Broken Hearted" (*C*, 54) and to Guinness in "Chain Gang" (*C*, 56), but it is the appropriation and rendering of "Night Train" into Dublin blues that seems to lead to their public success. And the reasons for that success would seem to point to another aspect of Jimmy's appropriation of an American musical form for the Dublin scene. What exhilarates the pub crowds is their delight when they hear a "classic" *American* song suddenly inflected with a specific, *local* Irish content. It is not that the local is suddenly made universal, but that it is heard in a way that makes it *sound* "American" (not African-American); that is, central, rather than peripheral; authentically, not uncertainly, modern; powerful, not a beggar's bowl rolling around on the kerb of Europe. The insertion of the Irish content into the American form reverses the historical relationship of the two cultures, the one-way, east-to-west flow, and challenges the notion of a passive Irish culture being consumed by a global American popular culture. The effect of the song is a kind of empowerment and authentication and the mania in the pubs is an exaggerated version of the uplifting effect Doyle shows the music-making, the "performing", to have on The Commitments themselves.

Band of Heroes

The popular success that *The Commitments* achieved — as both novel and film — would seem to be explained by its superficial novelty. The film also possessed a dynamite soundtrack. In a sense, it was the *novel's* "soundtrack" — its raucous dialogue — that was responsible for its notorious originality. And yet it can be argued that what really underpins both the novel's and the film's success, where they are most original, is in their manipulation of traditional — even archetypal — elements of plot and characterisation. One reason the novel was so easily "translated" to the screen is that its

narrative already drew heavily from popular film genres —
specifically, the contemporary musical and the "team" movie.
Doyle told Karen Sbrockey, in fact, that rather than a band
"It could have been a football team because I'm also very
fond of football, but I can't see football being . . . amusing on
the page. Also, it would have been restricted to one sex"
(Sbrockey, 1999). The "team" movie evolved out of the Second World War combat movie and if one considers the generic characters, conventional humour, scenic method, and
conventional plot of *The Commitments*, the parallels between
the novel and that film genre are obvious. Nor should this
surprise. As a novel about the politics of identity, *The
Commitments* explores the relation between the individual
and the group. This theme, as well as issues of action, responsibility, personal desire, guilt and shame recur in all
Doyle's works, and the theme of the individual and the
group is central to the war/team movie genres.

The Commitments begins with a "classic" scene — the
forming of the *ur*-group or "core": Jimmy, Outspan and
Derek, in the pub. In this scene as well we witness the articu-
lation of group identity, the assertion of a collective grievance,
and the identification of the group's task, all of which come in
the form of an inspirational speech from the emergent "natural" leader. The next stage is the selection of the other members from amongst a number of "recruits", some of whom
are known and some unknown to the original threesome.
Following the "interviews" in which Doyle describes Jimmy
turning away the unacceptables (*C*, 21–2) (the same convention is played for similar humour in *The Full Monty* [1996], a
film remarkably like *The Commitments* in theme and tone) the
first half of the novel is taken up with the formation of the
group. There is an inspirational song scene in which they listen to James Brown sing "Get Up, I Feel like Being a Sex Machine" (*C*, 17); because of Jimmy's speech in the pub, "get up"
has both an individual, personal and a collective, public conno-

tation — self-esteem and class-pride — as well as the obvious sexual suggestion. When Joey the Lips Fagan joins the group he is clearly the conventional figure of the wise old "veteran" who has already been where these youngsters will have to go. In an equally conventional scene, at first the band is incredulous; then he plays and wins them over and establishes himself as a figure of authority (*C*, 28).

The "bonding" scenes provide the novel with its thematic glue: Jimmy's lectures on soul, the acquisition of "equipment", the giving of the stage-names, the first rehearsal, the first scene in which the girls strut their stuff at the front of the group, the "suiting up", all mark advances in the group's preparation for its first "test". However, in this genre the adversary is not just external to the group — here, the public that needs to be "conquered" — there is always an internal adversary as well. Doyle's plot distributes this conventional foreshadowing effect through the whole group, but what is important is to recognise how his manipulation of this convention serves a thematic function in the novel which also determines its formal innovation on convention.

Formally, *The Commitments* has an hour-glass shape; first it presents the group gathering and coming together; then it shows it coming apart. Paradoxically, the band begins to come apart even as it begins to come together. The plot dynamic in *The Commitments* is a kind of centripetal-centrifugal tension that might be encapsulated in the archetypal binary of Eros/Eris, love and discord. The seed of discord is sown when the three women are attracted to Joey the Lips (*C*, 62–3). Then everyone begins to dislike Deco (*C*, 82) because he likes himself too much; as his self-regard becomes more and more obnoxious, it is also clear that his self-concern poses a threat to the group's long-term plans (*C*, 121–2). Deco is set up to be the Judas, but Doyle never brings his plot to such a point of narrative extremis.

When they are a hit with their local community at their first gig at the Community Centre, the first taste of success also brings the first real crisis, as Billy, the drummer, quits because of Deco. But when the nutter, Mickah Wallace, replaces him and turns out to be a superior drummer, crisis becomes growth in a conventional plot turn that sees the group advance closer to its real task — making it in the Dublin pub and club scene.

Of course, the band goes from strength to strength until it reaches the brink of "real" success, an offer of a recording session with Eejit records. This is where Doyle deviates from the conventional plot line. At the very moment when the prize is within its reach, the band implodes — not because of Deco's treachery or Dean's "selfish" jazz solos, but because of Eros/Eris again and the improbable but potent sexual allure of Joey the Lips. The novel ends with the original three Commitments, the "last survivors" of the band, the "vets" who will go on to the next "campaign" as "combat-hardened" Brassers. The point to stress is that Doyle's conventional plot is all about individual–group dynamics, the conflicts and tensions between individual and collective identity, personal needs and desires and the collective project.

The Commitments is not about family, but the focus on family in Doyle's second novel clearly follows from the view of Irish society in the 1980s that his story of the band presents in terms of the dialectic of individual and group. The individuals who form The Commitments join the band for all the reasons they give — to meet women and men, have a good time, and make some money — but most of all, to have a good time; they all agree it's great "crack". The story of the band is a narrative based on the heroic archetype of the *comitatus*. Deco must be "endured" not for the sake of the "surrogate family" (White, 2001: 61), but for the sake of the group "mission". The irony of Doyle's plot is that Jimmy wants people to commit themselves to the collective effort of a band and believes that in return for that commitment the experience will give them a new sense of self-worth, purpose, and personal integrity; the band then becomes a victim of its success. It is the emergence of individual desire and the discovery of personal integrity that ultimately bring the band down.

Going Solo: Soul or Jazz

Doyle's concern with individual identity, self-esteem and self-respect, and how these are influenced by the individual's relation to others, particularly in a specific collective formation like the family or, as in *The Commitments*, a band, runs like a spine throughout all his fiction. It is his exploration of the complex and ambiguous nature of the relation between the individual and the group that marks his importance as a novelist of the 1990s. In *The Commitments*, it should be emphasised, Doyle constructs a story about self-discovery and self-improvement through group action and the self-esteem that comes from solidarity with others — only to show the success leading to the break-up of the group. For a first novel, it is a very *savvy* book; it never lets the reader forget that it knows what it's up to.

When Jimmy makes his infamous claim to Derek and Outspan that "The Irish are the niggers of Europe, lads" (*C*, 9), the narrator intrudes to tell us that its revelatory effect strikes Jimmy as much as the others: "He grinned. He'd impressed himself again." Doyle's narrative voice distances itself from the characters so infrequently, its intrusion is worth considering. Jimmy is "impressed" by his rhetorical ingenuity. The narrator's ironic comment emphasises the improvisatory nature of Jimmy's language and behaviour. He is a "bullshitter", a "chancer", and "the niggers of Europe" analogy is a "con" — a "pitch"; and the narrator's deflation of Jimmy's rhetorical balloon should prevent anyone from ascending into the ideological ozone.

Jimmy is neither a social agitator nor a prophet; he forms a band not a social movement, and the cracks in the collective project begin to show as soon as Deco and Dean begin to build on the self-esteem and self-confidence the band experience gives them. Dean's case seems particularly symbolic. When he starts taking an interest in jazz, Joey is quick to reprimand him. According to Joey, jazz "is the antithesis of soul" (*C*, 124); jazz is "intellectual", middle-class and elitist (*C*, 124–26). But the real objection is that jazz is individualist. When Dean plays a solo that Joey describes as a "jazz solo" rather than a "soul solo", Joey describes him as "selfish": "Strictly speaking, Brother, soul solos aren't really solos at all. . . . Dean's solo didn't have corners. It didn't fit. . . . It wasn't part of the song. . . . It was a real solo. . . . That's what jazz does. It makes the man selfish. He doesn't give a fuck about his Brothers" (*C*, 134). Dean is not the only member of the band spreading his wings, of course; Deco has already announced he's going on a talent show to advance *his* "career" (*C*, 138–9). What is ironic is that, as with Deco, Dean's sense of individuality is a product of belonging to the group and his newfound self-confidence an instance of why Jimmy said they should form the group in the first place.

Doyle gives significant discursive attention to the "soul vs jazz" theme, but we should not conclude from this that he supports Joey's views. Joey the Lips deserves a novel to himself, and a different novel — or more mature novelist — would have given him more attention. To Doyle's credit, Joey remains an enigma in *The Commitments* — there is evidence that he is a fraud but also that he has told the truth. His support of the band is what is important, not his echoing of Jimmy's theorising about soul or his prejudice against jazz, which reflect his "mischievous" nature as Trickster. I doubt that Doyle was aware of the Trickster archetype at this point, but in narratological terms, Joey is the figure of the mysterious stranger who arrives in the community out of the blue, is attractive to the women and envied by the men, possesses a knowledge or talent the community or quester needs; instructs the latter, witnesses their success, and then departs as suddenly and mysteriously as he arrived. Joey the Lips is as old as myth and fairytale.

The Commitments introduces a theme Doyle explores throughout his career: the individual needs the support and nurturing that the group provides, but there comes a time when the identity the group provides becomes limiting. Jimmy eventually admits that he sees Dean's point about wanting more freedom to express himself and agrees that Joey the Lips is "full o' shi'e" when it comes to his "ideas abou' soul bein' the people's music an' tha'"(C, 144). It is not that the identity that comes from belonging to the group is limited in itself, but that it is different from another identity which the individual begins to sense is possible and which he or she is willing to risk realising.

Dean is not "selfish"; he is simply becoming *another* "Dean". When he explains himself to Jimmy, he says that he just wants to become a better musician and he acknowledges the role the band has played in awakening this desire: "I went through hell tryin' to learn to play the sax. . . . Now I can play it. An' I'm not stoppin'. I want to get better. . . . I express meself, with me sax. . . . That's why I'm gettin' into the jazz. There's no rules. There's no walls" (C, 143). The bond that unites and defines ultimately confines in Dean's case. The difference between soul and jazz that is made into a conflict for Dean is really the dynamic relation between the group and the individual Doyle shows to be the *medium* through which identity, esteem and confidence are forged.

Eventually, Doyle treats the complex dialectic of individual and collective identities comically when he has Jimmy think that all that was holding the group together was Imelda — all the males, including Jimmy, lusted after her. The apparent solidarity was an illusion and when Deco sees her kissing

Joey, the band self-destructs (*C*, 153) — but, of course, with each member emerging as a stronger individual. The extent of their commitment to "Dublin soul" and the band was contingent upon both delivering what each member needed from the experience; as they achieved that, or when they did not, their commitment ceased. As Gerry Smyth notes, *The Commitments* provides the reader with "adult", unsentimental entertainment, but it is also "a novel about fulfilment, about the possibility of exceeding expectations and realising potential" (Smyth, 1997: 71). Jimmy, Deco, Dean, and the rest are as successful as they could have been, but more importantly, they discover a self-potential they do not know they possess until they realise it. The effect of the humour in the novel is matched only by the moral uplift Doyle's plot delivers at its highpoint. But while Doyle puts "northside Dubliners" on the literary map with *The Commitments*, for all its vivid celebration of their vitality, spirit and humour, his novel does not romanticise their lives. At the end, characters are still out of work, looking for it, or in jobs they are not content with; this has been an "episode" — an important one, to be sure — in a "story" with much more to come.

Finally, it should be pointed out that one could read the soul vs jazz passage in *The Commitments* self-referentially. Is *The Commitments* a "jazz solo" or a "soul solo"? Joey, ironically, criticises Dean for being "selfish" and playing "a real solo"; that is, for expressing himself by pushing the envelope of the form. But this, I would suggest, is how Doyle begins the trilogy. *The Commitments* is extremely conventional, stylistically and formally, in its characterisation and plot, in its use of humour, in its scenic method. The novel has "corners", to use Joey's term: it is solidly "framed". But for all its solidarity with "northside soul", *The Commitments* also gives expression to an ambitious individualism that inevitably finds itself at odds with the solidarity of class and locale from which it derives its strength.

If there is a Commitment who most seems to reflect Doyle's situation as a novelist, it is Dean. Jimmy Rabbitte Jr may seem to be his creator's surrogate, with his managerial flair for motivational language and policy announcements, his enjoyment in lecturing others, and the delight he takes in his own rhetoric; but it is the Doyle who spent years scribbling away at the unpublished — and in his own judgement, un-publishable — *Your Granny is a Hunger Striker*, that one can hear in Dean's "I went through hell tryin' to learn to play the sax. . . . Now I can play it. An' I'm not stoppin'. I want to get better." Part of Doyle may be writing for his community; another is out "to express meself" by "gettin' into the jazz" which allows him to "solo" *as if* "There's no rules. . . . no walls." Perhaps this is how we should understand Doyle's explanation of his approach to language — "to use the ver-nacular, and not ignoring the grammar, the formality of it, to bend it . . ." (White, 2001: 181–2). It is the way Doyle "bends" the conventions that is significant.

The Performing Self

The Barrytown trilogy has been described as both realist and postmodern because of the way "it juxtaposes the ef-fects of mass international culture with a residual local cul-ture" (Smyth, 1997: 67). But Doyle's use of American pop music in *The Commitments* — and the trilogy as a whole — does not "juxtapose" alien and native cultures so much as synthesise them to show the hybridity that characterises contemporary Irish culture. Even so, Doyle's fiction shows a society and culture in a state of transition, not arrival. While Doyle represents individual identity in *The Commitments* as both self-invention and impersonation, his approach to char-acterisation in his first novel shows no deeper indication of what might be called the postmodern self.

The narrative device of a band of musicians and singers is a perfect vehicle for Doyle's purposes because "performing" contains the postmodern ambiguity of "acting" as both agency and imposture. Roddy Doyle is no John Banville, however. There is no ontological abyss beneath his characters. There is, instead, a self that searches for a style of being. Doyle is not postmodern in the sense that he shows identity to be *only* style, style without substance. Something abides after the event-specific t-shirt is discarded. The Commitments disband only to reassemble as The Brassers (*C*, 165). What abides is the connection to place and community and the fundamental sense of rootedness, of being in a time and place, that this provides.

Doyle does present a postmodern sense of "public" identity in *The Commitments* to the extent that he shows it to be stylistic, contingent, pragmatic, and willed. When Jimmy meets Derek and Outspan at the pub at the beginning of the novel, he criticises them for the songs they were intending to perform; he argues that *what* they sing will represent *who* they are in the sense of who they want to be *perceived* to be. In selecting the music they are selecting more than a persona; they are choosing a means to an identity. He tells them "It's not the other people's songs so much . . . It's which ones yis do" (*C*, 7).

It is important to recognise that the text shows Jimmy actually doing this himself as he makes his pitch to the boys, for Jimmy seems to discover his own role in the moment and process of inventing himself as a "manager" in the pub. The narrator describes Derek's and Outspan's response to his outburst about "doin' bad versions of other people's poxy songs": "That was it. He was right, bang on the nail. They were very impressed. So was Jimmy" (*C*, 6–7). That "So was Jimmy" is more than Doyle's imitation, perhaps, of Joyce's narrative irony toward Stephen in *A Portrait*; the comment conveys the improvisational nature of Jimmy's ar-

gument and its meaning as and within a "performance".
Jimmy doesn't seem to know what he's going to say or
where it will lead until he says it and arrives there. If we
recognise this about him — and his whole project with the
band and "Dublin soul" — from the beginning, then the anti-
climactic ending and Jimmy's reinvention of the survivors as
"The Brassers", a "Dublin country" (*C*, 165) group, should
not come as that much of a surprise.

Indeed, the ending is foreshadowed much earlier when
Dean catches Natalie and Joey making out and "For a few
minutes The Commitments broke up" (*C*, 63). The way the
narrator describes Jimmy's reaction is more than another instance of Doyle's ironic treatment of his protagonist: "Jimmy
snapped out of it. It happened when he went from the general
to the particular. It wasn't Imelda Joey the Lips had got off
with. It was Natalie. He didn't fancy Natalie. It was cool" (*C*,
63). Even for Jimmy, the band is more important as process
than product, as an activity that leads not just to feeling good
but to feeling good about oneself. For all his talk of solidarity,
Jimmy — like the others — remains an individualist.

Doyle's characters in *The Commitments* find their way by
impersonating someone finding their way; by finding, choosing
and then internalising an image and "modelling" it in front of
each other, and eventually, before a public. "Everyone in the
group becomes a personality," Jimmy says (*C*, 44). In a sense,
they emigrate to America, make their fortunes, return to Ireland, and spend it all in a matter of months — and without
ever leaving home. Fintan O'Toole remarks that "The whole
point of Doyle's novel . . . is that these Dublin kids are not
romantic Irish exotics. They have grown up with American
music. They either know the moves and sounds of Detroit
and Philadelphia already or they can learn them. They place
themselves, not in relation to the literary landscape of rural
Ireland, but in the unbounded domain of popular culture.
When they form a soul band they are becoming actors, im-

personating the roles of James Brown, Wilson Pickett, and The Supremes" (O'Toole, 1999: 37). At the end of the novel, Jimmy drops "Dublin soul" as fast as he invented it. He, Derek and Outspan happily reinvent themselves as "country-punk" (*C*, 163) musicians, their musical consciences not skipping a beat, while Doyle leaves the reader to revel in the continuing ironies of another contradictory hybrid. "Dublin soul" is as *disposable* as their identities as The Commitments, just as "Dublin country" will be dropped and their identities as "The Brassers" shed when the time comes.

Doyle's deployment of American soul music as the instrument of individual and group empowerment in *The Commitments* — as comical and ironic as it is — and the manner in which he represents the presence of American pop culture in general in Irish society in his other work, is problematic from any number of traditional or neo-nationalist perspectives. "Soul" circulates as a metaphor of identity throughout the history of Irish nationalist discourse and Doyle's ironic evocation and erasure of that tradition in *The Commitments* must be something of a red flag to readers who see the global proliferation of American culture as neo-colonialism. American pop culture — everything from Hollywood to MacDonald's to Microsoft, but especially music — is often identified as the instrument of American cultural imperialism, a force homogenising the world and marginalising local culture. Doyle clearly does not share this view or concern (see Paschel, 1997: 159); nor does he seem to have any significant investment in a *nation*-based sense of identity. The issue for his characters is not neo-colonialism but a reason for getting up in the morning, making some money, and getting some self-respect.

For all the novel's comic irony, self-respect is its one unambiguous theme. The repeated connection between soul and self-respect confirms the allegorical significance of the music as a trope for identity — although the *act of appropria-*

tion, making it one's own through performance, is more important than the music itself. An explicit theme in *The Commitments*, self-respect continues as an implicit theme in *The
Snapper* and *The Van*. The symbolic significance of "soul" for
the politics of identity in *The Commitments* is evident when
Jimmy talks about traditional political identities:

> Soul is the rhythm o' the people, Jimmy said again. –
> The Labour Party doesn't have soul. Fianna Fuckin'
> Fail doesn't have soul. The Workers' Party ain't got
> soul. The Irish people — no. — The Dublin people
> — fuck the rest o' them. — The people o' Dublin,
> our people, remember need soul. (*C*, 40)

The passage is important, not only because it expresses
Jimmy's generation's and class's disillusion with traditional
party politics, and because it expresses his post-national (or
perhaps anti-national), "city-state"-based sense of identity,
but because it expresses the sense that working-class Dubs
lack self-respect because they feel like second-class citizens
(see Paschel, 1998: 37). It is Jimmy who first interprets soul
as dignity in the novel. Jimmy Rabbitte Jr himself clearly
needs what he convinces the others they want. He enjoys
seeing his name in *Hot Press*, the local music magazine —
even if it is only an advertisement for auditions (*C*, 20); there
is a sense of empowerment that comes when he sees the
others enjoying his "lectures" and "policy announcements"
(*C*, 40); and he is irritated when Deco beats him to the
punch by inserting "local flavour" (*C*, 54) into "As I Walked
This Land of Broken Dreams" to make it "more Dubliny" (*C*,
54) — this tactic for making American soul into "Dublin
soul" had been Jimmy's idea and he doesn't like losing control over it. He stops them smoking dope, not because he is
against drugs but because "they hadn't got the go-ahead
from him before they'd lit up"; but he doesn't want to admit
this and so once again he improvises a grand idea: "We're

supposed to be bringin' soul to Dublin" and "Dublin's fucked up with drugs. Drugs aren't soul" (*C*, 73–4).

If there is an acceptable "recreational drug" in *The Commitments*, it is contemporary music — American, British and Irish. Throughout Doyle's fiction, pop music seems to signify a willed connectedness to a present in opposition to an involuntary, often imposed connection to the past. "America", in Doyle's fiction, as in Joseph O'Connor's, functions as a trope for an *otherness* attractive and accessible to the Irish which fills a contemporary Irish void — the heretically ironic lack of "soul". Or to use the word Doyle uses to introduce Jimmy Rabbitte Jr, America belongs to the "new": "Jimmy knew what was what . . . what was new, what was new but wouldn't be for long and what was going to be new" (*C*, 1–2). The play between "knew" and "new", knowledge and novelty, in this passage, points the direction the novel follows, as it describes a group of young people collectively and individually setting out to know themselves in a new way, and so to discover new selves. (It is fascinating to see how, in "The Deportees", a recent short story Doyle published in *Metro Éireann*, reprises this symbolic use of music as a *transformative* medium and experience in a new context. Jimmy, now married and the father of four, forms his first band since The Brassers. The Deportees' music breaks down the racial and ethnic differences between themselves and between them and their Irish audience. See Doyle, March 2001 – May 2002: 7.)

When Jimmy "interviews" prospective members of the band, he "judged on one question: influences" (*C*, 21). While this is played for humorous effects, it nevertheless points to a particular sense of being-in-the-world: who you are is who or what you allow to influence you, who or what you are "committed" to; and one version of an identity is the history of one's influences and commitments. Perhaps, to return to Yeats again, the most "radically innocent" aspect of Doyle's first novel is the subversive suggestion that begins to build from it and its centring trope of "Dublin soul" — a suggestion which grows in substance and effect in all Doyle's novels to follow — namely that for all the evident paraphernalia of modern life the characters are surrounded by, the life that is lived with and through them is not yet *intrinsically* modern, in the sense of modern and whole, that Irish society and culture are still in the process of *accommodating* the modernity to which they committed themselves with the first Whitaker Plan at the end of the 1950s.

Commitments — made, kept, and broken — run through Doyle's fiction. The name for the band that Jimmy proposes is another example of Doyle's dramatic irony. It would make sense for the band to be called after the music they will sing — "Dublin Soul", which certainly sounds "catchier" than "The Commitments". In fact, when he proposes it, the name does not sound like it comes from Jimmy at all — he has not used the word or talked about the concept (C, 9–10) — so much as from the governing intelligence of the novel, and its ultimate significance as a title actually contradicts Jimmy's meaning. Jimmy talks about the relationship between the individual and something in which they invest value — in this case, a kind of music; for him, the commitment is to a sense of relationship between the music, the musicians and their community. Their performance of this new kind of music will articulate and its reception authenticate the experience of a specific class and a particular place. But of course it is Doyle's novel that does this, not the music in the novel.

As the plot develops, the novel gradually exposes the irony of the band's name; there is no commitment in this group. Everyone has been out for themselves from the start. But that may be the point of Doyle's ironic treatment of his figures of commitment. For these young people the more important first step is the act of commitment itself, the

commitment to changing their lives, doing something different with their circumstances, "letting go" or, in James
Brown's terms, "gettin' up" (*C*, 18). What the plot makes
clear, *contra* Jimmy's rhetoric, is that the significance of the
band's name points *inward* to the relations between the band
members rather than outwards to the community or larger
society; but most importantly, towards the individuals themselves. Perhaps this is Doyle's point: no one is ready to make
a commitment, no commitment is worth taking seriously,
until there is basis for it in self-understanding, self-esteem,
and self-confidence. Doyle's young people make personal
progress in all three areas as a result of their commitment
to the group, but once those dividends of personal growth
have been collected, it's time to move on.

Conclusion: Rules and Walls

By the time he completed the Barrytown trilogy, Doyle was
seen as a novelist whose narratives present "typical" characters living in a distinct community and for whom the sense
of a communal reality is paramount. For some, this made
him an unwelcome "realist" of a new urban Ireland (see
Battersby); for others, his characterisation recycled traditional "Irish" stereotypes in a vulgar new garb (see Bradshaw). Such readings miss the tension between individuality
and group solidarity in Doyle's fiction, the dialectic that perhaps gives his novels their particular — and for some, particularly galling — purchase on contemporary Irish society.
In the trilogy as a whole, his representation of individ-
ual/group relations may be understood as a metaphor for
the relation between personal and class identities; taken together, the novels compose an informal allegory of the tensions and insecurities that follow when individuals set out to
reinvent themselves in the context of a society and culture
whose traditional identity-markers — history, religion, na-

tionalism, and relation to land — are felt to no longer possess the relevance or credibility necessary to structure the
narrative of individual identity.

It is difficult not to imagine Doyle chuckling to himself as
he wrote Dean's remark about soul music to Jimmy: "It's
good crack but it's not art" (*C*, 142). Perhaps Doyle was already thinking of "One of the big issues" his books would
provoke: "whether they are literary or not . . . [the] drivel
. . . that they are less literary because they use the vernacular . . . [and] images from television instead of books"
(White, 2001: 182). In Doyle's mind, the literary/non-literary
issue is clearly class-related: "I would like to think that the
first three books celebrate working-class life. I tried to capture and celebrate crudity, loudness, linguistic flair and slang,
which is the property of working-class people" (Costello,
2001: 91). If writing about what he does in the way he does
is considered "non-literary," it is because he is writing about
working-class people in a way that seeks to *approximate*
rather than appropriate their voices and *respect* rather than
patronise their perspectives.

In *The Commitments*, Jimmy Rabbitte Jr's project to create
"Dublin soul" is a metafictive symbol for Doyle's larger project of creating a presence in Irish fiction for his people and
his world. But Dean's dissatisfaction with soul music and his
preference for jazz signals an individuality that is feeling en-
cumbered by the group ethos that, ironically, has nurtured it
into a condition of rebellious self-confidence, and paradoxically, into a condition of greater and different need. If the
metafictive analogy holds, Dean's growth raises the question
of whether, as Doyle develops, one can see him, like Dean,
coming to need to "play" a form of fictive music other than
his "Dublin soul". At the very least, *Paddy Clarke Ha Ha Ha*
and *The Woman Who Walked into Doors* are serious jazz riffs
that push the "corners" he establishes in his first three books.

The literary/non-literary, jazz/soul, individual/group issues in Doyle's fiction lead to the class question in another
way. As Doyle writes about Barrytown, he becomes more
and more successful, but as he becomes more and more
successful, a distance opens between him and the world he
writes about — even though he may continue to live near
his old neighbourhood. The growing income and fame that
Doyle plays down in his interviews cannot help but make
him different from his neighbours. *Writing* about your world
already places you in a *different* relation to it — even if you
don't make a single cent from it — and it is possible to see
the trilogy expressing an increasingly complex or ambiguous
relationship to the class it represents. What Doyle may be
articulating *through* writing about his working-class characters going through processes of change is the experience of
his own *un-classing*, or as he describes it, his passing into the
"grey" area between classes that he says began in his family's
economic history but which he must also recognise has continued much more extremely in his own (White, 2001: 178).

In a discussion of the fiction of the Angry Young Men in
Britain during the late 1950s and early 1960s, Dominic Head
notes the "paradox . . . that the [working-class] individual
who becomes a writer also becomes something other than
working-class. The ideological tussle then centres on
whether to designate that individual a figure of transition, or
a figure of betrayal" (Head, 2002: 59). Significantly, in his first
play, *Brownbread* (1989), Doyle has one of the characters
conceal his middle-class background from his friends (*BW*,
26). Doyle's ambiguous representation of the group in *The
Commitments* may reflect, ironically, an ambivalence toward
working-class identity even as the surface of the text seems
to declaim it proudly. The novel contains figures of betrayal,
but more importantly, characters in transition, and it is the
latter which makes *The Commitments* the important water-
shed novel that it is.

Chapter Two

Sweating Perception: *The Snapper*

Doyle began writing *The Snapper* in the autumn of 1986, while he was writing a play for Passion Machine, and he didn't finish it until the summer of 1989. Of the three novels in the trilogy, it took the longest to write and the first draft ended up, in his words, "a huge big rambling mess of a thing with all sorts of characters" (Costello, 2001: 89). When he cut this to "the bare essentials", he ended up with a novel less than half its original length (Costello, 2001: 89). The "bare essentials" are Sharon Rabbitte's pregnancy and its effect on herself, her family, and most importantly, her father. Doyle told Caramine White that "One of the reasons I chose pregnancy was because I knew nothing about it and I wanted to see if I could create a world which had nothing to do with me but which would be convincing" (White, 2001: 152). The comical yet poignant scenes in which Jimmy Sr "reads up" on pregnancy thus connect the character to his creator, who "researched" the subject in the same way.

Another reason Doyle might have been led to his plot is that pregnancy and related matters — contraception, abortion, unmarried mothers — were much in the news during this period; 1985 had been "the year of the Kerry babies" and the Family Planning Bill, generally known as the "Contraception Bill". The Medico-Social Research Board reported that eight per cent of all births registered in the Republic in the last three months of 1984 were to unmarried women and that 3,026 Irish women had received abortions in the UK during that year (Gray, 1996: 314). Abortion continued to be a "hot" topic following a High Court ban on abortion-counselling referrals in 1987 and a report that from January to June of 1987, 1,850 women had travelled to the UK for the procedure (Gray, 1996: 324).

Moreover, when Jimmy Sr supports Sharon's decision not to marry the father of her child, we should sense the issue of divorce behind his thinking, or more generally, the social reality of unhappy marriages based on unplanned pregnancies and social coercion. He tells his best friend, Bimbo, who clearly believes otherwise, "Why should she? They've more cop-on these days. Would you get married if you were tha' age again these days?" (*S*, 64). Doyle has always been strongly committed to the right to divorce, and just months before he began to write *The Snapper*, the then Senator Mary Robinson had urged the government to adopt a more realistic and honest attitude toward marital breakdowns and to set a date for a referendum on divorce. Doyle supported the "yes" side in both the 1986 and 1996 referenda, actively campaigning for it in the second. Doyle's sentimental-comic resolution of a potentially home-wrecking situation in *The Snapper* is the second panel in a triptych that composes what he consciously intended to be "a new picture of Ireland" (White, 2001: 169). To the question, "how did you turn such a horrible thing into something so wonderful?", Doyle acknowledges that "There were at least two roads one could have gone, the bright and the dark. The dark is another reality", and for him, that other, darker reality belongs to Ireland's past (White, 2001: 152). The attitude toward unmarried mothers was changing, and most importantly, the child was "being accepted within the family"; he felt his treatment of the topic was warranted: "it's not a wonderful situation, but at least in many cases it's warm and accepting, and that's what I wanted to depict in the novel" (White, 2001: 153).

In relation to the trilogy as a whole, *The Snapper* is another facet of Doyle's image of a society and culture which in his view were breaking free from the dark institutional shadows of the past, but which were going to be haunted by them for some time to come. Jimmy Rabbitte Sr's reference to "these days" signals his awareness that he is living through changing times. But will Doyle's second novel — and perhaps the trilogy — which is so significant a work of fiction in terms of representing, explaining and questioning the changes coursing through urban Irish society and culture in the closing decades of the twentieth century, ironically, lose its comic edge once those changes have run their course? Or will that comic edge come to seem more comic-satiric? For while Doyle may have intended the pregnancy plot in *The Snapper* to be a vehicle for showing the positively changing sexual and social mores of "a new Ireland," a close reading of the novel finds an overall impact that is more ambiguous; a darker, more ambivalent humour emerges.

"You're wah'?"

The Snapper opens with Jimmy Rabbitte Sr's reaction to his daughter's announcement that she is pregnant, and so begins with the narrative focus on the character that preoccupies Doyle in this as well as the last book in the trilogy. Sharon's pregnancy is the plot catalyst in *The Snapper*, and she is a central character, but Doyle's interest in Jimmy Sr gradually overtook him during the writing process (see White, 2001: 154). *The Snapper* also begins an exploration of a certain type of Irish male that Doyle continues in *The Van*, except that he ends the trilogy, significantly, with a reversal of the darkness-to-light pattern of *The Snapper*.

In the opening scene, when Jimmy Sr admonishes Sharon for answering back — "Now, there's no need to be gettin' snotty" (S, 2) — it is the same reprimand he used with Jimmy Jr in *The Commitments* (C, 19). The phrase shows how Doyle constructs character-continuity through what Hugh Kenner, discussing Joyce, calls a "characterizing vocabulary" (Kenner, 1978: 17), but it also points to something significant about his characterisation of Jimmy Rabbitte Sr in the last two novels of the trilogy. The phrase means more than getting "uppity", in the sense of disrespectful; it also means acting "above" yourself in a relationship, forgetting who you are. Later in the novel, Sharon thinks her father is "getting snotty" when he acts hurt by her indiscretion (S, 151). In *The Van*, Jimmy Sr's relationship with Bimbo unravels when he begins to feel that an entrepreneurial Bimbo is acting "above his station", so to speak, in their longstanding relationship. Such seemingly unwarranted or inappropriate behaviour jeopardises the stability of a relationship because it foregrounds the culturally determined and sanctioned role-playing that sustains it and can make the parties suddenly self-conscious about the nature and strength of the bonds that hold the relationship together. Sharon's pregnancy upsets her relationship with her father because, like Darren's success with his Leaving Certificate in *The Van*, it unsettles — and in Darren's case, undermines — Jimmy Sr's sense of who and what he is. Two members of his family cross thresholds of experience that change his relationships with them, whether he likes it or not. But what Doyle shows is that by being forced to confront change in others, Jimmy Sr eventually is forced to examine himself. And this is where his character becomes most emblematic of an Irish society in transition.

Taken together, *The Snapper* and *The Van* show Doyle exploring the pressures being encountered by a traditional type of Irish male during the 1980s. In *The Snapper*, where the challenge involves less issues of sexual morality than of social "face", Jimmy Sr can appear to emerge as a new kind of "man" by the time his daughter gives birth because the text shows that the patriarchal delusion which underwrites Jimmy Sr's sense of self remains intact, if still a delusion; but in *The Van*, the challenge to his "manhood" is much more serious and ultimately proves destructive not only of friendship but of the central value in Doyle's fiction, self-esteem.

The *faux* crisis that develops in the Rabbitte household as a result of Sharon's pregnancy is indeed a consequence of Jimmy Sr "gettin' snotty". From the instant he learns the news, his ego obtrudes. Once he has concluded his manly/ fatherly performance around the kitchen table, unsuccessfully questioning Sharon about the father's identity, Jimmy's first thought is to get to the pub and his drinking buddies. A pro forma invitation to Sharon and Veronica results in his daughter accompanying him. In the pub lounge, both feel awkward; this is the first time they have drunk together. Knowing his friends are downstairs, Jimmy manipulates his way free of his daughter, and although he knows she knows what he's doing and does not mind, Jimmy feels guilty nevertheless; "so he got a fiver out and handed it to Sharon", saying, "It's not every day yeh find ou' you're goin' to be a granda" (S, 11). The narrator's comment is instructive: "He'd just thought of that now and he had to stop himself from letting his eyes water. He often did things like that, gave away pounds and fivers or said nice things; little things that made him like himself" (S, 12). Like Joyce's Gabriel Conroy, Doyle's Jimmy Rabbitte Sr is a "well-meaning sentimentalist" who appears, eventually, to be something like "the pitiable fatuous fellow" Gabriel sees in his mirror (Joyce, 1976: 216–17). Jimmy Sr likes to like himself. To do this, however, he must often be less than honest with himself. As Sharon's condition becomes public knowledge and the rumour of the father's identity circulates, Jimmy's pride takes a beating and he begins to take his embarrassment out on Sharon. This leads to the climax of the novel, a confrontation in which Sharon pretends to move out, a masterful performance that successfully shocks Jimmy out of his "snotty" behaviour and eases the plot towards its comic-sentimental denouement.

St Veronica

A neglected character in critical discussion of *The Snapper* is Veronica Rabbitte. From Doyle's remarks, it is clear that in his representation of the effect of Sharon's pregnancy on her mother, he was making a point. He told White: "it's the mothers — the girls' mothers — who are the victims"; for while the pregnancy may rob the child's mother of her youth, it robs the pregnant girl's mother — who will take on much of the burden of the infant care and child-raising — of her middle age (White, 2001: 153–4). Doyle presents Veronica Rabbitte as a woman who is trying to break out of the rut and routine of her domestic life, who seems to be growing disenchanted with the quality of her life. During the opening scene, we are told three times how tired she looks and feels (*S*, 1, 2, 4) and the scene ends with Jimmy Sr slamming the door shut and leaving with Sharon for the Hikers Rest as Veronica climbs to her bed. Her fatigue becomes a character-motif, and gradually, we sense her exhaustion to be more than physical. Jimmy Sr refers to her "moods" and she does not seem a happy woman beneath the surface of her domestic routine.

Although Doyle does not delve far beneath that surface — or any other, for that matter — in the novel, and although *The Snapper* is, to be sure, a comic novel in style and form, Veronica figures as something like a ghost at the feast. Pierre Macherey has argued that

> For there to be a critical discourse which is more than a superficial and futile *reprise* of the work, the speech stored in the book must be incomplete; be-

> cause it has not said everything, there remains the
> possibility of saying something else, *after another fash-*
> *ion.* The recognition of the area of shadow in or
> around the work is the initial moment of criticism. . . .
> It might be said that the aim of criticism is to *speak the*
> *truth,* a truth not unrelated to the book, but not as
> the content of its expression. In the book, then, not
> everything is said . . . (Macherey, 1978: 82–3)

To a large degree, the success of *The Snapper* turns on its un-
conventionally amoral treatment of a narrative subject that
traditionally evokes a conventional engagement with moral
norms. Doyle himself has asserted that "A novel is a novel.
I'm not a priest or a moralist, and I try to write within reality"
(White, 2001: 171). Of course, this does not mean Doyle's
novels do not raise moral issues or that the characters and
their actions do not have moral dimensions. What it means is
that Doyle expects the reader to engage the issues, morally
or not, without any overt coaching from him. (Although, as
we have seen, Doyle's narrator *does* put his thumb on the
scales at times.) To read *The Snapper* from a conventionally
moral perspective would be to read it very much against the
grain of the work. But while I do not intend to do this in a
strictly Machereyan sense, I do think that the absence of an
explicit moral perspective in the novel paradoxically *overshad-*
ows much of the narrative in a way that ironically *highlights*
certain features of narrative structure, characterisation and
language in ways that fracture its comic patina.

Doyle actually wrote two plays while he worked on *The*
Snapper, and he wrote the second, *War,* as he was finishing
the novel. The play premiered in September 1989. Sharon's
counterpart in *War* carries the name of her friend, Yvonne,
the daughter of her baby's embarrassing father, and Veronica
should be seen alongside Yvonne's mother, Briget Finnegan.
The Finnegans are a much darker version of the Rabbitte
family. It is as if Doyle decided to siphon off the darkness

that we glimpse in Veronica's character at the beginning of the novel and put it into her double in the play, and to do the same with Jimmy Sr and George Finnegan, in order to guarantee the comedic form of the novel. Thus *The Snapper* is a novel in which the "unspoken" takes the form of the repressed as well as the "re-directed".

Veronica functions in the novel as a kind of choked choric voice: she introduces the theme of shame. Throughout the opening scene in the kitchen, Veronica speaks only when she is spoken to; she seems to be waiting for Jimmy Sr to say something that will put Sharon's condition in a framework that will orient the family to its new circumstances. Clearly, for Veronica, there is a moral as well as emotional *gravitas* in the moment, but just as clearly, this is not felt by either her husband or her daughter. Veronica supports Sharon from the outset, but she also tells her that what she has done is "not right" (S, 6). Sharon's lame reply — "I suppose it's not" — accentuates the differences between them. When Jimmy moves to end the scene by announcing "A man needs a pint after all tha'", Veronica is "shocked" and speaks up: "–Is that all?" Jimmy is nonplussed. When she tries to explain herself, she cannot find the words:

> –It's a terrible — Veronica started.
> But she couldn't really go on. She thought that Sharon's news deserved a lot more attention, and some sort of punishment. As far as Veronica was concerned this was the worst thing that had ever happened to the family. But she couldn't really explain why, not really. (S, 7)

Veronica's immediate response is a sense of moral wrongdoing: Sharon's behaviour "deserved . . . some sort of punishment". But as we are given more of her feelings and thoughts, we recognise that it is more a sense of shame than of guilt that is working its way into Veronica's conscious-

ness. What seems to hit her hardest is what Sharon's actions have *taken* from the family. To say that this is her
sense of family dignity or honour is perhaps to intrude too
much upon the character, but her inarticulate disappointment that Jimmy has failed to recognise that the moment
"deserved a lot more attention" — and presumably a different quality of attention, as well — suggests that what Veronica is feeling is very different from what the other two are
feeling at the moment. When she does speak, she utters a
commonplace whose banality conceals as much as it reveals:

> —The neighbours, she said.
> —Wha' abou' them? said Jimmy Sr.
> Veronica thought for a bit.
> —What'll they say? . . .
> —You don't care wha' tha' lot says, do yeh? said
> Jimmy Sr.
> —Yes. I do. (S, 7)

Sharon's riposte that "anyway, I don't care" (S, 8) is a moral
trump card, as far as Jimmy Sr is concerned: "An' that's the
important thing", he tells Veronica. But "Veronica didn't
look convinced". Nor does Jimmy's argument that young
girls are getting pregnant all around them carry much
weight. The bravado of his concluding "Fuck the neighbours"
gives her no comfort. "Veronica tried to look as if she'd
been won over. She wanted to go up to bed."

A gap opens between Veronica and the others at this
moment which remains for the rest of the novel. It is not a
rift or fissure but a subtle separateness that attends her in
every scene, even if only comically, as when she tells Jimmy
Sr to make his own cup of tea or rolls her eyes at his patho-
logical use of the f-word, or more ironically, as when she
proves a more effective defender of Sharon's honour when
she punches Doris Burgess in the nose. At the end of the
opening scene, Jimmy's parting joke, as he leaves with

Sharon, "Cheerio now, Granny" (*S*, 9), is not funny at all; it merely confirms the distance between his wife's sensibility and foresight and his own moral and emotional obtuseness.

Jimmy Sr is a disappointment to Veronica in the opening scene, and he fails again later when she asks him to explain to their younger daughters, the twins, Tracy and Linda, that what Sharon did was wrong. He equivocates; but his concern that any such unequivocal language might affect the twins' attitude toward the baby barely conceals his real reason for not wanting to have a scene with the younger children: he wants to get off to the pub. However, his conversational "end-game" does point the reader toward an understanding of how this novel is not just showing but also questioning the changes occurring in Irish society and culture as modernity challenges tradition:

> Jimmy Sr was standing up, ready to go. But he didn't want to leave Veronica unhappy.
> —Times've changed, Veronica, he said.
> —I suppose so, said Veronica. —But do we have to keep up with them?
> Jimmy Sr didn't like questions like that. (*S*, 49)

Jimmy Sr's reluctance to think deeply or at all about such questions makes his apparent "pro-modern", "liberal" attitude to the changing times suspect, not thought out but simply based on a suddenly convenient acceptance of new social mores. Nor should the reader conclude that Veronica is a closet traditionalist. She is questioning, not rejecting, the new ways: "Are they better for us?" is what she's asking. But Jimmy Sr doesn't like questions like that.

Sweating Perception: Jimmy Rabbitte Sr

As Doyle wrote more books, the Rabbittes started reading more books, from *Everywoman* in *The Snapper* to *Lord of the*

Flies and *Great Expectations* in *The Van*. At first Jimmy Sr is not much of a reader, nor is Sharon, who can manage only three pages a night and has difficulty with words like "sensuality" and "perception". Not to worry, though, for she can always ask her father to explain:

> –Wha's perception? Sharon asked.
> –Wha?
> –What's perception?
> –Sweat, Jimmy Sr told her. –Why?. . .
> –It says my perception might be heightened when I'm pregnant.
> –Yeh smell alrigh' from here, love, said Jimmy Sr.
> (S, 15)

By the end of the novel, Sharon's pregnancy will exercise Jimmy Sr in ways he has not been stretched before. But whether he sweats his way to greater self-perception is a matter for debate.

Jimmy Sr's apparent liberalism about sexual relations outside marriage does not extend to racial relations, however. During his questioning of Sharon,

> he thought of something and he had to squirt his tea back into the cup. He could hear his heart. And feel it.
> He looked at Sharon.
> –He isn't a black, is he?
> –No!
> He believed her. The three of them started laughing.
> –One o' them students, yeh know, Jimmy Sr explained. –With a clatter o' wives back in Africa. (S, 6–7)

Jimmy seems to find things African either frightening or amusing. Later, when Jimmy Jr jokes that their skinny pup,

Larrygogan, is from Ethiopia, "Jimmy Sr, Linda, Tracy and Sharon laughed but Veronica didn't" (S, 25). Jimmy Jr seems particularly amused by the plight of the Ethiopians, who become his generic term of reference for the poor and disadvantaged (S, 37), an attitude that repeats his father's view of "piccaninnies . . . in a refugee camp somewhere" (S, 38). Probably neither father nor son's knowledge of Ethiopia includes an Ethiopian proverb that is, ironically, very relevant to *The Snapper* and its themes: "Where there is no shame, there is no honour" (Honderich, 1995: 825).

Veronica's traditional sensibility is informed by a concept of guilt and feelings of shame. Sharon's character presents a new sensibility, new values. Guilt and shame simply do not figure in her character the way they do in her mother's. Jimmy Sr sides at first with Sharon only to behave later as if he is closer to Veronica's outlook; eventually, perhaps, he emerges with a third perspective, perhaps combining the better qualities from his wife's and daughter's outlooks in his newfound respect for the "fuckin' miracle" of childbirth (S, 179).

When Bimbo reminds Jimmy Sr, "Havin' a baby's the most natural thing in the world", Jimmy "loved" him for saying it (S, 66) because to be reminded of the "natural" or the "human" during a time of radical social change is comforting. However, such change destabilises these concepts by calling into question the values and assumptions they rest upon. This is how Sharon's pregnancy in *The Snapper* functions as an allegorical metaphor for the rapid social and cultural change that has characterised Irish life since the 1960s. Jimmy Sr is comforted, perhaps, by his intuitive understanding of Bimbo's cliché: there is a bedrock of basic human values beneath the circus floor of the contemporary which is immune to changes in technology and taste. For some, this bedrock is the rock of faith, but not for Jimmy Sr — nor for any of the Rabbittes.

Nor is it for Doyle himself. As he told White, "There's no religion in me own life, for certain. I've no room for it at all" (White, 2001: 168). And so its absence in his novels is a personal statement; he adds: "I wanted to get away from the clichéd view of Ireland. . . . Priests in working-class parts of Dublin are peripheral figures. . . . It's a new picture of Ireland" (White, 2001: 169). But what Doyle places at the centre of his picture of the new Ireland is the very traditional love of family. At the climax of the novel, this is what Jimmy Sr reaffirms against the self-love that brings on the novel's climax. Thus, for all its topical contemporaneity, *The Snapper* contains both the "new" and the "old" Irelands in a way that represents a society and culture in a state of troubled transition. This is what lies behind Veronica's question: what are we giving up by accepting the new values? Is it a worthwhile exchange? What are the new assumptions and what do they say about who we are becoming?

At the end of the novel, Jimmy Sr looks over his family, once again gathered in the kitchen: the twins have been in a ballroom dancing competition, Darren in a bike race, and in the background, he hears Jimmy Jr's voice over the radio, introducing James Brown's "Living in America". "We're some family all the same, wha'", he proudly remarks (*S*, 211). Then Sharon starts into labour. Despite its humour and comic resolution, there are too many ironies in *The Snapper* for the reader to share unequivocally in Jimmy Sr's proud complacency. The pointed allusion to the song title recalls the economic issues broached in *The Commitments* and is a reminder that forced economic migration remained a reality in the late 1980s and early 1990s.

Although Jimmy Sr does come to feel a sense of shame over Sharon, it is not clear what sense of honour this feeling might reflect. He is mostly concerned with "keeping face", with his image as paterfamilias. Ironically, he evades Veronica's request to have a serious talk with the twins about sex because "They'd only laugh at me. I'm only their da. Anyway, it'd sound better comin' from a woman, wouldn't it?" (*S*, 49).

Jimmy Sr's understanding of what it is to be a father-figure is grotesquely figurative, an antiquated macho self-fantasy that is as thin — and banal — as a beer-mat. When Veronica physically disciplines Les and he storms out of the house, she prevents Jimmy Sr from going after him, but "Jimmy Sr couldn't leave it just like that. He'd lost, in front of Darren, the twins, Sharon — them all. He was the head of the fuckin' house!" (*S*, 46). For Jimmy Sr, paternal authority and respect are all about "winning" and "losing" and these come down to keeping up appearances, which is not always easy to do because life's priorities can get complicated. When Bimbo tells him over a drink that George Burgess has talked about Sharon as "a great little ride" (*S*, 79), Jimmy will not confront the man because of his fear of being barred from the pub. The tears he sheds, which appal Bimbo, seem wrung from the conflict of values — his daughter's honour or secure access to his local — as much as from a sense of hurt. When he eventually does have a run in with Burgess, weeks later, successfully intimidating him without having to fight, as he walks away "He wanted to whoop. He'd won. . . . George looked like a beaten man. And that chuffed Jimmy Sr a bit more" (*S*, 97).

When the truth gets out that George Burgess is the father, Jimmy Sr and Veronica are mortified:

> —She could've had more taste, said Veronica.
> —That's righ', said Jimmy Sr, glad to be able to say it . . .
> He was feeling sorry for himself; he knew it. And now he was letting his eyes water.
> —It's only yourself you're worried about, Veronica told him . . .
> —I can't even go ou' for a fuckin' pint. (*S*, 120–1)

Jimmy Sr feels embarrassment, not shame. The significance of his daughter's pregnancy essentially boils down to its consequences for his drinking in social comfort (*S*, 125). Although no one believes Sharon's story about the Spanish sailor, Jimmy Sr allows himself to appear to be convinced that it is true by Bimbo, Bertie and Paddy. Bimbo speaks for them all: "–The way I see it, said Bimbo, –just cos Georgie Burgess ran away an' said he got some young one pregnant an' Sharon is pregnant, yeh know, tha' doesn't mean it has to be Sharon" (S, 134). The face-saving exercise is painfully — one might say, shamefully — dishonest, and yet deeply sincere. The core of the group's solidarity is each man's personal investment in their collective version of the male ego: if one loses face, everyone's stock is devalued.

The theme of shame, embarrassment and face comes to a comic-ironic head when Jimmy Sr's obsession with other people talking about him leads him to pick a fight at the pub. He goes home to Veronica with a bloody nose but she soon twigs that it is Sharon whom he wants to bear witness. "–Look, Sharon, said Veronica. –Your father's been defending your honour. Isn't he great?" (S, 145). But Sharon does not oblige him with the response he was expecting. As she berates him, "He was nearly crying. . . . He was liking himself now" and boasts "as long as yeh live in this house I'm not goin' to let bollixes like them say things about yeh" (S, 146). Then, when Sharon suggests she should move out, Jimmy Sr realises "Something had gone wrong". He has lost control of the scene. He is not "winning"; he is "losing". Unlike Bimbo and the lads, Sharon refuses to cater to her father's male ego, to let him use her as an excuse to feel sorry for himself. This forces the issue for him — and marks a new level in characterisation for Doyle:

> All Jimmy Sr had wanted was value for his nose-bleed. But something had gone wrong. A bit of gratitude was all he'd expected. He'd felt noble there for a while before Sharon started talking about leaving, even though he'd been lying. But she'd attacked him instead.

> There was more to it than that though. . . .
> Jimmy Sr stayed there, sitting in the kitchen. He
> was busy admitting something: he was ashamed of
> Sharon. That was the problem. He was sorry for her
> troubles; he loved her, he was positive he did, but he
> was ashamed of her. Burgess! Even if there WAS a
> Spanish sailor — Burgess! —
> There was something else as well: she was making
> an eejit of him. She wasn't doing it on purpose . . .
> That wasn't what he meant. But, fuck it, his life was
> being ruined because of her. . . . He was the laughing
> stock of Barrytown. It wasn't her fault — but it was
> her fault as well. It wasn't his. He'd done nothing. (*S*,
> 147)

This is one of the longest passages of focalised narration in
the novel. It is as close as we get to the representation of
the character's thought processes. But again, even with the
focalised narrator Doyle maintains an ironic distance from
the character. The moment has left Jimmy Sr "miserable":

> He'd admitted shocking things to himself. He'd
> been honest. He was ashamed of Sharon. He was a
> louser for feeling that way but that was the way it
> was. He could forgive her for giving him all this grief
> but it would still be there after he'd forgiven her. So
> what was the point?
> He did forgive her anyway.
> A bit of gratitude would have been nice though.
> Not just for himself; for Veronica as well. (*S*, 147–8)

Perhaps it would — especially for Veronica.
    In the figure of Jimmy Rabbitte Sr, *The Snapper* skewers a
certain type of Irish male. While he is an exaggerated
stereotype, it is the ironic excess of Doyle's characterisation
that generates his synthesis of comic entertainment and social commentary (see Paschel, 1998: 39). Even when he is

"honest with himself", Jimmy Sr confuses honour with ego-
tism, shame with embarrassment. He begins to wallow in
self-pity: he "knew he could snap out of it but he didn't want
to. He was doing it on purpose. He was protesting; that was
how he described it to himself." But he also knows that
"What he was doing was getting at Sharon. He wanted to
make her feel bad, to make her realize just how much she'd
hurt her father and the rest of the family" (S, 149).

At last, Jimmy Sr has arrived where Veronica began, but
his position is insincere because of the narcissism we know
underlies it. Sharon soon sees through him. She knows his
feelings have changed towards her but, as she thinks, "it was
a bit late to be getting snotty now" (S, 151). By echoing
Jimmy Sr's admonition to her at the beginning of the novel,
Doyle turns the tables on his main protagonist. Jimmy Sr's
behaviour is unwarranted; he is acting "above" himself, as if
he has lived a life and achieved a character that he has not.
He consciously sets out to make life miserable for Sharon at
home and ludicrously hides his spite behind a moral screen:
"it was for her own good. She had to be made to realize all
the trouble she'd caused, the consequences of her messing
around" (S, 153). This is his low-point in the novel. What
breaks the impasse between him and Sharon, and what frees
Jimmy from his delusion that he is being honest with himself,
is a ruse. Unfortunately, the ruse involves Sharon pretending
to be honest as well.

The Snapper pivots towards its comic resolution on a
performance of false contrition that ultimately elicits an act
of true contrition. An insincere daughter pretends to be
sorry before her self-absorbed father so that he can then
forgive her and feel good about himself. As we know, Jimmy
Sr likes to like himself. The scene is quite theatrical: Sharon
actually sits at her father's feet and disarms him with her
"softened" voice; the living room becomes a confessional,
with Sharon saying all the things she knows the pseudo-

patriarch wants to hear: "I've disgraced the family. . . . –I've been stupid . . . –An' selfish. I should've known" (*S*, 156–7). The *coup de théâtre* comes when she announces: "If I leave it'll be the best for everyone." Jimmy Sr protests; Sharon exits unmoved. Both have performed their parts perfectly. Sharon "wondered if it would work. . . . She wondered if she'd be here next week. God, she hoped so. She didn't want to move into a flat. . . . She didn't want to be by herself, looking after herself and the baby. She wanted to stay here so the baby would have a proper family and the garden and the twins and her mammy to look after it so she could go out sometimes" (*S*, 157). For his part, Jimmy Sr is exultant: "Victory: he'd won. Without having to admit anything himself, he'd got her to admit that she was the one in the wrong. She was to blame for all this, and he'd been great. She said it herself. . . . He'd won. He'd got what he wanted" (*S*, 157–8).

The only thing greater than Jimmy Sr's capacity for self-delusion is Sharon's ability to deceive and manipulate him. It is when she pretends to carry on with her intention that Jimmy Sr breaks down and admits "I've been a right bollix, Sharon. I've made you feel bad an' that's why you're leavin'. Just cos I was feelin' hard done by. It's my fault. Don't go, Sharon. Please" (*S*, 162). Sharon works her father through the full process: she gets him to admit that even if the baby "looks like Burgess's arse" he will love it. By the scene's end, she has indirectly admitted that Burgess is the father; but it no longer matters: "They were both laughing. They'd both won" (*S*, 163). Meanwhile, throughout this scene, Veronica has been downstairs watching Jimmy Jr rinse his vomit from the dishes in the kitchen sink.

Jimmy Sr does adopt a new attitude towards the imminent arrival of his grandchild, and there is much to be commended in that new attitude, but it is still the superficial — and probably temporary — adjustment of a profoundly superficial man. Basically, Jimmy Sr decides to become Sharon's child's surrogate father rather than its grandfather — to be, in short, the kind of father that none of his children has had. To show earnest, he starts up a cycling club for Darren and his mates, "the Barrytown Wheelies Under 14 squad", except he cannot manipulate the stopwatch — nor instruct them on the need for responsible "ridin'", one assumes. He decides to cut the grass in front of his house because "The new short grass would be a sort of announcement: there's a new man living in this house, so fuck off and mind your own business" (S, 193–94). In his own mind, "He was a changed man, a new man" (S, 193).

Of course, it is all little more than a fantasy in the end: he gives up trying to cut the grass and decides to pay Leslie to do it, and apart from badgering Sharon about her diet and hormones and other such things which he picks up from his library books, he is clearly relieved when she declines his offer to assist at the birth. Jimmy Sr may believe that "A strong active man in the house, a father figure, would be vital for Sharon's snapper" — and that even his own children, Leslie, Darren, and the twins, "were still young enough" for him to affect them differently, but the fact is Jimmy Sr possesses neither the will nor the know-how to be any different from what he is — a well-intentioned "oul' bollix" (S, 193). The reader realises that Jimmy Sr's "new man" project is simply more self-delusion as soon as we're told that he now thinks "There was more to life than drinking pints with your mates" (S, 193). Needless to say, this is an apocalyptic thought that never makes it past the portal of Jimmy Sr's lips. The film version makes this clear: where the novel ends in Sharon's hospital room, the film ends with Jimmy entering a pub across the street to celebrate the birth.

Doyle's technique prevents the reader from identifying closely with Jimmy Rabbitte Sr. Paradoxically, the humour that continuously amuses likewise keeps him at a distance. His sentimentalism and naive concern about Sharon and the baby at the end of the novel compose a satisfying denouement to the story, but overall his character remains unchanged and there is much about it that is repugnant. His casual racism, for example, points to an aspect of his "new picture of Ireland" that Doyle takes up in his writing after *A Star Called Henry*. Jimmy Sr's response to a TV news story about child abuse in the UK — "At least it's not goin' on over here" (S, 109) — is ingenuous, to say the least. Doyle may have been composing a comic scene when the family enjoy Jimmy Sr's riff on Jimmy Jr's crack about the Ethiopian poor, but the novel does not permit us to ignore the deeper irony in Veronica's quip — "You're not fit to be a father" (S, 38). Similarly, Doyle may have thought he was composing a summary scene of familial harmony at the end of the novel, as the family congregates in the kitchen to listen to Jimmy Jr on the radio, but when Jimmy Sr starts singing "–OH YEH-HESS — I'M THE GREAT PRE-TE-HENDER" (S, 210), the novel will not let us ignore the irony. To ignore it would limit the novel's range of achievement to a superficial entertainment whose overall significance was less than the sum of its comic parts.

Sharon: "A Modern Girl"

While Jimmy Sr holds centre stage in *The Snapper*, Sharon, the catalyst of the plot, becomes in a sense the antagonist in the novel. All the other characters have "supporting roles". (In Veronica's case, this "role" seems to become increasingly problematic, which leads to her growth as a character in *The Van*.) But if the novel ultimately asks us to see Jimmy Sr as more than a "Dub" Homer Simpson, what does the novel lead us to see in the character of Sharon Rabbitte? If Jimmy Sr and Veronica represent an older generation that is being hauled into a new Ireland whether it wants it or not, what does Sharon represent?

There is a difference between shame and guilt. The feeling of guilt comes after a process of self-examination and self-judgement; the person recognises and accepts their responsibility for some perceived moral or legal wrong-doing, feels remorseful, and desires to expiate the wrong done. The feeling of shame is just as deeply personal but it originates outside the self and is then internalised: the feeling of shame arises when the person believes they have broken a common trust, let others down, disappointed those whose respect they value. Like the feeling of personal guilt, shame is a consequence of an act of self-judgement, but the person who feels shame has judged themselves by looking at themselves from the point of view of the group or community. Anthropologists distinguish between shame-cultures and guilt-cultures; the former tend to be pre-modern, heroic-classical (although Japan is commonly described as a shame-culture in the modern period), while guilt-cultures are modern, developing out of the Judaeo-Christian tradition. Catholic Ireland obviously would be considered a guilt-culture.

While different, shame and guilt are also clearly linked. The feeling of shame should follow from the feeling of guilt, but Sharon feels neither when she discovers she is pregnant. What she feels is *embarrassed*, as does Jimmy Sr, later. Embarrassment has nothing to do with shame and everything to do with pride and vanity. Sharon's interiority does not extend beyond the surface of her mirror, Jimmy Sr's beyond imagined or reported insults. To describe them as shallow characters, however, would not be fully appropriate — if apparently accurate — because Doyle, either from choice or inability, does not construct any dimension of significant inwardness in the novel within which shallowness could be measured. He does not approach characterisation or narration in this way in the trilogy as yet.

Doyle juxtaposes the two scenes in which Sharon tells her friends and Jimmy Sr tells his. In the former, the most serious moment is not serious at all: "Jesus though, Sharon, said Jackie, but she was grinning. . . . –I know, she said. –It's terrible really" (S, 53). With Jimmy Sr, Bimbo is the only one who seems to consider the situation more than pub chat. He asks "Is she gettin' married?" Jimmy Sr's reply makes clear he is easy with Sharon's decision: "No . . . –Why should she? . . . Would you get married if you were tha' age again these days?" Bimbo's reply sets him apart: "I'd say I would, yeah" (S, 64). He seems to be the only one thinking about the *child's* future, and considering the title of the novel, it is odd that there is actually no serious considera-tion given to the "snapper" as a human being who will soon be among them. From start to finish, the significance of the child for Sharon and for her father is its embarrassing origins and the impact of those origins on their social images and their relationship. Right up to the closing lines of the novel, the baby remains an "it" in Sharon's mind.

This evasion of the baby's actual humanity is summed up in Paddy's question to Jimmy Sr: "Who did the damage?" (S, 65); in a sense much of the story that the novel tells is Jimmy Sr's and Sharon's attempts at "damage-control". At the pub with the lads, it is clear Jimmy Sr has not given much thought, if any, to the future. Paddy remarks that Jimmy Sr will be responsible for the baby's financial support, to which he replies: "I am in me hole. . . . –Hang on, though. Maybe I will be. He thought about it. –So wha' though. I don't care" (S, 65). Bimbo applauds Jimmy Sr's tentative discovery of his generosity and represents the commonsense view that the baby should be loved unconditionally. His pronouncement — "Havin' a baby's the most natural thing in the world" — strikes the moral-emotional keynote of the novel.

Yet the text itself does not allow the characters such an easy time of it. While Bimbo's common sense and basic hu-manity prepare the mood for Jimmy Sr's toast — "To Sharon, wha'" (S, 66), the mother-to-be is getting "pissed" in another room in the Hikers. (This seems to be the only way Sharon knows how to drink.) Intentionally or not, Doyle's narrative structure does not present Sharon in a very attractive light at this moment. Following the toast, the scene ends quite ambiguously. Bimbo says: "D'you know wha' Sharon is, Jimmy? . . . — Wha'? –She's a modern girl. –Oh good fuck, said Paddy" (S, 66–7). Immediately, the next section begins with a description of the "modern girl" lying in her bed, "a bit pissed. But not too bad", going over her night out and contemplating the consequences of her disclosure. "Fuck them. Fuck all of them. She didn't care. The girls had been great" (S, 68).

In a statement that bears on the theme of shame in the novel, Doyle says his intention with Sharon was to construct and evoke the sense of "this yawning big hole of embarrassment . . . and the knowledge inside that must be kept secret. The awfulness is as much the fact that the man is so inelegant — a friend of hers — not the Spanish sailor she creates. I suspect that it is not the first time she has had sex against the car when she has been drunk" (White, 2001: 151). By not recognising the *antagonistic* function of Sharon's character, Caramine White's construction of her as a "heroine" is particularly misguided. It also leads to the unintentionally comic formulation that "Sharon is an unwitting participant in her own maturation"; according to White, "the pregnancy itself had little to do with Sharon's maturation; the circumstances around it are what spark her growth" (White, 2001: 69).

One needs blinkers — and a peg on the nose — to see Sharon as "not calculating . . . extremely competent" and the victim of "something that could happen to anyone" (White, 2001: 64). We recognise Sharon's abilities as a "calculator" as soon as we are introduced to her and told that she had informed her mother of her condition before telling her father in order to have Veronica on her side. And her manipulation of Jimmy Sr toward the end of the novel, when she pretends to move out, is precisely calculated — down to enlisting her friend, Jackie, in a supporting role. She may be trying to bring the curtain down on Jimmy Sr's impersonation of a morally wounded father, but the charade within a charade only points up the empty moral bank balances of both characters. Too drunk to remember the act, Sharon, to her embarrassment, does remember who impregnated her. "It was mad, but she wished she'd had sex a lot more often. Doubts about the father would have been very comforting; lovely" (S, 43).

The irony of Bimbo's christening Sharon "a modern girl" cannot be ignored. If, by the phrase, is meant an educated, independent, self-reliant, competent woman, then Sharon is obviously anything but. (It could be argued, as well, that this primarily American cultural stereotype is generally not associated with the image of a pregnant woman so much as a woman "on the pill".) And by altering the idiomatic "modern woman" to "modern girl" Doyle's text draws attention to Sharon's difference from this media construct. But Bimbo's description does bring to the foreground the theme of modernity and cultural change. It is Bimbo who reminds everyone that unmarried daughters have been getting pregnant since time immemorial, implying that families have always accepted the situation as "part of life". Of course, the reader knows that the social history of illegitimacy is more complex than that — in Ireland as elsewhere. Bimbo's attitude represents an unreflective use of modernity and modernisation as, in a sense, both a new moral language and a metaphor of explanation to present this perennial situation in a non-"traditional" way, and in a way that condones it. The well-intentioned gesture should be connected to Jimmy Sr's glib remark earlier that "Times've changed" (S, 49) — and we should continue to hear Veronica's question in reply to both: "But do we have to keep up with them?" (S, 49).

According to White, Sharon is to be commended because she "refuses to humiliate herself because others may think her actions wrong" and because "By asserting her rights as an adult, she forces her parents — and the reader — to acknowledge those rights"; apparently, what we witness in Sharon's behaviour in the novel is the evolution of "a self-sufficient character" (White, 2001: 65). No one should expect Sharon to "humiliate herself because others may think her actions wrong", but what about her own sense of wrong? At no time in the novel does she engage in anything like moral reflection. Her experience and its consequences have absolutely no effect, for example, on her drinking habits. It is business as usual before, during, and presumably, after the pregnancy. Of course she has rights, but has she no responsibilities? What Sharon "forces" her parents to accept is that while living under their roof and eating at their table, she has a right to get drunk and pregnant and expect them to support — emotionally, financially and physically — the consequences of that right. Not once in the novel does Sharon give a thought to her mother's rights — or even, for that matter, her unborn child's as she drinks herself sick more than once during her pregnancy.

As for Sharon's "self-sufficiency", this does not extend beyond making her own way to her doctor's appointments. Sharon does not think as a "modern woman" when she quits her job out of frustration and discomfort, nor does she seem self-sufficient when, lying in bed in the mornings, she enjoys hearing the sounds of other "girls dashing to work" knowing "she wasn't one of them. It was brilliant" (S, 198). She doesn't worry about her lost wages. "She'd be getting her allowance after the baby was born and her daddy was going to give her some money every week, once he'd sorted it out with her mammy. She'd only have to stay in the house a bit more often and she'd be doing that anyway because of the baby. So it was great" (S, 198). Presumably, she would be back at the Hikers with Jackie in no time, upstairs from where Jimmy Sr would be downing pints with the Bimbo and the lads, while Granny Veronica stays at home minding the snapper.

Sharon's immaturity — her expectation and reliance on her "daddy" and "mammy" to provide her with an allowance — underscores Doyle's image of the family rallying around one of its own in unconditional love. The drama that results from Jimmy Sr's struggle to accept the fact that his grandchild has been sired by someone he does not like is hardly *high* drama, nor does Doyle play it so. It remains situation comedy from beginning to end. Neither Sharon nor Jimmy Sr possesses enough depth to make serious drama possible. There is never any convincing threat of serious emotional hurt or credible moral outrage. Far from it, morality, as such, seems part of a lost communal consciousness in the novel, vaguely remembered only by Veronica.

The fact that Sharon is bringing a child into the world goes largely unconsidered; her whole attention is focused on keeping the embarrassing identity of the baby's father a secret. "The baby was nothing" (*S*, 119); what concerns her most is that the identity of the father will make it difficult for her to continue with her usual social routine of drinking at the Hikers. The parallel between father and daughter is exact. Toward the end, Sharon suddenly does have what to most will seem like a long overdue "normal" thought: "She hadn't thought about what the baby would be like before; only if it would be a boy or a girl. God, she hoped it would be normal and healthy and then she nearly stopped breathing when she realized she'd just thought that" (*S*, 176). But it is difficult to reconcile Sharon's concern for the foetus with the image of her "pissed" and vomiting into her handbag just days before she delivers (*S*, 206).

The novel ends with Sharon's tears of laughter over her naming of her daughter: "Georgina; that was what she was going to call her. They'd all call her Gina, but Sharon would call her George. And they'd have to call her George as well. She'd make them" (*S*, 215). She names her child after its father as a joke. A joke the whole community will enjoy, of course, but it is not just at Burgess's and his family's expense. If shame derives from the sense of having "let down the side", Sharon's final act of independence is not so much a testimony to her indifference to that community — and even her family — as to the aggressive side of the narcissism that characterises her. The community may be laughing at her, but she will have the last laugh — even if it is at her daughter's expense. Doyle gives no sign that Sharon is any different at the end of the novel than at the beginning, except for being a few pounds lighter. The reader can see no growth in her character because we have no knowledge of her *before* her pregnancy and the image of her puking into her handbag days before she delivers does not suggest she is about to become a model new mother but, sadly, a somewhat conventional class stereotype.

Conclusion: "I don't think they lead meaningless lives at all"

> Meet the Fuck-its. But sure they're a gas. . . . Nobody gives out about Sharon being pregnant. It's all part of life's rich pattern. And, sure it's a bit of a gas, anyhow. Not all the time, mind: Sharon heaves into the toilet bowl, racked with morning sickness — an Irish fictional first? But mostly, nobody comes to any harm, really. There is no suffering, only the occasional nuisance. . . . There is a strong sense that the natives survive because they are good at heart . . . drawing directly on an essentially uncontaminated and uncodified moral-emotional core. . . . (George O'Brien, quoted in Paschel, 1998: 68–9)

George O'Brien's hostile review of *The Snapper* points to aspects of the novel which the foregoing discussion also singles out, but I want to conclude here in a way that makes clear that I do not share this negative view of Doyle's second novel. The heart of the issue behind O'Brien's remarks is Doyle's combination of unconventional realism, exaggerated stereotypes, and the conventions of traditional comic-romance. Clearly, the result for some is a superficial and gratuitously offensive realism. Shades of the *Playboy* riots gather; Synge's ghost coughs in the grave.

The Snapper is "offensive" but not in the sense of insulting as much as the opposite of "defensive". This second instalment in the Barrytown trilogy is an even more aggressive representation of Doyle's "hidden Ireland" than *The Commitments*. Doyle has emphasised that *The Snapper* is "not a sociological tract — it's a story about people. . . . A version of reality" (White, 2001: 153), but he is more than an urban naturalist. His concern with showing the persistence of "love and warmth and affection" (White, 2001: 154) in a family under pressure and also the particular pressures faced by the middle-aged wife who has already done her mothering but who is more or less forced by circumstances to pick up her daughter's responsibility is as moral as it is mimetic, an expression of a deeply felt set of values and a sensitivity to the everyday circumstances and sacrifices that curtail individual freedom and thwart personal desire. When challenged with the view that the lives of his characters in the trilogy are unvaryingly meaningless — "They get drunk, aren't educated, have meaningless sex, steal, watch too much TV" (White, 2001: 170) — Doyle turned the question back on the interviewer:

> What's meaningless about that? . . . So why don't they talk about politics? Talking about politics is about as meaningless as talking about sex or talking about football. I don't see any difference in a bunch of kids talking about politics or talking about Manchester United Football. It's just conversation — it's filling gaps. So their lives are not meaningless but are filled with meaning. Their conversation is not deep — so what, whose is? This conversation is not normal . . .

> we are not having a chat on the bus. But when you do
> have a chat on the bus, like when I was on my way
> here today, I stopped and chatted with the caretaker
> at the local school about the weather, and then later
> someone stopped me and we talked about a match
> that was on the telly last night. So these are normal
> conversations. That's what I wanted to record. In a
> lot of conversations, it's what they don't say that is
> more interesting than what they do say. I don't think
> they lead meaningless lives at all. (White, 2001: 170)

For Doyle, *real* meaning is found in social life and meaningful/
meaningless is relative and a judgement that is usually class-
based. To describe Sharon's life as meaningless is perhaps a
combination of middle-class or academic snobbery, and as
Jimmy Sr says, "there's no need to be gettin' snotty". That
being said, however, it does not mean that the "meanings"
we find in Doyle's representation of Sharon's life in *The
Snapper*, or of the lives of the characters in his other novels,
will or need be what Doyle intends. After all, eventually he,
too, is only another reader of his novels and their ultimate
significance in relation to the society they describe is something that is still to be debated.

The drinking scenes in the Barrytown trilogy, however,
are scenes in which Doyle carefully — and I would say, re-
spectfully and even lovingly — represents the social experience of his characters, the bonds, consolations, support, that
they draw from the relationships and conversations. Sharon
doesn't go to confession to tell her problem, she goes to the
pub and tells her friends. The effect is the same: she leaves
to begin the long and complex process of dealing with the
consequences of her actions in her own way. It may not be
everyone's way, but there is a difference between being
"moralistic" and "moral". There is a moral dimension to
Doyle's depiction of lives of connection and alienation, coherence and confusion, suffering and endurance, warmth and

love. *The Snapper* does not condone Sharon's behaviour, but neither does it condemn it. That is not Doyle's view of the novelist's responsibility; nor, in his view, presumably, should a reader need or expect direction in that respect. The novelist's responsibility is "to write within reality" (White, 2001: 170) and to be truthful in the fullest sense to the world of appearances but also to the world of silences, to record both what is said and what is not said by his characters.

The latter occurs, interestingly enough, in Doyle's use of the TV in his fiction, particularly in *The Snapper*, *The Van*, and *Paddy Clarke Ha Ha Ha*. Watching the "telly" in these novels is a social-familial ritual; it is not as passive an activity as most "high-brow" commentators would suggest it is; family members react to and remark about the images, and their reactions elicit further reactions and comments. The TV programme functions as a catalyst for self-expression and "coded" communication within the family group and particular relationships within the family. (The same applies in the social situation of the pub, in *The Van*, when the crowd watches the 1990 World Cup soccer match between Ireland and England.) Declan Kiberd has noted that, following the institution of the national service in 1962, "Television became the device by which a long-repressed community learned once again how to talk to itself; and in the process that society was forced to confront much that had long gone unadmitted" (Kiberd, 1996: 567). Doyle domesticates the point. In at least two important senses, Doyle's generation of novelists is the first generation of "TV-novelists" in that their world-views have been informed — as well as formed — by television as both a medium and a socio-cultural phenomenon. The ways they write about their society build — and rely — upon that foundation of openness which Kiberd suggests the medium introduced, and their approach to narrative technique and characterisation has been influenced by the conventions encountered in weekly TV series, sit-coms and serials.

As Doyle understands and practises fictive realism at this point in his career, dialogue is the main armature of his narrative machine. What the characters say to each other reveals them to each other, to themselves, and to us. Doyle wrote two plays while he was writing *The Snapper,* and the novel often seems more theatrical than dramatic. Like *The Commitments,* it is structured with unnumbered sections which cohere individually as "scenes", the vast majority of which are "interiors" — the kitchen, living room and bedrooms of the house in Barrytown; the lounge and bar in the Hikers Rest; the Burgess house. What few exterior settings there are — Sharon on the street approaching her house, Jimmy Sr in front of his house — still possess the static quality of a theatrical set. Moments of insight or change occur *in* and *through* conversation.

All of this contributes to both Doyle's strength and weakness as a novelist in the trilogy. The emphasis on dialogue becomes the hallmark of his style, "Barrytownese" his "trademark" voice. Along with the characters, the humour, idioms, slang, vulgarity and profanity provide the novels with their distinctive élan. But if this need not limit the scope of exploration, it does limit the scope of expression — and ultimately, limiting how something can be said will curtail what can be said. An important critical question for Doyle's development will be the extent to which he develops his characters' interiority, either by constructing a greater balance between, in a sense, dialogue and soliloquy, or by developing a more expansive narrator.

In *The Snapper,* the traditional plot of a pregnancy "out of wedlock" becomes a means of exploring the changing nature of contemporary Irish society. Doyle may have intended to write a story in which a family emerges from the challenge faced by this "crisis" by refusing to accept it as a crisis, by affirming familial loyalty and "folkish" commonsense as well as new liberal-secular attitudes as opposed to the guilt-laden and hypocritical Catholicism of traditional Irish society. But the novel itself is not that simplistic. It shows more subtly the more complex trade-offs that occur when a society evolves away from longstanding traditional mores.

Ultimately, what connects *The Snapper* most dramatically to its time is the theme of guilt and shame it so obliquely, and problematically, unfolds. The confusion between shame and embarrassment encountered in varying degrees amongst the Rabbittes may reflect a confusion in Doyle himself, but it is only partially correct to say there is no sense of guilt or shame in Barrytown (Donoghue, 1994: 4). Even Sharon's embarrassment has a trace of shame in it and Veronica does seem to feel that Sharon is guilty of wrongdoing. What is true is that these characters' sense of embarrassment is a version of shame that is not a consequence of traditional *Catholic* guilt. The sincere shame Jimmy Sr feels as he apologises to his insincere daughter derives from his realisation that he has jeopardised his family by being selfish; he has allowed his pride to bring the family to a point where its unity is about to be broken, the circle breached. Doyle's concept of shame — what he himself refers to as "embarrassment" when he explains that he intentionally constructed Sharon's predicament around "this yawning big hole of embarrassment" (White, 2001: 151) — is strictly *secular*. For Doyle, the concept and experience of "family" are religious and spiritual. In *The Van*, Jimmy Sr begins to feel ashamed when his unemployment means he can no longer provide for his family and he feels guilt over his behaviour with Bimbo. Darren, too, feels guilt over his feelings and behaviour toward his father. But this is a guilt and shame generated by the bonds of family and friendship.

The real "yawning big hole of embarrassment" in *The Snapper*, "the knowledge . . . that must be kept secret", paradoxically, by being paraded in comic disguise, is the absence of a traditional religious-spiritual ethos in Doyle's fictive world and "new picture of Ireland". This is the point where this novel impinges most painfully upon its historical and cultural moment and where certain readers will be most challenged. For Doyle, the Catholic Church — Catholicism — is no longer central but marginal in his "Ireland". It would be a mistake to see this as part of a class perspective, however; rather, it would seem generational. The Catholic Church and institutional religion belong to a history that Doyle finds irrelevant or bogus, a backward-looking, hypocritical and constraining tradition that simply does not figure in the contemporary lives he has chosen to represent.

The Snapper continues Doyle's representation of an Ireland in change. After the focus on issues of self-esteem and individual identity among the younger generation in *The Commitments*, the second novel in the trilogy shifts focus to the working-class family and the challenges it faces when it attracts the attention of the community. The tension between individuality and the need for acceptance continues in Doyle's characterisations of Jimmy Sr, Sharon and Veronica; however, with Jimmy Sr and Veronica, Doyle begins to explore the theme of modernisation and cultural change more explicitly as a challenge to an older generation set in its ways and unclear as to how to move beyond them. He will complete this in the final novel in the trilogy, in which the challenge to Jimmy Rabbitte Sr's self-esteem comes not only with his unemployment, but with his wife's budding ambitions, Darren's academic success, and the positive developments in Jimmy Jr's life after he leaves home.

Chapter Three

Messin' with Normal: *The Van*

If unemployment remained the "biggest single economic problem facing Ireland" in the 1990s (Gray, 1996: 337), then *The Van* concludes the Barrytown trilogy showing Doyle with his finger on the pulse of his society at the beginning of that decade. The novel opens in the weeks before Christmas, 1989. Jimmy Rabbitte Sr has been out of work for some time and the effects on the family budget, his self-esteem, and his relations with his wife and children are beginning to tell. He soon has a companion in misery, however, when his best friend, Bimbo Reeves, is made redundant from his job at the bakery. When Bimbo decides to buy a derelict chip van with his redundancy money and go into business for himself, with Jimmy as his partner, Jimmy thinks he can finally see some light at the end of the tunnel. However, the business partnership, while initially successful, is doomed. Often hilarious, *The Van* is not a comic novel. Obstacles are overcome, the fallen pick themselves up, and the future looks promising. But the novel ends with a divorce, not a marriage; as Doyle says, "their friendship is over. . . . It'll never be the same and that is a big loss" (White, 2001: 158). And of course, it ends with Jimmy unemployed again, but this time the cause is not the Irish economy but his *character*.

The last novel in the trilogy is, paradoxically, the most outward-looking in its action and settings and yet the most inward-looking in terms of characterisation. Doyle himself described it as "a darker book by necessity" than *The Commitments* and *The Snapper* — "there's no room for a little sequel at the end" — and his remarks seem even darker than anything the novel itself intimates because he implies that Jimmy Rabbitte Sr is probably never going to have secure employment again: "It's just [for] a lot of people in Ireland — unemployment is a reality for the rest of their lives. They missed the modern education system and they're not qualified to do anything else. They missed the re-education threshold. Basically, the rest of their lives is filling their days. There's hundreds of thousands of people in Ireland like this" (White, 2001: 154).

The themes of education and of the new economic order are central to *The Van*, which presents a segment of the Irish population that enjoyed little more than the droppings of the Celtic Tiger. Considering Doyle spent so many years as a secondary school teacher, the presence of education in his fiction should come as no surprise. Education, modernisation, and identity are clearly interconnected for him. *The Van* points to divisions opening in Irish society as it modernises by enacting them on the level of family relations and friendship. A rift opens between Jimmy Rabbitte Sr and his son, Darren, which is more than just the age gap that is to be expected during adolescence. Darren studies for his "Leaving" (*V*, 276) throughout the novel and at the end we learn he achieves honours standing in all his subjects. Veronica, who has been taking two Leaving Cert subjects at night school, is also successful. Jimmy hears of his family's achievements as he lies in bed nursing a hangover so bad "he couldn't even get up to congratulate them" (*V*, 277). What the novel intimates is that Jimmy — and men like him — are being left behind.

Doyle's explanation of Jimmy Rabbitte Sr's condition in terms of his belonging to a "bad luck" generation is not the whole story, however; the novel itself shows that even when old dogs learn new tricks, they are still the same old dogs. Jimmy Rabbitte Sr is a victim of his times but even more a victim of his character. When discussing *The Snapper*, Doyle had admitted that "There were at least two roads one could have gone, the bright and the dark" (White, 2001: 152) and that he consciously chose the former. In a sense, *The Van* represents his going back to the road not taken in the previous novel. Joseph O'Connor has remarked that "there is a darkness in Doyle's world . . . which existed long before . . . *Family* ever hit the screens" and points to Doyle's sympathetic imagination of the situation of a child in "an unhappy marriage" (O'Connor, 1995: 143) in *Paddy Clarke Ha Ha Ha*. But the darkness in Doyle's fourth novel really emerges from the end of the trilogy. The breakdown in the Clarke family is a fuller and, admittedly, richer treatment of the issues and pressures Doyle first depicts in the Rabbitte household, and even the violent Charlo Spencer of *Family* can be glimpsed erupting, Hyde-like, from a drunk Jimmy when he suddenly feels vicious toward Veronica (*V*, 41).

The longest novel in the trilogy, *The Van* is also the most complex. Doyle wrote it, in his own words, "very quickly" (Costello, 2001: 88), finishing it in December of 1990 (White, 2001: 152). Structurally, this is the most carefully plotted of Doyle's first three novels. Being "on the labour" (*V*, 67) has Jimmy Rabbitte Sr's nerves wearing thin and his self-esteem plummeting. As Christmas approaches, even Veronica cannot hide her frustration with him. But Doyle complicates his protagonist's financial anxieties by giving him a mid-life crisis as well.

Doyle does this so subtly that Jimmy's growing interest in having a fling with another woman emerges realistically as an expression of the desperate state of his self-esteem rather than of boredom with Veronica, and by setting the scene of his would-be philandering where he does, Doyle integrates the episode's significance both with his characterisation and his themes of modernisation and identity in an Ireland and a Dublin of increasingly "big divides" between the rich and the poor, the working and middle classes (Paschel, 1997: 158). Jimmy's pathetic attempt to pick up a woman in a wine bar on Leeson Street occurs on the night he and Bimbo try to patch up their seriously damaged friendship; the pick up and the patch up are both fiascos and Jimmy's sense of failure and frustration lead to behaviour that is at times ugly and vicious, silly and childish, conniving and cruel.

Overall, the form of *The Van* is, in a sense, cruelly ironic towards its protagonist because the theme of change which is evident in the stories of all the characters — from Jimmy Sr through Bimbo and Maggie, Veronica, Darren and Jimmy Jr — reveals Jimmy Sr's ultimate collapse, as a childish man into his wife's maternal embrace, to be the consequence of his inability to change, to grow. Ironically, the childish Jimmy Rabbitte Sr lacks what all children have in abundance — imagination.

The Man in the Iron Mask: Jimmy Rabbitte Sr

While Veronica is working on *The Lord of the Flies* for her night course, Jimmy tries to read *The Man in the Iron Mask*. Veronica's attention to her studies impresses him but also seems to make him insecure. He tells himself — and her — that perhaps he will enrol next winter. No one should have any great expectations in that regard, however, because Jimmy is too fixed in his ways and his character to embark on any such project. Doyle's use of Dumas's novel is ironically significant in that respect, for Jimmy Rabbitte Sr is a man trapped behind a mask of male identity whose strength may seem to be an iron-hard resilience in the face of adversity, but whose real weakness is its inflexibility and resistance to change, as well as its contradictory facets in respect to work and unemployment. In *The Snapper*, we see Jimmy struggle with this mask, fiddling with it as the consequences of Sharon's pregnancy and the identity of the child's father begin to pinch his social face. In a sense, however, all he ends up doing is repositioning himself beneath it, regaining a desired comfort-level given the new circumstances; the mask remains. In *The Van*, the mask leads to Jimmy's deterioration because unemployment proves a much more serious blow to it and the "fit" between it and the man beneath.

Jimmy hides behind the mask of the tough guy. Although he is going to pieces inside, he pretends to others that nothing is bothering him. After Jimmy Jr gives him a fiver to buy a few pints, Sharon catches her father upstairs in a kind of trance, appearing "miserable, and small and kind of beaten looking" (*V*, 30). He denies there's anything wrong, but in fact he was having a kind of panic attack: "He'd thought his teeth were going to crack and break; he couldn't get his mouth to open, as if it had been locked and getting tighter. And he'd had to snap his eyes shut, waiting for the crunch and the pain" (*V*, 30–1).

Jimmy's unemployment has been thrust upon him and with it a "role" he must perform — that of the man living on the dole, looking for work but not too strenuously, enjoying the leisure, living within his means, concerned but not in any overt, "unmanly" way. Although he has been more active around the house than usual, Jimmy spends most of his time babysitting his granddaughter, Gina, playing pitch 'n' putt, or hanging out in the ILAC Centre. His drinking routine at the Hikers has been cut back to two nights a week, and he has to plan his arrival to be close enough to closing that he will not be required to buy more than one round. The gift of the fiver from his son is welcome but hurts his pride: "he'd been really grateful . . . delighted, and at the same time, or just after, he'd wanted to go after him and thump the living shite out of him and throw the poxy fiver back in his face, the nerve of him" (*V*, 31).

Daily life is full of reminders of either his "fallen" condition or his failure as a "provider" and as Christmas approaches, he and Veronica begin to argue over what they will have to do without. (*V*, 15). Eventually Jimmy accuses Veronica of blaming him for their situation (*V*, 56).

Worse than Jimmy Jr's generosity, however, is Darren's cruel wit. An apparently innocent bit of dinner-table slagging about Jimmy's physical shape turns nasty and hits him hard:

> Jimmy Sr wasn't going to take that from him, not for another couple of years.
> He pointed his fork at Darren.
> —Don't you forget who paid for tha' dinner in front of you, son, righ'.
> —I know who paid for it, said Darren. —The state.
> Jimmy Sr looked like he'd been told that someone had died. (*V*, 102)

He leaves the table and doesn't recover until he has a few pints later with his buddies. He recalls that "For a while after the dinner, he'd had to really stretch his face to stop himself from crying. And that passed and he'd thought he was going to faint . . . (*V*, 105). Jimmy interprets Darren's behaviour as "a phase young fellas went through, hating their fathers" (*V*, 105), but what Darren is going through is more complex than this. Already wondering "why Darren wouldn't talk to him properly any more" (*V*, 7), Jimmy cannot see that it is because Darren is beginning to imagine a different way of being in the world than that modelled by his father. He still enjoys his friends on the soccer team but at the same time is starting to think their carry-on about drinking "was a bit fuckin' childish though; not the slagging, the subject matter. The theme" (*V*, 23). His application of that final, school-derived word to his friends' behaviour signals his difference from them, but more importantly, from his father, for whom the subject of drink is a favourite "theme". Darren is dating a young girl, Miranda, to whom he is attracted physically but also because "she had a mind of her own" (*V*, 25). What Jimmy sees when he meets her is that she's "a ride" and more attractive than any girl he ever dated (*V*, 53).

Doyle explicitly uses the language of change to dramatise the growing difference between father and son. When Darren disagrees with Veronica over her support of the school policy that forbids the twins wearing make-up to classes, he says: "If everybody had that attitude . . . nothing would ever change" (*V*, 47). Jimmy doesn't know how to react to his son's budding independence: "He liked hearing Darren talk like that, but he was being cheeky as well; to his mother. There was something about the way Darren spoke since his voice broke that left Jimmy Sr confused. He admired him, more and more; he was a great young fella; he was really proud of him, but he thought he felt a bit jealous of him as well sometimes; he didn't know" (*V*, 47). Throughout the novel, Darren is seen doing his homework, studying, serving drinks at the Hikers rather than drinking them, sitting and chatting with Miranda in the front room, helping out Bimbo and Jimmy in the van, and finally, successfully earning a place at Trinity. While he still obviously loves Jimmy, there is a sense that Darren clearly does not want to end up like him.

The changes in his relationship with his son only exacerbate Jimmy's sense of a topsy-turvy world. Routinely, in *The Snapper*, Veronica went up to bed while Jimmy went off to the Hikers. In *The Van*, this is reversed. Veronica goes off to her night classes and Jimmy goes up to read on their bed (*V*, 16–17). Veronica emerges as a much stronger character in *The Van*. Like Darren, Doyle develops her in relation to the themes of change and education. Even more than in *The Snapper*, she begins to assert her impatience with Jimmy, but now a new independence as well. When he mentions that he is thinking of going to night school with her next year, she knows immediately she does not want that: "she wanted to do it on her own, even going up to the school on her own and walking home; everything" (*V*, 16). When he asks her to put off studying to watch Gina, so that he can play golf, she refuses outright (*V*, 27). Like Darren, Veronica still loves Jimmy, but a distance has opened between her and her husband that was not there in *The Snapper*. She does not avoid reminding him that he is not bringing enough money into the house for their needs and is not averse to hitting below the belt when provoked. When a drunk Jimmy stumbles in the bedroom trying to take off his shoe and wakes her:

> Veronica sat up and turned on the lamp beside her . . .
> —Can you not tie your laces properly yet?
> And she put his foot in her lap and got going on the knot. He nearly fell off the bed turning for her.
> —You're useless, she said. —You really are.
> For a split second he was going to straighten his leg quick and put his foot in her stomach, the way she spoke to him like that; for a split second only. Not really. (*V*, 41)

What upsets Jimmy is not Veronica's treating him as a child — she does this elsewhere, for example, when she offers to buy him "an Airfix" for Christmas (*V*, 51); he likes that. What strikes a nerve is her calling him "useless", because he has already been thinking this of himself (*V*, 28) and to hear it from Veronica hurts.

Doyle's characterisation shows Jimmy's inner problems to be a consequence of an identity that is as much constructed for him as by him. His culture infantilises him as much as it encourages Veronica to mother him. If drink reduces the man to the grown-up infant that Veronica is expected to nurse, so, too, does unemployment. For the working-class Jimmy Rabbitte Sr, gainful employment is the prime guarantor of his manhood; the job and wage signify to himself, his family, and society that he is a "real man". His dispensing of fivers for Choc-Ices and Twixes in *The Snapper*, sudden cash for Veronica to buy something for herself in *The Van*, and so on, is also the only way he knows — when sober — how to express his love for his family. When he stops bringing money home, every week of unemployment sees him drawing on his short reserves of self-confidence and self-worth. Eventually, even his wife and family begin to act as if he is a patriarch on credit.

Both Jimmy and Veronica are victims of the same patriarchy in the sense that both are subjected to the limited subjectivities their culture offers them. There is an economic dimension to the construction of gender (see Jeffers, 2002: 11) and Jimmy is as much a victim of the patriarchal and working-class construct of "man–father–husband" as Veronica is of "woman–mother–wife". This construct is the "iron mask" of his working-class male identity that Doyle shows is beginning to suffocate him in his present circumstances:

> There were days when there was this feeling in his guts all the time, like a fart building up only it wasn't that at all. . . . there was a little ball of hard air inside in him, getting bigger. It was bad, a bad sort of excitement, and he couldn't get rid of it. It was like when he was a kid and he'd done something bad and he was waiting for his da to come home from work to kill him. He used to use his belt, the bollix. . . . Waiting for it was the worst part. If he did something early in the day and his mother said she was going to tell his da, that was it. . . . He'd go through the whole day scared shitless. . . .
>
> And that was how he sometimes — often — felt now, scared shitless. And he didn't know why. (*V*, 53–4)

Jimmy may not understand the connection between his current anxiety and his memories of his father's discipline, but Doyle's text associates the unconscious guilt Jimmy feels because of his unemployment — it is as if "he'd done something bad" — with his equally unconscious sense he must be punished for it by the patriarchal society — the "machine at work" (*V*, 53) — which dispenses and disciplines identity. This passage, moreover, shows how Jimmy's mask of manhood ironically sustains the "child" within him that Veronica — and the rest of his family — are expected to indulge. It is no coincidence that Jimmy describes the "guilty" pleasures he enjoys with Bimbo when Bimbo joins him on the dole — including the pleasure he takes in the fact that Bimbo has lost his job — with a metaphor from childhood: "He couldn't wait to get up and out in the mornings, like a fuckin' kid on his summer holliers" (*V*, 86).

Messin' with Normal

When Jimmy accepts Bimbo's offer of partnership in "Bimbo's Burgers", he takes on a challenge he is incapable of meeting. It is a challenge to his character that results in any openness to change he may have being closed off by a more powerful fear of change, and in which any capacity for growth he may have is stifled by his intractable narcissism. If Jimmy seems to grow in character in *The Snapper*, in *The Van* he regresses. The final image of him sitting on the side of his bed and plaintively asking Veronica, "Give us a hug . . . will yeh. I need a hug" (*V*, 311), is a poignant but pathetic emblem of his defeat.

Jimmy Rabbitte Sr is not a malingerer. Doyle addresses any such misunderstanding of the character when he has Jimmy recall the pleasures of a well-earned cup of tea during his labours as a plasterer (*V*, 46). Jimmy has become so demoralised by his unemployment that he has begun to "settle" *for* it as well as into it.

> You got used to it. In fact, it wasn't too bad. You
> just had to fill your day, and that wasn't all that hard
> really. . . .
> The worst part was the money, not having any of
> it . . .
> Unless, of course, he got work between now and
> then.
> Only, it was easier to cope if you didn't think
> things like that, getting work. You just continued on,
> like this was normal; you filled your day. (*V*, 67–8)

After the resignation, after the insulation from false hope
and bitter disappointment, *like* normal becomes normal.
When Bimbo loses his job, Jimmy "felt good . . . felt happy"
(V, 87), not because he took any pleasure in his friend's mis-
fortune but because by sharing his situation Bimbo made it
feel even more "normal" and not his fault. Jimmy's strenuous
objections to Bimbo's application for a job at MacDonald's
are a compellingly realistic confusion of a frayed and fragile
sense of dignity and a robust capacity for self-delusion:

> Jimmy Sr knew Bimbo; if he was offered one of those
> jobs he'd take it. . . . And Veronica would ask him
> why he couldn't get a job like Bimbo — but that
> wasn't the reason he wanted Bimbo to cop on to
> himself. Veronica knew that if Jimmy Sr ever got of-
> fered proper work he'd jump at it, even if it was less
> than the dole. He couldn't let a friend of his — his
> best friend — allow himself to sink that low. A man
> like Bimbo would never recover from having to
> stand at a counter, wearing a uniform that didn't fit
> him and serving drunk cunts and snot-nosed kids
> burgers and chips. (*V*, 97)

The obvious dramatic irony here is that this is precisely
what Jimmy himself ends up doing in Bimbo's van. What we
need to recognise about Jimmy Rabbitte Sr is not that he
would rather continue as "a man of leisure" (*V*, 96) on the

labour than take a job, but that he sees himself as a plasterer and Bimbo as a baker: that's what they do, that's what they are, and the idea of settling for any job is too unsettling to Jimmy's sense of who and what he is. His reluctance to encourage Bimbo to buy the van should be seen in the same light; it derives less from his fear that Bertie is taking advantage of his friend than from foreseeing — correctly, as it turns out — that the purchase will change them in ways Jimmy does not want to be changed.

"Jimmy Sr didn't know why he didn't want Bimbo to buy it. It just sort of messed things up, that was it" (*V*, 118). "Messing things up" is an important motif in the novel. Later, as the business begins to run smoothly and Jimmy gets used to the money coming in, he starts to feel irritated by Bimbo's wife's business initiatives; he wants to complain to Bimbo but "He didn't want to do anything that would mess everything up" (*V*, 228). The problem is that what he would be "messing up" is a situation in which he has been taking advantage of his friend — and Jimmy seems to know this, if not admit it (*V*, 228).

After Bimbo puts him on a salary, Jimmy admits to himself that "It was his own fault in a way; some of it. He should have bought the half of the van when he'd thought about it. . . . He thought he'd been cute, deciding not to bother; there was no need. He'd just been greedy" (*V*, 278). Jimmy's lack of self-knowledge compounds his reluctance to be honest with himself, and both feed what seems to be a deep-seated fear of change, of "messing up" a situation he has gotten used to — even if it is not completely to his liking.

The irony is that while the money from the business has solved Jimmy's problems on the home front — "Back to normal then, said Jimmy Sr –Wha'. –Yep, said Veronica" (*V*, 176) — the partnership destroys the friendship. To try to patch things up, Jimmy proposes "A night on the batter" (*V*, 249). His hope is that "Away from the van, and Maggie, and the pressure and the rows and all the rest of the shite, they'd have their couple of pints and a good laugh, get locked, and they'd be back to normal, the way they used to be; the way they'd stay" (*V*, 251). But by this point Jimmy is not sure what he wants or why he wants it. Their "night on the batter" ends with him battering Bimbo with a toilet door and the two of them going home in the back of a taxi without speaking to each other, sadly foreshadowing "the way they'd stay" at the end of the novel.

"Am I makin' sense?" Jimmy Sr in Nighttown

The full significance of Jimmy and Bimbo's great adventure on the southside depends on seeing it in relation to an earlier scene at the Hikers where Jimmy and Bertie lecture Bimbo on who should be allowed to drink where. The obvious relation between the scenes shows the growing disorder within Doyle's protagonist. When Jimmy leads Bimbo down into the wine bar, he is descending to his personal low-point as a character in the novel. This is where he loses sight of whatever moral compass has guided him and starts thrashing about in a desperate bid to strike out for some illusion of a self he could never be. The plan to recover their former bond is doomed by the fact that Jimmy is no longer the man who was once Bimbo's best friend. For all his fear of change, Jimmy Rabbitte Sr, sadly, has changed and Doyle constructs his protagonist's gradual dissolution by adapting the pop culture convention of the mid-life crisis.

The clues appear in the earlier scene at the Hikers in a way that makes Jimmy's behaviour in the wine bar all the more ironic. As he joins Bimbo and Bertie at the Hikers, he notices "three couples, all young and satisfied looking" and voices his disapproval: "They should be upstairs" (*V*, 32). This leads to a discussion in which the easy-going, democratic and hospitable Bimbo defends people's right to drink

wherever they want — as long as they're "not messers" (*V*,
34). Bertie argues that the people Jimmy has singled out
have no more right to be in the Hikers bar than he, Bimbo
and Jimmy would have to be in a southside disco: "It's not
our scene, said Bertie. He swept his open hand up and
across from left to right, and showed them the room. –This
is our scene, compadre, he said. –Fuckin' sure, said Jimmy
Sr" (*V*, 35). While the catalogue of their "scene" that Bertie
proceeds to give is humorous, Doyle's point is serious. Bertie and Jimmy are really talking about how the Hikers not
only contributes to their sense of who they are, but confirms and sustains it. As Bertie talks, Jimmy thinks:

> He only came up about two times a week these days
> . . . but it wasn't the gargle he was dying for: it was
> this . . . the lads here, the crack, the laughing. This was
> what he loved. (*V*, 34)

This is more than an attempt to explain working-class "pub
culture" after the critical reaction to *The Snapper*. The issue
is a sense of identity based on knowing who you are by
where you belong: "We fit here, Bimbo, said Bertie –An'
those fuckers over there should go upstairs to the Lounge
where they fuckin' belong" (*V*, 36). The inclusive-exclusive
outlook that Jimmy subscribes to here reflects his need for a
stable social milieu in the microcosm of the pub to counter
the unstable world he experiences outside it. By the end of
the novel, Jimmy will have broken his own rule, of course, in
actions that reflect his increasing confusion as to who he is
and where he belongs, and his anxiety over where his life is
— or more likely, is not — heading.

When Jimmy reminds Bertie that he was once in a disco
bar, however, the integrity of the speaker — if not that of his
viewpoint — is seriously impugned, and their interrogation of
Bertie about his experience in Limerick leads into the topic
of extramarital sex — a different form of being where you

don't belong. Jimmy suspects he knows why Bertie would have transgressed his own rule but is not sure. Unlike Bimbo, he'd like more details. Bimbo wants to believe Bertie is "only messing" (*V*, 40), fooling around about "fooling around". But this kind of "messing" is connected to the earlier senses of the idiom, meaning upsetting an order or equilibrium — "messing things up." The contrast between Bimbo's and Jimmy's attitudes towards Bertie's story points up Jimmy's "wandering eye" in the novel (he is wondering if *he* could do what Bertie claims to have done) and foreshadows the contretemps that will unfold later on their night out.

Doyle carefully constructs this development in Jimmy's state of mind. In the section immediately following this, Veronica speaks to Jimmy as if he was a child and he almost hurts her (*V*, 41). At Bimbo's house on Christmas day, he is attracted to Vera, Bertie's wife, noting how unlike Veronica she is (*V*, 58, 60, 63). On a sojourn to Dublin city centre he sits by the Ha'penny Bridge and "counted fifty-four great-looking young ones going by in only a quarter of an hour; brilliant-looking women now, and all of them dressed beautifully, the height of style" (*V*, 69). When Jimmy Jr announces his engagement to Aoife at dinner, Jimmy Sr questions him about his future mother-in-law: "Jimmy Sr really did want to know what Aoife's ma looked like. He didn't know why; he just did — badly" (*V*, 102). He takes to watching the young factory girls who walk by his house to and from work (*V*, 111). At the Hikers, when Bertie starts talking about an attractive sixteen-year-old shop-girl, Jimmy joins in so enthusiastically he suddenly becomes self-conscious: "He wondered if he should have been talking like this, if he was maybe giving something away" (*V*, 76–7).

On their night out, Jimmy is and is not himself and the night spins out of control because of the confusion within him. He has suggested the excursion as a way for them to get "back to normal, the way they used to be" (*V*, 251) and yet as they stand drinking in the Palace, Jimmy's motives seem more revolutionary than recuperative: "Jimmy Sr wanted something to happen" (*V*, 253). He *thinks* that what he wants to happen is to "click with a woman" (*V*, 256), but what he really wants is to feel better about himself and his prospects. That is what is behind his desire to return to the way things were between himself and Bimbo — before the van, before he became unemployed, before the thought of the future made him "scared shitless". Unlike their relationship at work, on their night out Jimmy is in charge. When he proposes moving on to another bar, Bimbo replies "Okay . . . You're the boss," and Jimmy thinks: "That's right . . . I am the boss. It had always been that way. . . . Jimmy Sr'd always been the one who'd made the decisions" (*V*, 254) in their relationship. But his unemployment and the van had "messed" with all that. Now, Jimmy wants to assert his "natural" right to be the "boss" in their relationship, seeing as Bimbo, quite unfairly in Jimmy's mind, has become his boss in the van. Jimmy is not out for sex, he simply wants his self-respect back:

> What he wanted was to see if he could manage a young one or one of these glamorous, rich-looking, not-so-young ones. He'd back off once he knew it was on the cards; actually getting his hole wasn't what he was after at all — he just wanted to know if he could get his hole. . . . (*V*, 256)

When Jimmy fantasises taking "one of these kind of women" to a hotel, it seems the idea of the hotel room excites him more than the prospect of sex: "Jimmy Sr had never been in a hotel room" (*V*, 257). Once again, the focalised yet ironic narrative voice has fun with Jimmy. He is/isn't serious, he would/would not take the opportunity, and so on, but behind the fun is the clear sense of Jimmy's unhappiness. The man in the iron mask is struggling to remove the mask. Ignored by a passing woman, he thinks "All he needed was a bit of practice.

If she came back in an hour or so he'd get off with her no problem. Not that he'd want to get off with her. . . . He was just messing . . ." (*V*, 256). Jimmy is "just messing" because he is so "messed up" himself. He doesn't want to "mess everything up" (*V*, 228) between Bimbo and himself, but in "messing" (*V*, 265) with the women in the wine bar, Jimmy risks "messing everything up" in his life. When he suggests going on there after closing time, it is clear that he — and Bimbo — know what Jimmy is hoping for: "Jimmy Sr's heart was loafing his breast plate. So was Bimbo's" (*V*, 261). Jimmy knows it is not in Bimbo's nature or character to do what he is implicitly proposing, but he badgers him to go along with him because what Jimmy is really out to do is to re-establish the former hierarchy in their relationship; that's what getting back to "the way they used to be" means for Jimmy.

By taking the lead and showing what a "ladies' man" he is, Jimmy is not out to be unfaithful to Veronica but to be faithful to his sense of his own self-value, and to put Bimbo back in his place. In the wine bar, when they finally get two women to talk to them, Jimmy becomes very aggressive very quickly. This is the Jimmy Rabbitte Sr we saw in *The Snapper* — the man who needs to win (see earlier, *V*, 137). When he sees Bimbo getting on like a house on fire with Anne Marie, he becomes desperate to one-up him with Dawn. He tries to impress her by buying the wine — "If he didn't get his hole after forking out twenty-five snots for a poxy bottle of wine he'd —" (*V*, 267) — and by telling her he's the "boss" of a catering business. But when Bimbo tells Anne Marie about the van and she tells Dawn, Jimmy looks and feels a fool. Doyle is particularly cruel to his protagonist here. He has him expose himself as a crass, vulgar, insecure "gobshite", but most ironically, and paradoxically, he has Jimmy show the falsity of his earlier belief that people should stick to their "scene" by showing him to behave so "out of place" in the wine bar not because it is "out of his class" but simply because Jimmy Rabbitte Sr is a crass, vulgar, insecure "gob-shite". Even with a wad of cash in his pocket, Jimmy remains what he is, which has nothing to do with being working-class. The contrast between Jimmy and Bimbo in the scene — and throughout the novel — makes this point; Bimbo is as authentically working class as Jimmy. The ironic relationship between the episode in the southside wine bar and the earlier scene at the Hikers strengthens the connections between Jimmy's sense of identity, the erosion of his self-confidence and self-esteem over the period of his unemployment, his interest in other women, his observations of the growing gap between the rich and the poor, the working class and middle class in the city, those who are benefiting from the economic changes sweeping over Ireland and those who are not (*V*, 68–9, 254), and the sense that he is being left behind by Jimmy Jr, Darren, and even Veronica, and becoming an "outsider" in his own city. When he looks over and sees "Bimbo and Anne Marie . . . chewing the faces off each other", "He wanted to cry, and go home. . . . –His nickname's Bimbo, he told Dawn." But there's no way Jimmy's going to win this night. When Dawn finally rebuffs him, Jimmy thinks: "he was fuckin' hopeless" (*V*, 271), and the thought recalls his earlier self-judgement, when he felt defeated by Dumas: "He was useless; couldn't even read a book properly" (*V*, 28). Out of frustration he follows Bimbo into the toilet and tries to hurt him. When he attempts to explain his actions, he blames Bimbo for spoiling his chances, but Bimbo hits back with the truth: "–You messed it up yourself. It's not my fault if — if she didn't like yeh, is it?" (*V*, 273).

Throughout the novel, Doyle presents Bimbo as the "straight shooter" (if not someone with the sharpest arrows in his quiver) and here his response to Jimmy's usual self-deceit is right on the mark. The often apparently "simple" Bimbo is by far the more mature, sensible and decent man — as well as being the better friend. Jimmy's night of messing has brought their friendship to a new low-point, not "back to normal" as he'd hoped, and Bimbo's patience finally gives out:

> —Is it not good enough for you now? Bimbo asked him.
> —It's not tha' —
> —It pays your wages, Bimbo told him.
> Jimmy Sr was lost.
> —If you don't want to work in it, said Bimbo, —you can leave any time yeh want to. — An' good riddance. . . .—I'm sick o' you an' your bullyin' —, sick of it — (V, 273)

The poignancy of the moment derives in large part from one friend misunderstanding another who does not understand himself. "Jimmy Sr was lost" sums up the climax of *The Van* as well as the condition of the protagonist at the novel's end.

As in *The Snapper*, Doyle uses dramatic contrast between scenes to accentuate their thematic significance. The "morning after" the Leeson Street fiasco has an ebullient Veronica delivering the news of Darren's — and her own — Leaving Cert successes to a hung-over Jimmy, who is too incapacitated to come down and congratulate his son. It is a shameful moment and he knows it (V, 276), and it leaves Jimmy feeling even more "useless" (V, 277). But it is the way the juxtaposition of the night before and the morning after brings the themes of education, change, and self-transformation to the foreground in conjunction with the character of Jimmy that should be recognised: "Darren would be going to university now. He'd applied for Trinity, Jimmy Sr thought it was, to do something or other. University. For fuck sake. And Veronica —" (V, 277). Darren is moving on. Veronica is doing something for herself. And all Jimmy can think of is trying to "get a leg over" with a married primary school teacher he has met in a wine bar. The juxtaposition of these scenes accentuates the narrowness of his horizons, his lack of imagination. When he tries to get out from under the iron mask, he is simply accepting another mask his class and society offer him; and his impersonation of a middle-class businessman is as incompetent as his macho-masculinity is inauthentic.

The final phase of Jimmy's "messing" (*V*, 286) with Bimbo sees him become increasingly petty, childish and obstructive. He poisons the atmosphere in the van, takes "breaks" when customers are lining up for service, leaving Bimbo to carry on alone, and insinuates that he is going to join a union. But after he "acts the prick" (*V*, 283) like this, Jimmy comes to realise, ironically, that he has truly "lost" because Bimbo is enjoying acting like a boss with him (*V*, 283–4). Jimmy seems unable to stop himself from trying to destroy what he and Bimbo have built up:

> He'd the best of both worlds now; his days to himself and a job to go to later. He got a good wage on Thursdays, and he'd none of the responsibilities. The hours weren't bad, just a bit unsocial. He was a lucky fuckin' man; he had no problem believing that. He believed it.
>
> So he really couldn't understand why he felt so bad, why at least a couple of times a day, especially when he was hungry or tired, he was close to crying. (*V*, 284)

As in *The Snapper*, Jimmy sees himself as the aggrieved party: "He was lonely. That was it. . . . Lonely. It was like he'd learnt something, worked it out for himself. He even smiled" (*V*, 284–5). The smile brings tears. Depressed, he begins to feel even more sorry for himself. Like a stubborn child, convinced he is in the right and everyone else in the wrong, Jimmy holes up in his room where he is "safe enough" to cry without being seen or heard. Ironically, while his money worries have gone, Jimmy finds himself back where he was before Bimbo bought the van in terms of his state of mind:

> There was a ball inside him, a ball of hard air . . . It
> nearly hurt sometimes. It made him restless, all the
> time. . . . And he knew there was nothing physically
> wrong with him, even though he could feel it. And
> he knew as well that he'd felt this way before; it was
> kind of familiar, definitely familiar. He couldn't re-
> member exactly —. But when he'd noticed himself
> feeling this way, tight and small and exhausted, he'd
> recognised it immediately. (*V*, 285)

The language echoes the description of him as "miserable,
and small and kind of beaten looking" (*V*, 30) when Sharon
discovers him in his bedroom after Jimmy gives him the fiver.
But whereas his unemployment beat him down before, he
has only himself to blame for his current malaise.

Towards the end of the novel, the metaphor "lost" is as
important as the idiom "messing". Jimmy feels he has "lost"
his way at the end of the night out with Bimbo; he feels he
has "lost" to Bimbo in the van war; and finally, he feels he
has "lost" Bimbo as a friend. When the Health Board inspec-
tor shuts down the van operation, Bimbo accuses Jimmy of
informing on him. Then the physical violence that has always
been just below the surface in Jimmy erupts. When Bimbo
hits back at him, Jimmy thinks "This was terrible. They were
coming up to the end" (*V*, 303), but that doesn't come until
Sharon arrives with Gina. Bimbo yells at her and Jimmy goes
for him: "there was no mending anything now" (*V*, 305).

Not that Bimbo does not try to patch things up between
them, or at least understand what went wrong. Unable to
fight any more, they go for a pint, but when Bimbo asks
"Wha' happened, Jimmy? . . . It took Jimmy Sr a while to understand. —Fuck off, would yeh, he said. He didn't care what
had happened anymore. It was over and done with. He'd no
time anymore for that What Happened shite" (*V*, 307–8). For
Jimmy Rabbitte Sr, it seems, the unexamined life is not worth
thinking about. And although the drunken Bimbo apologises

abjectly and begs him to come back as a full partner, he refuses and "acts" the aggrieved party to the bitter end. Even after Bimbo has "killed" the van by driving it into the sea, he rejects his overtures. Jimmy's "Forget it, pal — I've learnt me lesson" (*V*, 309) is the most ironic line in the whole trilogy, for Jimmy Rabbitte Sr is shown to learn very little over the course of *The Snapper* and *The Van* — other than how to peel potatoes and make a mediocre batter.

Conclusion: "A Naay-Shun Once Again"

A striking feature of the Barrytown trilogy is the way the vivid present that preoccupies each novel is disconnected from any significant — or significantly represented — past, and the future is either specifically goal-defined (a recording contract, giving birth, finding work) or only vaguely suggested. Doyle's characters' consciousness of time is as circumscribed as their physical movement within Barrytown itself. Other than James, no one in *The Commitments* has any long-term plans or goals. While Darren seems to be on his way out of Barrytown, eventually, and Veronica is doggedly working — as Jimmy Jr would say, "to be different . . . to do somethin' with [herself]" (*C*, 6), the image of the van stuck in the sand and slowly disappearing beneath the incoming tide seems a grim emblem of Jimmy Rabbitte Sr's situation and prospects.

The Rabbittes represent a traditional urban working-class Irish family in the late 1980s caught in the meltdown of the stable economic and social order that historically defined their individual and collective identities. The economic changes that come to victimise Jimmy are offset by the new educational advantages available to his children, just as his own inability to change is accentuated by both of his sons' determination to make different lives for themselves. Jimmy Jr figures in *The Van* most obviously as an image of the inversion that sadly has occurred in their roles. Jr supplants Sr as he gives his father drinking-money and makes plans for his marriage to Aoife — a woman very unlike his mother in her ways (*V*, 29). Although Sharon and the twins seem to have chosen to follow in their father's small footsteps (*V*, 49), their mother, at least, seems to want more from life than Jimmy is prepared to settle for — or more precisely, to want more from herself.

The Van ends on a sour note; the humour does not soften our sense of Jimmy's evident smallness and his overwhelming limitations as a man. He is narcissistic, spiteful, hypocritical, conniving and cunning. He takes advantage of Bimbo by turning his strengths — his innocence, honesty, simplicity, and decency — into weaknesses. Doyle's text is unequivocal. The final image of the man-child begging his wife-cum-mother for a hug is deep-fried bathos. One wonders how soon it will be before St Veronica crosses that threshold of boredom with her domestic martyrdom which will find her looking back at someone she suddenly realises she has left behind. It is not that Jimmy's character is childish or adolescent that is important; it is that it is arrested. He is the only family member in the trilogy who proves he has reached his limits and is standing still, while the others are moving on — including, of course, his creator.

In time, the comic dimension of the Barrytown trilogy, as entertaining and as integral to the success of all three novels as it is, will recede in relation to the novels' other qualities. It is the increasingly rich, complex and dark body of characterisation and plot upon which the comedy floats that makes Doyle's first three novels central to any critical account of the "new wave" in Irish fiction at the end of the twentieth century, and which makes them important as both entertaining and disturbing reflections of a society and culture in transition.

In *The Van*, much more than in either of the previous novels, Doyle not only includes references to the larger world of contemporary politics — to the Guildford Four and the collapse of the Berlin Wall, for example — but he points more explicitly to what he has described as the "big divides" opening up in Irish society, evident as much in the broken streetlights of Barrytown (*V*, 31) as in the over-crowding in the Rabbitte household (*V*, 42) and the government's "Action Pack for the Unemployed" that Jimmy sees advertised but, significantly, unavailable in the ILAC Centre library (*V*, 13).

The division that Doyle draws repeated attention to in his novels is that between the north and south, but it has nothing to do with the thirty-two counties and everything to do with one city. In fact, the issue of "one Ireland" seems to be a non-starter for Doyle. The nationalistic dimension of the 1990 World Cup episode in *The Van* is played for humour and treated ironically — "It was great for business . . ." (*V*, 176). The significance of the episode seems to be that nationalism is simply another mask people subject themselves to, even though in this instance, it is a mask that allows Jimmy Sr to tell Jimmy Jr that he loves him, something he could only do under the influence of drink and under the cover of a collective expression of emotion (*V*, 182). But that seems to be Doyle's point. The only national party that could attract Jimmy Rabbitte Sr's attention would have to be a piss-up, not a political party — like the celebrations after the Irish win over Romania. The significance of this episode in the novel, as with so much in Doyle's narrative technique, also derives from the anti-climax it sets up. "And then they got beaten by the Italians and that was the end of that" (*V*, 183). Soccer-fever is as illusion-fraught as any other fever; the euphoria is as ephemeral as Jimmy's and Bimbo's partnership. National identity is insignificant in comparison to identities that derive from family, class, and generation — the identities that centre Doyle's characterisation.

The economic divide between working-class and middle-class Dublin that Doyle points to in *The Van* is evident when he has Jimmy notice the difference between the wealth and confidence exuded by the young people he sees on Grafton Street and what he sees in his own community: "Not like the young ones in Barrytown; these young ones were used to money. They were confident, more grown up; they shouted and they didn't mind being heard — they wanted to be heard. They had accents like newsreaders" (*V*, 254). This contrasts sharply with what he knows about the problems with Barrytown youths drinking and out of control at the seafront (*V*, 81), the pick-pocket he watches lift a woman's wallet (*V*, 89), the "knacker kid, a tiny little young fella, crouched in against the granite all by himself, with a plastic bag up to his face . . . sniffing glue" (*V*, 190), the language the young children use to them at the van (*V*, 232), but most powerfully, it contrasts with "The Living Dead":

> There was a gang of them that hung around the Hikers carpark, young fellas, from fourteen to maybe nineteen. Even in the rain, they stayed there. They just put their hoodies up. Some of them always had their hoodies up. They were all small and skinny looking but there was something frightening about them. The way they behaved, you could tell that they didn't give a fuck about anything. When someone parked his car and went into the pub they went over to the car and started messing with it even before the chap had gone inside; they didn't care if he saw them. Jimmy Sr once saw one of them pissing against the window of the off-licence, in broad daylight, not a bother on him. Sometimes they'd have a flagon or a can of lager out and they'd pass it around, drinking in front of people coming in and out of Crazy Prices, people that lived beside their parents. It was sad. When they walked around, like a herd migrating or something, they all tried to walk the same way, the hard men, like their kaks were too tight on them. But that was only natural, he supposed. The worst thing though was, they didn't laugh. All kids went through a

phase where they messed, they did things they
weren't supposed to; they smoked, they drank, they
showed their arses to oul' ones from the back window on the bus. But they did it for a laugh. That was
the point of it. It was part of growing up, Jimmy Sr
understood that; always had. He'd seen his own kids
going through that. If you were lucky you never really
grew out of it; a little bit of kid stayed inside you.
These kids were different though; they didn't do anything for a laugh. Not that Jimmy Sr could see anyway. They were like fuckin' zombies. When Jimmy Sr
saw them, especially when it was raining, he always
thought the same thing: they'd be dead before they
were twenty. Thank God, thank God, thank God
none of his own kids was like that. Jimmy Jr, Sharon,
Darren — he couldn't have had better kids. Leslie —
Leslie had been a bit like that, but — no. (V, 187–8)

This is the longest paragraph in the novel. (Nor is it the end
of The Living Dead; Doyle describes in detail one of their
assaults on the van (V, 189–90, 241).) If Barrytown has a
heart of darkness it is the Living Dead, schoolteacher Doyle's
greatest nightmare — a lost generation of urban youth. The
only other social issue to receive more attention than this in
the novel is unemployment. The Living Dead have parents,
presumably, and Jimmy's rumination about these kids opens a
messy can of socio-cultural worms. The fact that Bertie's son
was going in this direction and that Jimmy's son, Leslie, seems
to have gone even closer, insinuates a disturbing irony into
the passage. Jimmy's denial — "Leslie had been a bit like that,
but — no" — may be just that: *denial*.

Jimmy is visibly troubled when Bertie and Paddy are aggressively disrespectful to the guards outside the Hikers (V,
85–6), but he does engage in illegal barter with Bertie in The
Snapper and does not even think to get *off* the labour once he
starts bringing hundreds of pounds home from working in the

van. This leads back to the question of Jimmy as a "fit" father that was raised in *The Snapper*. Eventually, it may be that the cumulative effect of all the ironies in the Barrytown trilogy far outweigh any conscious intention Doyle may have had to use the books to celebrate working-class culture. This is not to say that the books ultimately compose a satire of that culture, its values and perspectives; far from it. But it does suggest that there is a facet of Doyle's representation of the Rabbittes — and particularly of Jimmy Sr, and perhaps of Sharon — that forms a *critique* of their mores, values and behaviour.

The characterisation of Jimmy Rabbitte Sr in *The Van* is Doyle's most complex in the trilogy because it is so rounded and because of the greater interiority provided by the focalised narrator. Jimmy emerges as a character with strengths and flaws but most importantly, as a character whose strengths and flaws the reader is able to understand. If a more critical image of the protagonist emerges, Doyle has constructed a solid enough figure that he can bear the scrutiny without being reduced to a single, unambiguous moral value.

Through the contrast between Jimmy and Veronica in *The Van* — a contrast begun in *The Snapper* — the last novel in the trilogy expresses Doyle's sense of a growing divide between the genders in contemporary Irish society — a theme that will come to centre his next two novels. Again, it is important to recognise that this division emerges from economic and class issues, which in turn, feed into the issue of identity. *The Van*, too, shows individuals being formed through the dialectic of personal and collective loyalties, individual and group integrity — the need to belong and be accepted, and the need to be different and free to become whatever one is capable of becoming.

Jimmy's unemployment in *The Van* is a metonym for the economic changes and conditions occurring in Ireland during the 1980s, in the same way that Sharon's "illegitimate" pregnancy in *The Snapper* is a metonym for the erosion of traditional social and cultural values. The van may not be a symbol of "the valiant illusions of Barrytown" (Fitzgerald, 1991: 16), but there is a sense in which the hilarious yet sad story of "Bimbo's Burgers" is an allegory of the Thatcherite ideology of self-help and independent initiative that western governments subscribed to during the period (see Appelo, 1992: 15). People have to learn to walk before they can run and Doyle shows economic toddlers being allowed to jump into the race before they're ready and without any support. However, it would be imperceptive to see *The Van* as strengthening the stereotype that "the working-classes cannot take care of themselves and need to be led by people outside the working-class community" (Paschel, 1998: 100). Jimmy and Bimbo are represented as childish men mothered by their wives, but this has nothing to do with their working-class marriages; it has to do with their characters, their wives' characters, and the relationships that have developed between them. With Bimbo *and* Jimmy, Doyle also shows generous, hard-working, self-sacrificing, loving, family men. Similarly, Doyle represents much that is to be praised about the world of the Rabbittes and Reeveses, from the "religious" centrality of the Hikers to the strength of the family bond, as well as much that is flawed and clearly getting worse. The view that Doyle's representation of Barrytown and its inhabitants romanticises this segment of contemporary Irish society and culture has less to do with a close reading of the novels than with extra-textual cultural politics.

Doyle describes himself, his family's class background, and his generation in the same way and with the same language in all his major interviews (Paschel, 1996; White, 2001; Costello, 2001); in a sense, he seems to be constructing a personal myth. He describes himself as one of "hundreds of thousands of people who occupy a grey area between . . . working class and middle class. . . . the products of free education . . . introduced [in] the late 1960s [and] the first of our families to go

to university" (Paschel, 1997: 151). He believes this in-
between-ness is a source of strength for him as a writer:
"when I'm sitting down to write I feel quite familiar in both
these camps, the working class and the middle class (Paschel,
1997: 151); "it's that grey area that most of my work inhabits"
(Costello, 2001: 92). Growing up "with a foot in each class"
placed him in "a useful position . . . as a novelist" because
"People who have grown up solidly working class seem to be
hopelessly lost in a different version of reality. Whereas being
from a grey area, you seem to be a little more street-wise"
(White, 2001: 178). This explains, perhaps, why Jimmy Rabbitte Sr comes across as being very adept at finding his way
around the streets of Barrytown, but is lost when he crosses
"enemy lines" (V, 13) and ventures south of the river. Doyle's
remark not only suggests that there may be a narrowness, a
limitation, built into his characterisation, but also why.

It is not necessary to adopt a psychoanalytic or narrowly
autobiographical approach to his fiction to observe the
oblique mirroring that seems to occur when Doyle's representation of the Rabbitte family is juxtaposed with his remarks about his own family background. Doyle's breaking
from his career and identity as a successful secondary schoolteacher and his reinvention of himself as a novelist link him
imaginatively to Jimmy Rabbitte Jr's generation and what he
describes as its energy and self-confidence. But in the same
way that he contrasts Rabbitte *père et fils* in terms of those
qualities, saying Jimmy Sr lacks "his son's energy or resources
or education" (White, 2001: 154), Jimmy Sr's paralysis is an
extreme version of the in-between-ness or "greyness" that
Doyle describes as his own condition, having crossed from
his working-class origins to the solidly upper-middle-class life-
style of the internationally successful novelist-filmmaker.

In *The Commitments*, the real objection that Jimmy has to
Dean's turn to jazz is not musical or ideological, but social.
He is put off more by the fact that Dean is reading *The Ob-*

server. The problem is not that Dean is becoming an individual but that he is outgrowing his roots. It might be said, then, that in as much as Doyle is representing aspects of his own class background in his novels, through his writing he is also "negotiating" his changing situation in a changing society. This, too, is what makes his fiction so significant in relation to the "new Ireland" of the 1980s and 1990s.

Doyle told Costello that he enjoys alternating between writing fiction and working on films because "It's nice to get out . . . and to negotiate with people and to choose who is going to act the parts" (Costello, 2001: 90). In both the fictive and the "real life" worlds of the author, "negotiating" has to do with moving between or bridging worlds and classes. The difference between Jimmy Rabbitte Jr and Jimmy Sr is that the latter does not have the will, energy, or character to "negotiate" his way into the new Ireland, which his son has done. In *The Van*, Jimmy Sr's excursion to the southside is a fiasco; his "negotiations" with everyone — from bartenders to women to his best friend — are dismal and demeaning failures.

Doyle's turn toward character with *The Snapper* does not represent a divergence from a path so much as the curve in his evolution as a novelist that was latent from the start. The change in tone from the first to last novels in the trilogy is a consequence of the shift from what could be described as a broadly mimetic narrative intention to a more pointedly character-driven fiction. Doyle told Costello that he considers character more important than plot (Costello, 2001: 96) and admitted that, after *The Commitments*, he wanted his second novel to be "more intimate" (Costello, 2001: 88); that he wrote *The Van* because "the father was taking over *The Snapper*"; and that *The Woman Who Walked into Doors* originated while he was writing the last episode of the TV series, *Family*, and he suddenly "felt strongly that [Paula] had an awful lot that she could say . . . and I could imagine her sitting down when she had free time . . . and she would start writing and explore her past" (White, 2001: 156). Doyle's growing interest in Jimmy Sr in *The Snapper* signalled the change in direction for his fiction.

The tension between the mimetic and the expressive, between "depicting a reality" (White, 2001: 54) and giving voice to a character, is a reflection on the level of style and form of the thematic dialectic between the group and the individual which is a constant in Doyle's fiction. Beginning with *The Commitments*, his novels increasingly depict individuals coming into conflict with their communities or the ethos of the group from which they take their identities, particularly the family.

In *The Commitments* and *The Snapper*, it is a character's discovery and assertion of their individuality that precipitates the narrative crisis and provides the overall shape to the narrative form. There are a number of moments in *The Commitments* in which the enterprise Jimmy Rabbitte Jr has built is threatened when someone in the band begins to assert his or her individuality, but it is Dean's gradual disenchantment and his confession to Jimmy that playing in the band "doesn't stretch me. . . . It's limitin'" (*C*, 142) which is most significant. In *The Snapper*, Doyle presents a similar process but inverts it in his representation of Jimmy's egotistical crisis brought on by Sharon's pregnancy. The support he takes from his drinking buddies ironically only confirms his fundamental weakness of character, a weakness that the changing circumstances of his life will continue to prey on in *The Van*.

In the last novel of the trilogy, Bimbo's efforts to make a go of it with the chipper are a reprise of Dean's desire to escape the initially liberating yet ultimately "limitin'" identity afforded him by membership in the band. Jimmy's increasing discomfort with his best friend's ambition is a reflection not only of his own limited horizons but of a fundamental fear of change, a fear which in large part derives from his lack of imagination. Unlike Jimmy Jr, who eventually admits that he sees Dean's point, Jimmy dares not follow Bimbo's lead and attempt to fashion wings from chip bags and fish batter in order to fly out of the nets of routine and habit. At first unconsciously, but gradually more and more intentionally, Jimmy sabotages not only his friend's dream, but ironically and sadly, both their friendship and his own potential for change. This is perhaps the saddest aspect of his situation at the end of *The Van*.

The Barrytown trilogy has an hour-glass shape. Doyle told White that "the storyline [of *The Van*] parallels *The Commitments*, instead of a band it's a small business enterprise which falls apart at the end" (White, 2001: 154). The parallel is also an inversion, however, in tone — *The Van* is harsh and unambiguously pessimistic, *The Commitments* hilarious and indefatigably optimistic — and in the way each novel treats the dialectic of individual and group. In *The Commitments*, the band implodes as individuality in all its forms — creative, destructive, egotistic and erotic — wreaks its hilarious havoc; but there is a generosity in the young people (not to deny their obvious self-concern) that is perhaps also an expression of their self-confidence (or it may be vice versa) and that does not perceive independence as a threat. In *The Van*, however, individuality and independence, while they evoke a combination of mockery, vandalism and patronage from the community, draw resentment, anger and spite from the main character. It is true that humour and humanity pervade Doyle's first three books, but that does not mean that they gloss over the darker features of contemporary Irish life or conceal the mixture of light and shadow that make that life both complex and rich. It is this coincidence of light and dark that makes all Doyle's novels distinctively his own, and deeply, rather than superficially, realistic.

Chapter Four

Growing Pain:
Paddy Clarke Ha Ha Ha

Doyle won the Booker Prize for *Paddy Clarke Ha Ha Ha*, which to date remains the only Irish novel to win the prestigious prize. Its popular and critical success, as well as the international audience that the prize brought him, consolidated his reputation as the pre-eminent novelist of the "new Ireland" of the 1990s. But while the comic realism that makes the trilogy so entertaining continues to ground Doyle's narrative style, after three novels, two plays and two screenplays, Doyle was a much more experienced writer and *Paddy Clarke* is a much more "polished" work. It is also Doyle's saddest story. It is the story of a little boy who watches and listens as his mother and father bring their marriage and his childhood to an end. That ending coincides with the beginning of the "new Ireland" that Doyle examines in the Barrytown trilogy.

What strikes a more *literary* chord in *Paddy Clarke* is the interiority that Doyle achieves as a result of extending the focalised narrative technique of the trilogy into, the first-person narrative voice of the protagonist, a narrative method he refines even further in *The Woman Who Walked into Doors*.

Dominic Head explains "the general trend . . . towards a first-person 'confessional' style" in post-war British fiction as a reflection of "the special capacity of narrative fiction to capture personal moods in an increasingly fragmented historical period" (Head, 2002: 10) and to interpret Doyle's turn to narrator-protagonists in his last three novels as a conscious or unconscious reflection of a sense of living through a period of increasing fragmentation in Irish history fits with the overall reading of his fiction in this study. But the quantum leap forward Doyle makes in *Paddy Clarke* and *The Woman Who Walked into Doors* has as much to do with his evolving moral imagination as with his increasing narrative skill. The construction of the characters of the ten-year old boy and the abused alcoholic wife, exclusively through narrative voice, required a considerable "stretching" of the imagination, first in terms of generation and then gender. But in both novels, Doyle shows the moral and imaginative "preoccupation with characters who are weak or marginalized" (Donnelly, 2000: 25) that has marked his writing since *The Commitments*.

Building Sights

The Barrytown setting in *Paddy Clarke Ha Ha Ha* is nothing like that in the trilogy. The story takes place during the mid-1960s when the estate was first being built; as well, the Clarkes are a lower middle-class family. But there is a continuity between *Paddy Clarke Ha Ha Ha* and *The Van* in its domestic theme. The character of Paddy's father has his roots in Jimmy Rabbitte Sr and is growing towards the Charlo Spencer of *The Woman Who Walked into Doors*. Paddy's mother also seems a version of the longsuffering Veronica of the trilogy and the story of the dissolution of the Clarke marriage and the estrangement between Paddy and his father emerges from plot elements latent in *The Van* and in the relationships between Jimmy Sr, Veronica and Darren.

Doyle's narrative technique in *Paddy Clarke*, however, marks a new sophistication in his approach to narrative structure as expressive form, specifically, involving the imaginative, emotional and epistemological dimensions of memory, nostalgia and recollection. He complicates the base linear chronology of the narrative by having Paddy's associative mental processes move backward, then forward, then backward in time. Emotional power builds through incremental surges in pathos and thematic unity is maintained through a continuously linked series of evolving image patterns. Overall cohesion and forward momentum are provided by Paddy's voice and Doyle builds the reader's vision of the novel's world, characters and themes in a narrative dominated, significantly, by the imagery of literal building sites.

While the story of a young boy in his ninth and tenth years, *Paddy Clarke Ha Ha Ha* is not a traditional coming-of-age novel. Set well before the onset of puberty, Paddy's growth over the period covered by his recollections is that of a young boy who will pass into adolescence and manhood with the basis of character established during these years. By focusing on this particular formative period, Doyle's novel diverges from the emphasis on adolescence in Joyce's *A Portrait of the Artist as a Young Man*, and emulates more the example of his favourite author, Dickens, in *Oliver Twist*. While the traditional novel of growth or education of the hero provides the template, it is Doyle's modification that is significant in *Paddy Clarke*. All the traditional themes are present: the settings, relationships, and worlds of family, school, and play are vividly detailed and fully developed. Doyle also writes explicitly about religion for the first time in his fiction.

The Bildungsroman, or novel of growth, has been described as "the 'symbolic form' of modernity" because of its "focus upon mobility, change and development" (Connor, 1996: 6–7). The form "offers the promise of a reciprocal mirroring between the individual and society" and society in the novel of growth "becomes visible as the enabling field of operations for the individual, and the individual as the actualisation of social possibility" (Connor, 1996: 6). While *Paddy Clarke* does not cover a long enough period in Paddy's life to be a full-fledged novel of growth, it is worth considering it as a reduced or "arrested" example of the form and Paddy's story as ultimately a narrative of reduced or arrested "social possibility".

Where the traditional climax of a Bildungsroman usually involves the protagonist's triumphant confrontation with an adversary, successful response to a challenge, or solution of a troubling mystery, all of which are evidence of the protagonist's maturation, self-knowledge, and understanding of the world in which he must make his way, a resolution often symbolically represented in the marriage of hero and heroine, *Paddy Clarke* ends with a marital break-up and the protagonist's unrelieved mystification by the seemingly intractable problem of trying to understand why his parents no longer love each other. The image that closes *Paddy Clarke* is much darker and much more upsetting than that which concludes *The Van*. A numbed Paddy shakes hands with a father who has become a stranger, who returns at Christmas bearing gifts like a distant relative, and who greets his little boy with a handshake, not an embrace. "His hand felt cold and big, dry and hard" (*C*, 282). Paddy's reply to his greeting, "Very well, thank you", is uncharacteristically formal and in a sense comes from a cold, dry and hard place inside him that did not exist at the beginning of the novel. In terms of plot, theme and imagery, forms of building and destruction compose the narrative dynamic of *Paddy Clarke Ha Ha Ha*. Throughout the story, Paddy's surrounding landscape is in a state of continuous upheaval as land is cleared and new houses and streets are built. His experience of the human landscape is also one of building and destruction — the continuity, change and dissolution of relationships.

The relation between identity and place in this novel differs from that in *The Commitments*, in which Jimmy Rabbitte Jr proclaims his Barrytown identity as a working-class north Dubliner. The Barrytown that Doyle presents in *Paddy Clarke* is not yet the homogenous working-class estate the Rabbittes call home; rather it is based on the Kilbarrack of his own childhood, "bang at the edge of the city" (White, 2001: 176):

> It was sort of semi-rural when I was a very young child. I tried to capture that development in *Paddy Clarke Ha Ha Ha*, this idea that an area was bought out and built up, and in the process it became a more solidly working class area. I never gave much thought to class until that. I suppose my own upbringing was lower middle class. . . . My father's background would have been more solidly working class, my mother's more middle class. (Paschel, 1997: 150–1)

This suggests that much of the sense of identity in Doyle's fiction derives from his experience of the physical transformation of a landscape and the social transformation of a human community (see also, Doyle, 1988: 28). The important point is not that the Barrytown he describes in *Paddy Clarke* is pre-urban, but that Paddy's experience of it is one of loss. Building sites displace Paddy's and his friends' sights of unfilled but not empty space, of place inhabited by the proprietary imagination of childhood, surveyed, mapped and colonised by the pioneering adventures of imaginative play. Much of the poignancy of Doyle's novel derives from the pathos created by the gradual erosion of Paddy's youthful sense of imperium as both his territory and home succumb to forces he can neither control nor understand.

It is important to recognise the recollective character of the narrative voice in the novel, the "nice balance between the adult's recollection and the immediacy of childhood perceptions" (Donnelly, 2000: 25). Doyle said: "I wanted a sort of a continuity, but sometimes at a sort of an unconscious level. The plot was to be there, but not too apparent at the beginning. . . . I didn't want the joints to be seen" (Sbrockey, 1999). The significance of this seamless narrative structure is its expressive effect. By emulating the associative process of a recollecting mind, Doyle conveys a sense of how that mind is built through experience over time. While not the explicitly stereoscopic voice of Pip, for example, in *Great Expectations*, whose adult self looks back, often ironically, at the experiences of his youthful self, the narrative voice in *Paddy Clarke* is similarly self-conscious. There is obvious prolepsis, for example, in his anecdote about hiding in the sewer pipes with Kevin, when Paddy remarks "These were the last moments. Me and Kevin" (*PC*, 108), and it is also a much older narrator who informs us — and reminds the reader of the trilogy — that "There was no chipper in Barrytown then" (*PC*, 36). So when the narrator remarks "Sometimes when nothing happened it was getting ready to happen" (*PC*, 33), it is not a lapse in realism but a moment, dramatically ironic in retrospect, when the adult Patrick is heard rather than the ten-year-old Paddy. It is the voice we hear in the last line of the novel and it is this modulation of the narrative voice that expresses the transformation of Paddy into Patrick Clarke during the months leading up to his parents' separation.

Doyle said he wanted the first half of the novel "to seem haphazard — winding memories, and by degrees the winding memories become straighter and straighter as the parents' marriage becomes worse and worse" (White, 2001: 161). Thus, moments of understanding that occur late in the narrative — for example, when Paddy recognises that "they'd been fighting for years — it made sense now" (*PC*, 256) — or of self-understanding — as when he realises that his brother, Sinbad, can see through him: "He'd found out; he'd found out. . . . He knew: I was frightened and lonely, more than he was" (*PC*, 260) — occur as boy and man attempt to straighten out "the winding memories" of this period in his childhood. This new sophistication in narrative method also reflects Doyle's increasing involvement in film and his adaptation of film technique to his writing. He had already experimented with a "cinematic" shifting between narrative present and past in his play, *War,* and he described the non-linear technique of *Paddy Clarke* as intentionally "meandering" in the manner of "*Amarcord,* my favourite film" (Sbrockey, 1999).

The associative method that Doyle employs imitates "the way a kid's mind would work" (White, 2001: 161) by showing, for example, how Paddy can only understand what is going on with his parents by "reading" their faces and "translating" the tones of their voices into experiences he is already familiar with: when his father overreacts to Paddy's question about wearing jeans on Sunday, Paddy observes how "My ma looked at him with a face, like the look she had when she caught us doing something; sadder, though" (*PC*, 61). Such associations also produce telling juxtapositions. Paddy recollects an incident with his mother involving tar stains on his trousers: "She made me lift my other foot . . . She slapped the side of my leg and opened and closed her hand. I put my foot into it. She looked at the sole. . . . She let go my leg. She always said nothing when she was being annoyed. She clicked and pointed" (*PC*, 125). Immediately after this, he describes his father:

> He made his hand open and close like a beak, the fingers stiff, right into her face.
> —Nag nag nag.
> She looked around and then at him.
> —Paddy, she said.
> —The minute I get in the door. . . .

> I knew what Paddy meant, what she meant the
> way she'd said Paddy. So did Sinbad. So did Cath-
> erine, the way she stared up at my ma and then,
> sometimes, my da.
>   He stopped. He took two deep breaths. He sat
> down. He looked at us, like he used to know us,
> then properly. (*PC*, 125–6)

The contrasting images of his mother's and father's hands develop Paddy's growing sense not only of the problem between his parents but of their different natures. Such associations show Paddy trying to make sense of what is happening at home and provide Doyle with the means to engineer Paddy's progress through the labyrinth of his childhood.

This associative method is both realistic and "poetic". It is what ties the novel together from section to section: from Paddy describing his hands after being strapped by Miss Watkins to describing his father's hands holding a copy of Mailer's *The Naked and the Dead*; from Paddy being terrified by the image of the giant jellyfish in *The Voyage to the Bottom of the Sea* on TV, to being "chased" by a Portuguese man-of-war at the sea front; from descriptions of the food and meals at Liam's and Aidan's motherless house, to Paddy's school lunches and his mother's cooking. It is a world of absolute childish truths (you can get polio from drinking sea water); gossip (Eddie Donnelly died in the barn fire started by "someone from the new Corporation houses"); and arcane lore corroborated by TV programmes (Paddy's father's lesson about fingerprints is confirmed by Napoleon solo on *The Man from U.N.C.L.E.*). There is a sense that Doyle has set out "to record and memorialize aspects of the Ireland of his own youth, a country whose cultural insularity is being infiltrated by the television set in the corner of the living-room" (Donnelly, 2000: 25) and the signs of Ireland's growing encirclement by a new gulf-stream of international capital and

American popular culture during these years are evident throughout the novel. The storm clouds of Vietnam and the Middle East darken the media horizons, and allusions to *The Fugitive, The Virginian, Mart & Market, Hitchcock Presents,* Daniel Boone, Geronimo, Norman Mailer and The Monkees remind 1990s Ireland of "the way we were". But the view that *Paddy Clarke* represents "a version of pastoral nostalgia, looking back . . . to a lost innocence that refers both to the immediate family unit (the Clarkes), and to the broader cultural context" (Cosgrove, 1996: 233) should be regarded with suspicion.

There is a nostalgia of place in *Paddy* Clarke, but to describe this as "pastoral" overstates the point and gives a misleading sense of Paddy's sensibility. The setting of the novel is not the pastoral "west" of Ireland but a lower middle-class suburbia bordering on farmland on the northern fringe of Dublin. Nor is the nostalgia for a lost sense of identity based on a history of family rooted in a specific place or a place with a history. Paddy's memories of running through the fields and startling pheasants in the deep grass compose more a nostalgia for *childhood* than for the place — the memories of endless summer days playing outdoors, the childhood games and adventures, the huge horizons, the life apart from parents, the child's world unto itself.

Nor does Doyle's text support the Romantic view of childhood as a lost innocence. From the opening paragraphs, in which Paddy and his friends talk about dead mothers, it is a world of ignorance more than innocence, and a world closely circumscribed by adult presences and absences. Furthermore, the constant physical violence and cruelty of the gang's play and of Paddy's treatment of his younger brother, Sinbad, prevent any reading of the novel through a green- or rose-tinted lens. It is important to emphasise that Doyle does not represent the Irish family or Irish culture in *Paddy Clarke Ha Ha Ha* in relation to some prior Golden Age that is displaced by a negative modernity. Doyle constructs Paddy's world of fears and superstitions, theories and absolute truths, as a childish version of a "heroic" world of myth, legend and folk-lore. Adults in this world can be giants, trolls, heroes and heroines — or eventually, just human mothers and fathers. Doyle's densely detailed construction of a child's world in *Paddy Clarke* thus comes to represent the heyday and passing of a heroic fantasy, a vanished world, and it is in this sense that "Doyle's attentiveness to the bric-a-brac of modern life as a significant factor in the shaping of character registers those late twentieth-century forces that were beginning to supersede the historical and religious lessons endured by Paddy Clarke in the classroom" (Donnelly, 2000: 25).

The conventional signifiers of the traditional Irish culture that has been challenged by modernisation — nationality, Catholicism and land — are all treated ironically or critically in the novel, in ways that presage *A Star Called Henry*. In *Paddy Clarke* the atavisms of nationalism and religion recur in domestic and educational settings. At school, Paddy comi-cally convinces himself for a moment that he has a 1916 martyr for a grandfather — until the teacher, the nationalist souvenir-worshipping Miss Watkins, recalls him to reality by strapping him until his teeth chatter (*PC*, 23). She does not "correct" other boys when they "blessed themselves" in front of this iconic tea-cloth. Doyle's scorn for a system that subjects children to such blatant ideological indoctrination is evident throughout the episode. The passages he quotes from the Proclamation of Independence sound grotesquely ironic, even sinister, given the setting: "In this supreme hour the Irish nation must, by its valour and discipline, and by the readiness of its children to sacrifice themselves for the common good, prove itself worthy of the august destiny to which it is called" (*PC*, 20). What Doyle proceeds to show, however, is a figure of authority representative of that na-tion physically disciplining actual children under a ludicrously reduced banner of its "august destiny." The description of Miss Watkins solemnly intoning this secular scripture while she makes her captive charges march in place beside their seats in the dilapidated portable classroom of the national school hits a satirical bull's-eye: "Irishmen and Irishwomen: In the name of God and of the dead generations from which she receives her old tradition of nationhood, Ireland, through us summons her children to her flag and strikes for her freedom" (*PC*, 21). The only thing Ireland "summons" and "strikes" at this moment are the outstretched hands of an eight-year-old boy. The "pre-fab" classroom is a brilliant touch, suggesting the flimsy, "ready-made" construction of the "Ireland" that was an ideological function of the state education system following independence.

Paddy's instant connection to the martyrs of 1916 also parodies, perhaps, those in the Republic who continue to need some "ancestral" connection to the heroic nationalist past in order to validate themselves or boost their views in the present. *Paddy Clarke* has been described as "a novel of code-switching" and Doyle uses the 1916 Proclamation in this scene in the same way that he uses Gaelic phrases in this and other classroom scenes to juxtapose the "dead' hieratic Gaelic language of the past" and the moribund nationalist myth which is imposed upon the children with the "the newly invigorated demotic language of popular and mass culture introduced largely via the media and particularly through the television screen" (Strongman, 1997: 35). Paddy and his friends argue more about the correct pronunciation of "Adidas" (*PC*, 30–1) than of any Gaelic word.

Doyle's representation of the Catholic religion in *Paddy Clarke* is also ironic and satirical. At school, he learns about the famous leper-priest, Father Damien, but the effect is not so much spiritual empowerment as a fantasy of power on Paddy's part — he coerces younger children to be his leprous worshippers. Much more seriously, and more darkly,

Doyle shows Catholicism failing Paddy as a source of solace
in his misery. Listening to his parents fight, he descends into
a psychological darkness whose contours mock the religious
master-narrative of his culture:

> All I could do was listen and wish. I didn't pray; there
> were no prayers for this. The Our Father didn't fit,
> or the Hail Mary. But I rocked the same way I some-
> times did when I was saying prayers. Backwards and
> forwards, the rhythm of the prayer. . . .
>   I rocked.
> –Stop stop stop stop — (PC, 154)

Doyle explains the absence of religion in the Barrytown trilogy as intentional: "There's no religion in me own life, for
certain. I've no room for it at all" (White, 2001: 168). But he
admits that "*Paddy Clarke* is filled with religion — a childish
version of it, because it's a different time, the 1960s"
(White, 2001: 169). But clearly, this "childish" religion reflects a view that there is something childish or "arrested"
about the kind of religious belief and institutionalised religion
that have dominated Irish society and culture for so long.

   For Doyle, it would seem, nationalism and Catholicism
form something of a composite monster at the centre of the
maze of Irish history; "labyrinth", in fact, is one of the words
Paddy, who is something of a precocious wordsmith, uses to
describe the building-site of the Bayside estate to the north of
Barrytown: "It was the shape of the place. It was mad. The
roads were crooked. The garages weren't in the proper place.
. . . The place made no sense. We went there to get lost" (PC,
148). However, the maze and monster in *Paddy Clarke Ha Ha
Ha* turn out to be social and domestic; specifically, the social
form of the family and the loveless marriage, heartache and
violence concealed within it. And what Doyle shows to be the
way out of the labyrinth of memory and grief in the novel is
the path of narrative itself, the process of narration, and the

guiding thread of language. The only love and relationship that do not disappoint or break in *Paddy Clarke Ha Ha Ha* are Paddy's love of words and growing mastery of their capacity to bring understanding to confusion and heartbreak. *Paddy Clarke Ha Ha Ha* looks ahead to *The Woman Who Walked into Doors* in this respect, in that it seems to mark Doyle's discovery of the myth of the healing power of narrative poesis, a myth central to Paula Spencer's narrative activity.

Something Happened

In the paradoxical world of Paddy Clarke, the tidal bore of home and school's everyday sameness ebbs and flows around sudden change and violent discontinuity. The boys try to assert themselves against the latter, comically and symbolically writing their names into the fresh cement, whenever and wherever they find it, only to find later "they'd been smoothed over". Paddy's world is one of vanishing territorial markers, childish rituals and relationships that dissolve even as they seem to be forming. It is a world of seeming stability. "The building site kept changing. . . . We'd go down . . . and it wouldn't be there any more, just a square patch of muck and broken bricks and tyre marks" (*PC*, 5). While there is an element of nostalgia in all of this, what is noteworthy is the total absence of sentimentality in the novel. Nor is it necessarily that Doyle's backward look comes from a colder, harder, drier sensibility; rather, it may be that it comes from Doyle's sense of ambiguous belonging, in-between-ness, of riding a wave more than standing on solid ground, a perspective that sees through metaphorical as well as literal bricks and mortar to the building sites they conceal, whether of Barrytown or of a Republic.

"Something had happened; something" (*PC*, 95): in the novel this phrase forms something of a motif (*PC*, 178, 220, 241) whose origins are in the narrator's observation that

"Sometimes when nothing happened it was getting ready to happen" (*PC*, 33). What happens is that Barrytown becomes a working-class estate, something Paddy sees as it happens, and his parents separate, something that he could not see as it was "getting ready to happen", but which in retrospect becomes clear to him. The building boom in Barrytown and its surrounding areas is that of "Corporation" houses (*PC*, 6) and it is Doyle's juxtaposition of these houses going up as Paddy's home comes apart that provides an intriguing thematic for aspiring allegorists.

"It was so brilliant being in a team called United . . ." (*PC*, 173). Paddy is a Manchester United fan and Paddy is a joiner. He loves belonging to his gang and being accepted by it. To a dyslexic culture, a "united" or an "untied" society would appear much the same. In *Paddy Clarke Ha Ha Ha* Doyle describes the time in which the fields of north Dublin were being bulldozed to make way for the new estate of Barrytown; but as Doyle describes it, this building is also a destruction. The novel begins, as it ends, with an image of a broken family unity. The "Missis Quigley" Paddy and his friends harass is a widow and, once Liam and Aidan O'Connell ride off home, he and Kevin Conway begin "talking about having a dead ma" like them (*PC*, 1). By the end of the novel, Paddy's parents will be separated from their spouses like Mrs Quigley and Mr O'Connell, and Paddy, his friendship with Kevin and the other boys broken, will find himself alone and the subject of their mockery:

> –Paddy Clarke –
> Paddy Clarke –
> Has no da.
> Ha ha ha! (*PC*, 281)

"I didn't listen to them. They were only kids," he says, but Paddy is only ten and still a "kid" himself.

It is domestic violence that ultimately unties the knot of relationship in *Paddy Clarke*, and to the extent that making sense of violence, past and present, is making sense of Ireland, this novel looks ahead not only to *The Woman Who Walked into Doors*, which examines domestic violence, but also to *A Star Called Henry*, which explores the origins of the nation state in revolutionary violence. There is a great deal of physical violence and emotional cruelty in the novel, and the image of childhood Doyle constructs is at times as exaggerated as his image of working-class life in the trilogy. To the question, "Why is Paddy so violent?" Doyle replied: "Because little boys are violent. Read *Lord of the Flies*" (White, 2001: 173). But the images of lighter fluid being forced into Sinbad's mouth and then set alight by his brother or of Kevin cracking an iron poker across the others' spines are just the most extreme outbursts of a violence Doyle presents as an underlying feature of a culture whose religion has an act of state execution and violent sacrifice at its ritual heart and whose history — including, obviously, the "birth" of the modern nation — likewise is steeped in violent death and the myth of martyrdom.

The few instances of non-violent bodily contact in the novel seem almost abnormal and are usually noted by Paddy for the special pleasure he takes from them. At home, Paddy's mother hits Sinbad for losing his shoe (Paddy hits him, too) and his father hits Paddy for complaining about a song he was forcing him to learn. In the latter incident, Paddy is as much surprised by his inability to read his father's body language as by the behaviour itself:

> Da hit me. On the shoulder; I was looking at him, about to tell him that I didn't want to sing this one; it was too hard. It was funny; I knew he was going to wallop me from the look on his face a few seconds before he did it. Then he looked as if he'd changed

> his mind, like he'd controlled himself, and then I
> heard the thump and felt it, as if he'd forgotten to tell
> his hand not to keep going towards me. (*PC*, 88–9)

The flat monotone of Paddy's voice, accentuated by the opening series of short phrases, projects the deflated spirit that is the consequence of the moment as well as communicating the sense of wrong that was done to the boy; the effectively controlled irony of the colloquialism, "It was funny", then frames the point of the episode for Paddy — the fact that he was tricked, that his father is beyond his interpretive skills, beyond prediction — a point painfully repeated at the end of the novel when he leaves home before Paddy himself can run away (*PC*, 280). Doyle's point is the adult's loss of self-control and a father's mistreatment of his son, but the way he has Paddy describe his father's action gives the sense of a mind–body breakdown, an involuntary disconnection between head and hand, heart and mind, a fragmentation which is repeated in the man's relationship with his wife and children.

At the beginning of the novel, Paddy is attracted to his father in part because of his mystery. Mr Clarke prefers to read rather than watch TV and always has a newspaper or book in front of him. Paddy loves to ask him questions and is proud that he is named after him. But from the beginning, Paddy also senses a darker side to his father: "He'd be mean now and again, really mean for no reason" (*PC*, 37). What he is noticing but not understanding, of course, is his father's unhappiness. Eventually, while Paddy comes to understand that this unpredictability in his father has something to do with how he feels about his mother, the fact that he might not love her remains a complete mystery to him, something that still eludes his understanding at the novel's end.

That Paddy notices things and accepts them as the way things are long before he understands them is evident from the way he describes the first instance of his parents' fighting in the story. Awakened by thirst — and perhaps their voices — he thinks there are burglars in the kitchen, but seeing that the TV is on and recognising the voices as his father and mother, he realises "They were having another of their fights" (*PC*, 42). As Paddy sits on the stairs listening to them argue, his teeth began to chatter in the same way they did after he was strapped by Miss Watkins. "I let them. I liked it when they did that" (*PC*, 42). Paddy is amused by what the reader recognises as a symptom of fear and strain, a tension that is a consequence in both instances of violence done to a child by adults; in the classroom, physically, and in the home, emotionally. In both settings, Paddy "catches unhappiness off those closest to him, the very people supposed to make him happy" (Lane, 1994: 92). Since this is "*another* of their fights", he has heard them before. He calls out to them to "Stop" and "There was a gap. It had worked; I'd forced them to stop" (*PC*, 42). One of the more poignant aspects of Paddy's premature growing up in the novel is his realisation of his powerlessness to affect his parents' unhappiness and prevent his own.

Paddy becomes an attentive witness to his father's increasingly petulant, irrational and violent outbursts with his mother. Doyle sharpens the pathos of the process by representing it as the son's gradual loss of his father. One day he revels in his father's antics when learning to drive the new car — "he was mad sometimes, brilliant mad" (*PC*, 90) — but the next is mystified by his truculence during a picnic to Dollymount. Paddy senses that "Something had happened; something" (*PC*, 95) but cannot explain it because he cannot "read" his parents' faces: "Ma said something to Da. . . . I could tell by the look on the side of her face, she was waiting for him to answer. But it was more than that, her face" (*PC*, 95). Throughout the episode Paddy's account of what is going on between his parents in the front seat of the car —

perhaps his mother has asked her husband if he still loves her — is intercut with his more certain and detailed description of what is going on in the backseat between him and Sinbad, as they eat their favourite biscuits and drink their Fanta. Doyle's method conveys how this sad normality is experienced by the child as both an ever-present background that occasionally moves to the foreground of his life, which otherwise is dominated by the hierarchy of priorities and sensory pleasures we would expect to preoccupy him.

Violence is a norm in Paddy's world. At school, Henno slaps, pokes and punches his charges towards responsible citizenship, and in the schoolyard and beyond, a Goldingesque tribalism prevails. Paddy refuses to let a new boy from one of the Corporation houses play football with him and his friends, and to impress them kicks him for good measure (and also because the boy was smaller). Violence, actual and imitated, features in all of Paddy's play activities, from setting Sinbad's mouth alight — "It went like a dragon" (*PC*, 8) — to playing war games and "Indians and Cowboys" on the building sites. "Dead legging" — kneeing someone in the thigh, usually someone smaller, like Sinbad — is one of his favourite pastimes. Other boys prefer "pruning" — squeezing someone's testicles until the victim drops to the ground.

Paddy does not try to make sense of his friends' or his own behaviour. And although he is anxious and mystified by the violence in his world — he becomes quite concerned by the newspaper headline "World War Three Looms Near" (*PC*, 24) and badgers his father for an explanation — it is the violence between his parents that Paddy wants to make sense of. It is realistic, of course, for Doyle not to have Paddy connect or even notice his own violence; but the reader must. Paddy doesn't begin to question his own situation until the situation in his home begins to reach its crisis. When Paddy, hoping to impress the hateful Kevin, picks a fight with Seán Whelan, a new "Corpo" boy at school, he is suddenly attacked by Charles Leavy, who comes to the aid of his street-mate. Afterwards Paddy notices that none of his friends, including Kevin, came to *his* aid: "it took me a while to get used to that, to make it make sense. To make it alright" (*PC*, 186–7). What life puts before Paddy at home and at school tests his need and ability to "make it make sense". Significantly, it is shortly after this traumatic event at school that Paddy actually hears his father hit his mother for the first time.

There are 117 sections organised into eight groups in *Paddy Clarke*, and the shortest grouping contains just one section, which presents Paddy's reaction to hearing the sound of his father's violence; it represents the central trauma in the novel before the final wound of his father's departure, a kind of emotional Rubicon which, once crossed, forever alters Paddy's relationship with his parents:

> The first time I heard it I recognized it but I didn't know what it was. I knew the sound. . . . My ma and da were talking.
> Then I heard the smack. . . .
> I recognized it now. I knew what the smack had been . . .
> He'd hit her. Across the face; smack. I tried to imagine it. It didn't make sense. I'd heard it; he'd hit her. . . .
> Across the face. (*PC*, 190)

Since Paddy has heard the sound before, the reader may conclude that this is not the first time Paddy's father has hit his wife. But this is Paddy's moment of recognition, his connection of the sound to a mental image. Now he understands the sound. But he still does not understand why his father has hit his mother. That "didn't make sense". Like his betrayal by Kevin and the others in the fight with Charles

Leavy, Paddy cannot understand this betrayal. The next section, one of the most powerful in the novel, begins: "I
watched. I listened. I stayed in. I guarded her" (*PC*, 191). The
ten-year-old boy assumes responsibility for his mother's
safety, never leaving her presence whenever his father is
home, staying awake all night to listen for any sound of trouble (*PC*, 232).

It is the domestic violence that eventually unties the
knot that binds the family — and specifically, father and son.
(His father leaves when he realises Paddy saw him hit his
mother.) But what Doyle also shows is that it is this untying
that binds — in the sense of seizing — Paddy's childhood,
marking its end and presumably determining much of his
future as adolescent and man. Paddy is slowly torn apart. "I
loved him. He was my da. It didn't make sense. She was my
ma" (*PC*, 191). He tries to get close to his father but cannot
scale the wall of newspaper he hides behind (*PC*, 202–8). He
plays the clown to manipulate his father's humour whenever
he senses things getting ugly: "There was a fight coming and I
could stop it by being there" (*PC*, 209); "I'd done it. It was
alright. Normal again. He'd cracked a joke. Ma had laughed.
I'd laughed. He'd laughed. Mine lasted the longest. During it,
I thought it was going to change into a cry. But it didn't. . . . I
wanted to go while it was nice. I'd made it like that" (*PC*,
210–11). Paddy's life becomes a hell of continuous vigilance
and paranoia. When his mother stays in bed one morning he
doesn't know whether to believe his father that she is ill or
to think she is hurt (*PC*, 220). Ironically, his school marks
improve because of the time he spends studying in her presence. But he cannot stop the inevitable: "They were fighting
all the time now" (*PC*, 221). "I didn't understand. She was
lovely. He was nice" becomes Paddy's mantra of perplexity
(*PC*, 222, 244).

Towards the end of the novel, Paddy desperately tries to
continue to be the neutral "ref" between his parents (*PC*,

257–59). The ten-year-old's black-and-white view of the world — his need for things to be black-and-white — collapses about him. He feels he should be able to identify someone in the wrong, someone to blame, to hate, but he cannot. "They were both to blame" (*PC*, 255) and he loves them both. Doyle's construction of Paddy through the carefully measured increments of anguish and perplexity that this voice conveys is an unequivocal *tour de force*. But it is important to recognise that through Paddy we also see how adults, going through this the way Paddy's parents do, put their children in an impossible situation.

Doyle wrote *Paddy Clarke Ha Ha Ha* in the period between the two divorce referenda. While set in the "Swinging Sixties", very little of that decade's "cultural revolution" makes it into the novel. Reading between the lines, one might conclude that Paddy's parents are being influenced by what they read, see, and hear about what is going on elsewhere at the time. But the novel presents a marriage coming apart for undisclosed reasons. Doyle's choice of a ten-year old as narrator might seem short-sighted here, but again, any frustration the reader may feel is a pale reflection of Paddy's own predicament. It is remarkable that not once in the novel is there a scene in which his mother or father sits him down and explains what is happening. But perhaps that would not have happened anyway in Ireland in the 1960s — or anywhere else. Doyle shows two adults carrying on as if the four children around them were little more than benign growths hanging from their bodies, while the children — even the baby — develop nervous tics, become silent and withdrawn, and pale from the lack of sleep. Like a scab Paddy keeps picking at, Paddy keeps coming back to the fact that he could not understand what was happening. Eventually, he gave up trying:

> Sometimes, when you were thinking about some-
> thing, trying to understand it, it opened up in your
> head without you expecting it to, like it was a soft
> spongy light unfolding, and you understood, it made
> sense forever. They said it was brains but it wasn't; it
> was luck. . . . It wouldn't happen this time though,
> ever. I could think and think and concentrate and
> nothing would ever happen. (*PC*, 256)

The heart of *Paddy Clarke Ha Ha Ha* — the core of the narrative consciousness — is the undoing and reforming of the
fragile, ambiguous, insecure sense of belonging, of feeling "at
home" in the world, which begins with the sense of identity
the boy takes from the rough nurture of his experiences
with the gang and from the security of his home life. Both
these sources of selfhood prove unstable and unpredictable.
Life in the gang becomes a constant strategy and challenge,
and family life becomes a continuous storm-watch. Paddy's
survival in both worlds depends on his interpretive skills.
Thus, the theme of language in the novel may be understood
in relation not just to Paddy's character, in the sense that he
might grow up to become a middle-class novelist with roots
in a working-class Barrytown about which he will write a
series of novels, but in the sense that Paddy's attraction to
language is related to his need to understand what is happening between his parents.

   Paddy recognises that language is the fundamental instrument of understanding, for making sense, and discovers
it can also be used to make peace. He also knows that language leads to narrative which leads to fiction. Paddy begins
to use his precocious talent with words to distract his
mother from her sadness and to defuse his father's mounting anger. As he becomes more attuned to his parents'
troubles, he is forced to develop an extraordinary talent for
recognising the fluctuations in emotional temperature when-

ever his parents are in a room together. In one such episode, he realises that Sinbad has misread his father's mood following an outburst. (*PC*, 126). Paddy deftly intervenes to save his brother by inventing a story about a boy being sick in Sinbad's class. "Da looked at Sinbad. . . . Da changed. It had worked. His foot was bouncing across his leg; that was the sign. I'd won. I'd saved Sinbad. . . . I'd beaten Da" (*PC*, 126–7). The scene shows the mounting strain under which Paddy is living. Reading his parents' faces, listening for the tones in their voices, decoding their body language, his life is lived on tenterhooks.

Growing Pain in the Years of Plenty

The 1960s may have been "the Golden Years, the first years of plenty" (Gray, 1996: 215), for some, but Doyle's representation of Ireland since the 1960s suggests that, like Ian McEvoy and Sinbad, Irish society has suffered "spurts of growing pain" (*PC*, 122) — in particular, the widening gaps between classes, regions, genders and generations. Some of these divisions are noted by Jimmy Rabbitte Jr in *The Commitments* as well as by Jimmy Sr in *The Van*. Paddy's and his friends' construction of the myth of the "Slum scum" (*PC*, 118) who live in the nearby Corporation houses represents the demonisation not of a racial, religious or ethnic "other", but of a different class.

Some of Doyle's critics have accepted this myth unquestioningly, believing that it is the "arrival of the members of the mainly working-class inner city communities" that threatens the "fairly stable social order of Barrytown" (Paschel, 1998: 83) and that "Charles Leavy and his ilk" are "the precursors of 'the living dead'", that "group of fearless, unfeeling teenagers who terrorize Jimmy Sr in . . . *The Van*" (White, 2001: 100). But it should be noted that Paddy's middle-class suburb is already fairly unstable before the dreaded

"Corpos" arrive and Paddy never suffers unwarranted violence from Charles Leavy or any other boy from the Corporation houses. In fact, it is Paddy who is shown being unnecessarily callous and cruel to the little boy who tries to join their soccer game, kicking him without reason. Leavy beats up Paddy for picking a fight with the pacifist and much smaller Seán Whelan; otherwise he leaves him alone. Nor does the novel ever present the boys from the Corporation houses engaged in the shoplifting, vandalism or harassment that Paddy and his friends carry out. Of course, they probably did, but the novel does not show this. What the novel presents is that open fields become house-lined streets, green horizons vanish, a new bridge replaces an old one, paved roads replace dirt roads, and a middle-class husband and wife stop loving each other.

It is his childhood's brief pastoral that Doyle seems to have drawn on most for the novel: "The place is mine; the time is mine. There are memories of my own, running through a field and seeing pheasants fly up, balls of dust under the kitchen table. But the story isn't mine. I'm glad to say. . . . It's fiction" (Rockwell, 1993: C1). However, the lack of details gives the Clarkes' break-up a "timeless" quality that suggests Doyle's 1960s plot is informed by his 1990s involvement in the social issues surrounding the right to divorce. It oversimplifies the novel to see Paddy's domestic and gang experiences as reflective of (or even, allegorically, caused by) the social changes in his "outside environment" (Paschel, 1998: 84); if the novel does "create a link between the negative change of the environment to the growing callousness of the children" (Paschel, 1998: 86), the "environment" created by teachers like Miss Watkins and Henno seems more to blame.

Paddy recalls a time of cocoon-like bliss when he used to hide in his "fort" beneath the dining-room table: "I'd sit in there for hours. . . . it was safe. . . . I woke up once and there was a blanket on top of me. I wanted to stay there forever" (*PC*, 103-4). However, Paddy goes on to describe how, coincident with the arrival of his brothers and sisters, he gradually couldn't fit under the table anymore. The lost sense of security that Paddy comes to feel is not exclusively the effect of his parents' break-up, but also from the natural process of growing up.

Paddy laments that "Our territory was getting smaller" (*PC*, 128) because of the development and the arrival of the Corpo kids: "There were no farms left. Our pitch was gone, first sliced in half for pipes, then made into eight houses. . . . There was another tribe there now, tougher than us" (*PC*, 147). He feels that he and his friends are being driven off the land like the Indians of nineteenth-century America. But the sense of place and the time of childhood are merged in his narrative and the boys' territory becomes smaller not only because their lower middle-class island is flooded by the rising tide of the working-class but also because the boys grow bigger and older.

The novel does not show Paddy or the others becoming more "callous" because they play in building sites or unconnected sewer pipes or kick a soccer ball around with boys like Chares Leavy and Seán Whelan. Rather, Doyle's source for the cruelty would appear to be his view that Golding was being realistic in *Lord of the Flies*: this is how nine- and ten-year-old boys behave — or behaved — on the shrinking suburban "island" he describes as the Barrytown of 1967–68. Nor does *Paddy Clarke* express "a nostalgia for the 1960s" (Kiberd, 1996: 611) in the sense that phrase usually conveys; *Voyage to the Bottom of the Sea* and *The Virginian* are hardly most people's highlights of that decade. What Doyle remembers fondly are details of domestic interiors and outdoor adventures which are timeless but located in the 1960s for him because he was born the same year as Paddy Clarke, 1958.

The "growing pain" in *Paddy Clarke* is the narrator-protagonist's mental and emotional torment as he is forced to listen to and watch his parents' marriage burn out. It is also the pain that Paddy feels as a result of giving up the identity gained from inclusion and acceptance by his gang, and from moving towards an identity he would have to define for himself. Paddy's turn toward that difficult process of self-invention is expressed through his unflagging interest in words and how he can use them in an identifiably personal way.

In the "naming ceremony", under Kevin's direction, the boys kneel holding hands in a tight circle around a smoking fire. As Kevin strikes each boy in turn with a poker, he must say a "bad" word, which then becomes their "name" in the gang until the next naming ceremony: "It had to be a bad word. That was the rule. If it wasn't bad enough you got another belt of the poker" (*PC*, 130). Kevin's priestly role is to confirm the self-naming by pronouncing "The word was made flesh!" He lays it on too thick, however, and after hitting him once too often, Liam breaks ranks and leaves the game. Paddy sympathises — "I wanted to go with him" — but doesn't move. "I'd take my punishment now, for the same reason that Aidan was staying. It was good being in the circle, better than where Liam was going" (*PC*, 131). Paddy then handles Kevin the same way he handles his father:

> There were two others left but I'd be next. I knew it: Kevin was going to take it out on me. . . .
>
> It took him ages. . . . It was dark now. I could hear the wind. I had to close my eyes again. My legs were hot, too close to the fire. He'd gone; I couldn't place him. I listened. He was nowhere.
>
> —The word was made flesh!
>
> My back was ripped. The bones exploded.
>
> —Fuck!
>
> —From henceforth thou will be called Fuck.
>
> It was over. . . .

> I'd done it. . . .
> It was all over now . . . It had been worth it. I was
> the real hero, not Liam. (*PC*, 131–2)

The scene draws together the themes of individual versus group identity, the relation between identity and place, the ingrained sense of sacrifice in a culture of violence, and the redemptive power of language. The "ceremony" encapsulates the complex and ultimately coercive ironies of identity-formation in society, the delusion of the subject's self-naming, the self-subjection that is a prerequisite for recognition by authority, and so on. Already, however, Paddy intuitively knows that he belongs with the rebel Liam, even though he is satisfied with his "top dog" status in the group.

Paddy experiences more violence in the gang as he begins to witness more violence at home, and as his family life becomes more worrisome, his need to belong to the gang seems to increase. He sees himself as "the real hero" not only because he says "The best word . . . The forbidden word" but because he stays in the circle. Eventually, though, he comes to understand that Liam *was* the hero that day. Paddy's childhood ends when he decides to leave the gang, Barrytown ceases to be the secure personal "country" (*PC*, 150) that it once was, and his father leaves home. As Kevin is displaced in Paddy's mind by Leavy and Sinbad, it is inevitable that some violent reckoning between Paddy and the gang will have to occur.

This surge in independence follows from the worsening conditions at home. His father has started coming home drunk and even not coming home at all. But worse is Paddy's sense that his mother is changing. During one fight, "She'd hurt him . . . that was what it sounded like" and Paddy's sense of order, of his father's and mother's roles, is challenged. "I didn't like it that she'd shouted. It didn't fit" (*PC*, 254). In the weeks before the fight with Kevin, Paddy becomes a nervous wreck. One moment he thinks he has imagined it all — "There was no proof" (*PC*, 245) — and the next is convinced that his family is going to join the other broken families in Barrytown — "We were next. I knew it, and I was going to be ready" (*PC*, 245). The fight with Kevin marks his crossing over to an identity no longer based in acceptance by others. "This was the most important thing that had ever happened to me; I knew it. . . . It would never go back to the same again. . . . I was on my own" (*PC*, 273–4). The echoes of Jimmy Sr's fight with Bimbo are intriguing. The fight signals Paddy's resignation to his separateness, an acceptance of the individuality he is and which, ironically, he has been driven into — prematurely — as a result of his parents' fighting. And he thinks he can make himself "ready" for both eventualities, the break with Kevin and the gang and the break-up of his parents by emulating the "tough" Charles Leavy. What particularly impresses Paddy is the way Leavy says "Fuck off":

> I wanted to say it exactly like him. . . . quick and sharp and fearless. I was going to say it without looking over my shoulder. The way Charles Leavy said it. His head shot forward like it was going to keep going into your face. The word hit you after his head went back. The Off was like a jet going overhead; it lasted forever. The Fuck was the punch; the Off was you gasping.
> Fuck awfffffff. (*PC*, 249)

Earlier Paddy thought the four-letter word was the "best" of "forbidden" words because of its aura of banned mystery and the thrill of transgression that uttering it brought (*PC*, 132); now he is attracted to the word's power, its capacity to project energy and aggression, anger or indifference, but mostly, the word seems to repulse, to enforce an isolation or put up a barrier between the speaker and whomever it is spoken *at*, and this seems to appeal to the fragile Paddy. What is also significant about this passage and its contrast with Paddy's earlier paean to the four-letter word, is that in the first, he was using the word in the context of the gang, as a way of dealing with Kevin's sadistic authoritarianism, his shame at not supporting Liam, and as a way of gaining respect and recognition from the other boys. But in the second passage, the word has become almost a "new" word for Paddy; it is Charles Leavy's word and Charles Leavy belongs to no gang, follows no leader, and certainly does not allow anyone to hit him with a poker. What Doyle shows here is Paddy changing from using language to ingratiate himself with others and to negotiate his acceptance and identity within the group, to using language to assert individuality, indifference to, and eventually rejection of the identity the group had given him.

Language, codes, identity, belonging and acceptance, understanding and being understood: all of these are central to *Paddy Clarke Ha Ha Ha*, as they were in Doyle's previous fiction. At the beginning of *The Commitments*, when Jimmy puts down his friends' ideas about acceptable music by calling it "art school stuff", the narrator tells us "That was the killer argument, Outspan knew, even though he didn't know what it meant" (*C*, 4). The point is humorous but also insightful. Doyle is showing how people are aware of *how* language means even when they are not sure *what* it means; how people function within a world of codes even though they don't always understand them. Outspan feels "trumped", so to speak, by Jimmy's put-down; he does not understand the trick but he knows he's been taken. Much the same happens with Paddy and his playmates in the gang. Again Doyle is exploring the individual's need to belong to something bigger than himself in order to feel his own significance reflected in the eyes of the others who acknowledge him. But that acknowledgement, acceptance and recognition must be constantly renegotiated and "formalised" by the group and the individual, and one of the ways this occurs, Doyle shows, is on the level of language, as in the "naming ceremony". *The Commitments*, too, has a "naming ceremony" in the scene where Jimmy gives the band its stage-names (*C*, 42–8). Later, when Dean tells Jimmy Rabbitte "There's too many rules in soul. — It's all walls" (*C*, 143), Doyle draws attention to the ambiguous nature of the inclusion that social codes perform and the *subjection* the individual must accept in exchange for the recognition of their subjectivity; for a while, those "walls" are protective, a source of security within an identifiable structure; but eventually they become confining, and the individual either acquiesces to remaining contained within them, or he or she must go outside them.

Like Dean, Paddy regards recognition and acceptance by the others as very important for a time, but eventually he comes to experience the limitations and deficiencies of collective identity. The group is set up to provide security in exchange for conformity and Doyle represents this economy of identity in the gang's patterns of violence — which is a kind of micro-economic version of what the novel shows to be a macro-truth — evident, to Paddy, as much in far-off Vietnam or the Golan Heights as in Henno's classroom or the language on Miss Watkin's tea-towel, that limp veronica of gift-shop nationalism she uses as a teaching-aid.

Conversely, the group punishes difference with exclusion, which can take the form of emotional or physical violence. When Henno puts Charles Leavy to sit with Liam, Paddy is delighted: "It was great. Liam was finished now; Kevin and me wouldn't even talk to him any more. . . . I didn't know why. I liked Liam. It seemed important though. If you were going to be best friends with anyone — Kevin — you had to hate a lot of other people, the two of you, together. It made you better friends" (*PC*, 182–3). The gang is not organised in order to nurture individuality but to repress it through its "tribal" laws. When Paddy begins to feel different and to be perceived as different, he becomes estranged from his former playmates. The linguistic and behavioural codes that previously organised, explained and expressed his sense of the world now seem a foreign language and an alien culture, evident in his response to the "Paddy Clarke Ha Ha Ha" chant at the end.

In the novel, the end of childhood is marked not only by the Copernican revolution in the child's consciousness as it comes to feel and know the truth of the unstable nature of the world of adults, a world that hitherto had been, paradoxically, both *other* than the child's and yet fundamental to its security, it is marked as well by the assumption of the burden of individuality that comes with this de-centring. Paddy's emergence into a more self-conscious individuality is one consequence of his experience of his parents' break-up, but so too is the erosion of his self-esteem and confidence about both himself and his world. Late in the novel, Doyle has Paddy sum up his frustration with his powerlessness to prevent his parents' separation and his inability to make any sense of their feelings. "I couldn't do anything. Because I didn't know how to stop it from starting. . . . I didn't understand. I never would. No amount of listening and being there would give it to me. I just didn't know. I was stupid" (*PC*, 255–6). Doyle leaves the reader to extrapolate from a comment like this — and from his idolisation of Charles Leavy — what sort of adolescence Paddy will have.

Everything about Leavy attracts Paddy: "I wanted to be like Charles Leavy. I wanted to be hard. . . . Charles Leavy didn't dare anyone; he'd gone further than that: he didn't know they were there. I wanted to get that far. I wanted to look at my ma and da and not feel anything. I wanted to be ready" (*PC*, 250). At night now, when he hears the fighting downstairs that he realises he is powerless to stop, he tells them to "Fuck off" but not so as they would hear. "I was crying now too, but I'd be ready when the time came" (*PC*, 250). What Paddy is getting ready for is to be abandoned by his father. Following his fight with Kevin his former friends all "boycott" him but Paddy thinks "They could only boycott me if I didn't want to be boycotted" (*PC*, 276). He is ready to be alone. What had drawn him to Leavy, ironically, was Leavy's apparent contentment with *his* aloneness (*PC*, 251).

As Paddy readies himself for his domestic apocalypse he is also drawn towards his little brother, Sinbad. Paddy wants to be "tough" like Leavy, immune from the pain his parents are inflicting on him, and he wants to protect Sinbad from what's coming: "I wanted to help him. He had to know; he had to get ready like me. I wanted to be able to stand beside him. . . . I wanted to get him ready" (*PC*, 242). But both Leavy and Sinbad rebuff him and Paddy is left feeling "alone" (*PC*, 239). With Sinbad, Paddy is reaping what he has sown. His brother ultimately drives him to tears: "Something happened: I started crying. I went to thump him and before I had a fist made I was crying. I hung on to his nose just a while longer, just to be holding him. I didn't know why I was crying; it shocked me. I let go of his nose. I put my arms around him. . . . He stayed hard and closed. . . . I was hugging a statue" (*PC*, 241). (Doyle reprises this view of sibling relations in his novella, *Not Just for Christmas*, which he wrote for the Open Door Series, a New Island Books literacy project. Danny and Jimmy also grow up in a similar setting to Paddy and Sinbad; see Doyle, 1999: 55). Obviously, Paddy is not the only one who will be permanently affected by his parents' behaviour. As matters reach their worst, Paddy wants to stand united with his brother against the coming disaster, but his cruelty toward him has long untied the natural bond they could have developed. Over the course of the novel, Doyle builds Paddy's growing sense of identity through his need to belong in three relationships — to his Barrytown gang, to his parents, and to his brother. By the end of the novel, each of these has come undone.

Conclusion: On Uncertain Ground

Paddy had planned "to run away to frighten them and make them feel guilty, to push them into each other" (*PC*, 269), but at the end, he recalls, "I was too late. He left first" (*PC*, 280). Paddy walks in on his parents and sees his father hit his mother. No one acknowledges what has happened. Nor does his father say goodbye, presumably out of shame. The hypersensitive Paddy simply "knows": "The way he shut the door; he didn't slam it. Something; I just knew: he wasn't coming back" (*PC*, 280). His father does come back, however, in Charlo Spencer, a more extreme version of the abusive husband, of course, and a petty criminal who occupies a social space between the traditional working class and the growing underclass of the perennially unemployed, destitute and shiftless.

The element of nostalgia in *Paddy Clarke Ha Ha Ha* may have its origins in the generational thinking that gradually gets stronger in the Barrytown trilogy, as the differences between Jimmy Sr and Jimmy Jr become more pronounced (see White, 2001: 154). But more than the nostalgia, Doyle's careful building of pathos in the reader for the lovable — if not necessarily likable — and beleaguered Paddy, clearly points toward his even more complex empathic representation of Paula Spencer in *The Woman Who Walked into Doors*, and confirms Joseph O'Connor's view that "The emotional landscape of [Doyle's] work is broadening all the time" (O'Connor, 1995: 143). Doyle has acknowledged that, with his success as writer and filmmaker, in terms of income he has passed over into the upper middle class, but if he set out to write about the middle classes, he admits that "in terms of emotions and tastes I would see myself on very uncertain ground" (Paschel, 1997: 151). There are no middle-class characters of significance in the Barrytown trilogy, and the only time Doyle places his working-class protagonists in contact with middle-class people, as in the southside episode in *The Van*, the occasion ends in disaster.

In *Paddy Clarke*, Doyle provides a more detailed and complex meeting between the classes, but the results are much the same, even though the classes are represented by children. Significantly, it is the middle-class boy who makes the overtures to his working-class schoolmate. But Doyle shows the gulf between them to be unbridgeable. Charles Leavy simply isn't interested. If class displaces nationalism in *The Commitments*, with Jimmy Rabbitte Jr's unequivocal rejection of "Fianna fuckin' Fáil" (*C*, 8), in *Paddy Clarke Ha Ha Ha*, Doyle replaces the traditional two solitudes of religion in Ireland with those formed by class division. The "uncertain ground" that Doyle himself seems to have encountered first was that of his own childhood and adolescence, as his neighbourhood changed all around him and his family's fortunes prospered. The image of the literally changing ground in *Paddy Clarke* is thus not only a descriptive but a significantly expressive metaphor. "Development" covers a spectrum of change — from real estate to personal growth — and Paddy Clarke's story involves both extremes. But if Paddy's changing suburban landscape represents Doyle's sense of his own working-class/middle-class origins, by revisiting that "uncertain ground" he also charts the territory from which he has developed as an individual and writer.

"Something had happened" between the 1960s and the 1990s, Doyle says, in *Paddy Clarke Ha Ha Ha*, but the novel also implies that a lot did not change. If the estate-building is "a synecdoche for modernity in general", that does not have to mean that the novel is "deeply troubled by the recognition that the price of modernity is high, and entails the loss of a recent past in which the individual could feel more happily at home, and more surely in touch with a self 'innocent' in its natural spontaneity" (Cosgrove, 1996: 239). The novel does not construct any such image of the "recent past". Whether imagined in terms of nationality, Catholicism or land, the past in *Paddy Clarke* is not represented in positive terms. The episode with Miss Watkins and the 1916 Proclamation is ironic-satirical; there is no lamenting of lost identity there. The representation of religion is likewise ironic, comical — or in the passage where Paddy recognises the failure of prayer to help him, explicitly critical. But Paddy is not shown to *lose* anything by this; Doyle has not shown religion *giving* him anything important to his sense of identity to lose. As for the depiction of land in the novel, the nostalgia is not for a historical, *Irish* place but a *child's* sense of place, possessed only by imagination and the centripetal delusions of childhood.

Doyle's text, for all its desultory bilingualism and heterogeneous cultural signifiers, does not problematise identity by showing a nationalist, Catholic and pastoral Ireland infiltrated and eroded by an international, secular, urban modernity; rather, it shows a period in which a new generation encountered a modernity that would require it to invent identities outside the traditional collective formations of nation, religion and eventually class. The break-up at the end of the novel is not just between Paddy's parents; what the novel points to is the generation gap that will open between Paddy and his parents. He will grow up into a very different sense of individual and collective identity than theirs.

Head concludes that "the loss of paternal stability for Paddy Clarke pitches him . . . into an implied post-nationalist world of unstable identities. The freedom from established patterns of nationalist affiliation, however, marks a significant historical moment" (Head, 2002: 144). This is insightful, but the loss of the father and the broken family circle in *Paddy Clarke* should not be considered apart from the changes in the boy's landscape, the open fields of north Dublin, as they are bulldozed, dug up and filled with the brick and concrete of the Barrytown estate in a kind of urban pathetic fallacy. If *Paddy Clarke* is read symbolically in relation to "Irish modernity", it is the synergy between this building and un-building that is the disquieting hypothesis behind the novel's disturbing pathos.

Paddy Clarke Ha Ha Ha seems to express the judgement that Irish society and culture opened up to modernity in the 1960s in ways which failed to negotiate it in anything more than superficial, material terms — a failure which led to a society without "soul", as Jimmy Rabbitte Jr says in *The Commitments*, and one that rejected the change in social policy represented by the first divorce referendum.

The Dublin of *Paddy Clarke Ha Ha Ha* is heading towards the city of *The Commitments*, *The Snapper*, *The Van*, *Family*, and *The Woman Who Walked into Doors*. A space was cleared and a place created, but neither meant human or social disconnection were bridged. Dublin becomes a larger city but not necessarily a better city. What happened to the Clarkes may be commonplace but it is also a reflection of a fundamental weakness in Irish society — the misery of adults and children incarcerated in a sham social form or expelled into the categories of the outlawed or damned. Paddy grows up by being broken, but perhaps, like the medical myth of the broken bone, he emerges stronger for his pain. Let down by the state religion, which failed to console or connect him to anything greater than his own imagination, and by the national(ist) education system which failed to inspire him more than it sought to indoctrinate and discipline him, ultimately Paddy, like his creator, seems to discover that memory, imagination and the art of fiction are his best hope for a life that is "self-delighting, / Self-appeasing, self-affrighting" (Yeats, 1983: 189).

Chapter Five

"What went wrong with Daddy?": *Family* and *The Woman Who Walked into Doors*

By 2003, only nine years after it was spotted, the Celtic Tiger seems to have been downgraded from economic miracle to stuffed animal. But well before such analysts as Denis O'Hearn, Peadar Kirby and others were presenting the statistical evidence to contradict the "received wisdom" (O'Hearn, 1998: 1) about the new Ireland, Roddy Doyle was demystifying the beast. *The Woman Who Walked into Doors* (1996) was published in the year that was described by one analyst as "'the triumphant culmination' of the new independent Ireland" (O'Hearn, 1998: 65). Along with *Family* (1994), Doyle's TV series in which Paula Spencer, the novel's narrator-protagonist, first appears, *The Woman Who Walked into Doors* was a grim reminder that for those already living on the economic and social margins of Irish society, the new prosperity merely pushed them further from the centre. As in the trilogy and *Paddy Clarke Ha Ha Ha*, Doyle shows a society and culture whose superficial modernity of supermarkets, Walkmans, home videos and the DART coexists with traditions of silence, acquiescence and denial. *Family* and *The Woman Who Walked into Doors* compose an obscene scream in the face of a complacent middle class that did not want to know about alcoholism, spousal and sexual abuse, professional blindness and institutional apathy.

The transition from *Paddy Clarke Ha Ha Ha* to *Family* would not have been difficult for Doyle; it was a return to the socio-economic class he was more comfortable portraying, if a lower level of that class; it was also a return to the contemporary period. Music features thematically and in relation to characterisation in the series in the same way it does in *The Commitments* and *The Snapper*, and there is much in *Family* that is simply an exaggeration of elements in the trilogy. Charlo not only deals in stolen merchandise like Bertie, we actually see him thieving; and Charlo's sexual escapade with his friend's wife is what Jimmy Sr almost brings himself to fantasise with Bertie's wife on Christmas Day. Charlo's refusal to listen to Paula's concerns about the children and her disgust at his influence on them recalls Veronica's efforts with the twins and Jimmy Sr's reluctance to help her out. Charlo and John Paul's love of soccer recalls Jimmy Sr and Darren in *The Van* and the scenes at the Spencer dinner table also recall that setting in the trilogy. Nicola Spencer could be one of the young factory girls that Jimmy Sr spies on as they pass in front of his house in *The Van*, and John Paul ends up becoming another of his class's "disappeared", like Leslie Rabbitte.

Doyle wrote *Family* as he was finishing *Paddy Clarke* and John Paul in the series is not much older than Paddy and like Paddy hangs out with a gang of school friends. The two scenes in which John Paul gets out of bed at night and stumbles upon his parents fighting (on one occasion, wetting himself in fear) recall similar scenes in the earlier novel. The scene in which Paddy's parents argue at the dinner table and Paddy starts rocking back and forth becomes the scene in which Paula and Charlo argue in front of their children and the asthmatic John Paul is driven to use his "puffer". John Paul runs away from home for a night, whereas Paddy plans to but is pre-empted by his father's departure; and very much like Paddy, John Paul is shown being torn between his love for his mother and for his father. Both *Paddy Clarke Ha Ha Ha* and *Family* come to a climax with the departure of the father.

In 1997, Doyle said that he was "most proud of" his screenplay for *Family* (Paschel, 1998: 154). He wrote the TV drama at the invitation of Michael Waring, a BBC producer whose *Boys from the Black Stuff*, written by Alan Bleasdale, had impressed Doyle when he saw it in the early 1980s (White, 2001: 155). Using the Ballymun estate in north Dublin as the setting, *Family* is very much in the same vein as the Waring-Bleasdale series — an uncompromising, "in your face" urban docu-drama. Doyle describes himself as "socially committed and politically engaged" and has admitted that he has no qualms about upsetting and outraging people (Costello, 2001: 91). Following the screening of *Family*, he received a letter from an outraged priest telling him, "In your own words, fuck off" (Fay, 1996: 19). While Doyle has repeated more than once that, as a novelist, he is a story-teller-entertainer and not a moralist — "I have no manifesto or agenda myself" (Paschel, 1997: 153) — his comments about *Family* and *The Woman Who Walked into Doors* suggest otherwise. It is a clearly moral "should" that we hear in his statement that "I feel [*The Woman Who Walked into Doors*] should have been written and I'm glad I wrote it — in an Irish context, it says things that should be said and haven't been said before" (White, 2001: 173). The same could be said for his recent short stories published in *Metro Éireann*.

Like *Paddy Clarke Ha Ha Ha*, *The Woman Who Walked into Doors*, is a retrospective narrative. The structure is more complex in the later work, however, because Doyle has Paula "unpack" different compartments of her memory

— the period of Charlo's death a year before she begins writing; the year before that, following her eviction of him from the family house; their courtship and seventeen-year marriage; and her own childhood and adolescence. Then, she was Paula O'Leary, born only two years before Paddy Clarke; she is the Paula we do not see in *Family*. She is also the construct of the narrator's memory in *The Woman Who Walked into Doors*. Like Paddy, Paula is the narrator-protagonist and with all the obvious differences of age, gender and class that separate them, they have one characteristic in common: both tell their stories as a way of trying to understand a central event in their lives. For Paula, the mystery is what attracted her to Charlo, what kind of man he really was, and whether he was ever what she thought he was — someone worthy of her love. The structure of her narrative implies that the answers she seeks are not to be found in any one compartment of her past but are scattered throughout, and particularly in her memories of childhood, her family, and her experience in the school system.

Because she is representing herself, Paula comes off better in the novel than in the series. The second episode of the series ends with Paula going to casualty to find an unconscious John Paul having just had his stomach pumped; the doctor is upset and becomes irritated with her because she will not acknowledge the seriousness of her son's condition and what his behaviour is saying. She simply refuses to face it. In the novel's hospital scenes, however, Paula represents herself as a double victim, first of her abusive husband and then of an indifferent medical bureaucracy that sees her as a "hopeless case", a social stereotype and not an individual. *Family* presents more vividly the society and world Paula inhabits, and especially the impact of her disastrous marriage to Charlo on her children — John Paul and Nicola, in particular. The novel presents the interior world of the character from which much of her behaviour issues and which is profoundly

damaged by the reactions it elicits from her husband, an interior world that remains hidden and inarticulate in the TV
series. But when we learn in the novel that John Paul has left
home and is a heroin addict living on the streets, this comes
as no great surprise to the series viewer. When we hear
Paula talk about her adolescence and her experiences at
home and at school, then her original attraction to Charlo —
which is difficult to imagine in the series — is understandable.

Paula: Facing Up

The character of Paula Spencer emerges from *Family* in the
same way that Jimmy Rabbitte Sr came out of *The Snapper*.
As he wrote the series, Doyle gradually became more interested in Paula's character and had begun to think about the
novel by the time the fourth episode was broadcast (Jeffers,
2002: 54); in a sense, the opening frames of that episode
show the birth of the novel, as we watch a drunk Paula talking to her reflection in her bedroom mirror: "My name is
Paula Spencer and I am an alcoholic. . . . My name is Paula
O'Leary, no . . . my name is Paula Spencer and I am an alcoholic." The camera is focused on the mirror image and then
slowly pulls back to reveal Paula from behind, but Ger Ryan
speaks her lines looking into the camera, as if she were
looking out from the mirror, as if she were a prisoner in the
glass as well as of the bottle. In *Family*, Doyle could only
show a few months of Paula Spencer's life, and so the novel
came not only out of a sense of unfinished business with the
character, but of incomplete presentation: "The book allowed me to give the full woman" and "confirms the choices
you see in the broadcast because it allows her to explain"
(White, 2001: 157). The novel tells the story of how Paula
O'Leary became Paula Spencer, but whether her narrative
contains an "explanation" of that process is an important
critical question for readers and the answer is perhaps best

searched for in the difference between her narrative and her narration. For while the facts of Paula's story are significant, it is the self-consciousness that grows within her as a result of the processes of memory, imagination, and narration, and the life-story she constructs for herself through those processes, that mark the progress she makes.

In *Family*, there is a conventional linearity to Paula's story. Over the four episodes we see her dire predicament but we also see her emerge from it step by step, beginning with her eviction of Charlo from the family home, her rejection of Ray Harris, telling the yuppie in Howth whose house she cleans to "fuck off", defending John Paul's right to have a tattoo against the school authorities, and finally, resisting Charlo's attempt to insinuate himself back into the family. The final scene in the series, in which Paula surprises her children at the dinner table by asking John Paul to say grace, leaves the viewer with a sense of a harried woman under great stress but coping and over the worst of it. The novel tells a different story, even though at the end of it, too, in Doyle's view, "There is room for hope" (White, 2001: 155). Paula may have survived the marriage and Charlo, faced up to her alcoholism, gained her independence, and begun to feel some pride in herself, but the focus of her narrative is much more on the past than the future, as if the key to her future is lost and waiting to be found there.

This dramatic and moving story of an abused woman not only shows Doyle's growing moral imagination, it also expresses a quantum leap in his self-consciousness as an artist. His most morally intense novel is also his most self-consciously metafictive. This latter quality also points toward his next novel. The questions about memory, imagination and truth that Paula raises in relation to her personal history are clear precursors to the narrative and critical issues that Doyle raises in *A Star Called Henry* about modern Irish history, nationalist historiography, and the representation of the past. Paula's struggle to come to terms with her history, a struggle from which the "story" of her life emerges, is an emblem for the larger society and culture which contain her and of which she is a representative. Breaking free of Charlo does not just happen with his expulsion from the home, nor even with his death; two years later, Paula must go on her Orphic journey to the past, not to bring the dead back to life, but to bring herself — or a "new self" — to life. Her narration is as much a rebirth as a recovery.

Paula must tell a story about herself that will satisfy two profound needs: the story must provide a convincing explanation of how she has come to be in the situation she finds herself, and yet the reconstruction of the past which this entails must also clear a way for her to move ahead with her life unencumbered by that past. The difficulty she faces is that at either end of the spectrum of "histories" she might tell are accounts of her life that would leave her psychologically crippled and emotionally paralysed. One possible "true" version of her story — that Charlo never loved her because she is not worthy of being loved — might make sense but would destroy her. Another — that Charlo *did* love her and was basically a good human being who "went bad" — is unconvincing and would require such energies of self-delusion that its effect would be the same — an inability to get beyond the past. Somehow she needs to find a "truth" between these extremes that will not destroy her but which also faces the "facts" of her life.

Paula's problem is, of course, Doyle's problem. More so than in *Paddy Clarke Ha Ha Ha*, he put himself in a box when he opted to use a first-person narrator-protagonist for this novel. The challenge in *Paddy Clarke* was to create the voice and sensibility of a ten-year-old boy going through a year in which he witnessed the break-up of his parents' marriage. Doyle managed this by telling the story in the past tense, which allowed him to subtly inform the boy-narrator's voice and naïveté with occasional ironies and a growing pathos that derive from the implicit presence of the older self that shadows the narration. These two dimensions of the narrative voice cohere through Doyle's use of the central motif of the narrator's struggle to understand his father's change of heart.

But in *The Woman Who Walked into Doors*, this same kind of challenge is complicated because Doyle must not only imagine the experience of a thirty-nine-year-old alcoholic wife and mother who is the victim of chronic abuse, which is daunting enough, but he also must construct a voice for this narrator-protagonist that will do more than simply "tell the story" but not violate credibility by doing that "more". To put it bluntly, he risks constructing a character whose behaviour suggests that she is too "stupid" — or in her own words, "brainwashed and braindead, a zombie" (W, 176) — to be able to tell the story of her life in any way that will make sense of it other than by representing it as the life of a very stupid woman.

Doyle extricates himself from this box by turning his problem into Paula's problem. By manoeuvring her into a situation of conflict with her older sister, Carmel, over the "real" truth about their father and their childhood, for example, Doyle allows her to raise, in a realistic manner, issues about memory, imagination and truth, and become self-conscious about her own undertaking. A further reason that Paula's self-consciousness seems realistic is that it emerges from a constant resistance to her sister's account of their family life that seems like denial. Recalling the occasion when her father saw her wearing mascara and called her a slut, Paula remembers how the older "Carmel was always fighting with him":

> I remember the screams and the punches. She remembers them as well but she refuses to remember anything else, the good things abut home and my father. (W, 46)

Throughout this recollection, Paula records her mother's passivity. When her father plays "horsey-horsey" with her and her younger sister, Denise, and orders Carmel to go and make tea, he tells his wife: "It's for her own good" and Paula remembers: "She nodded. She agreed with him even though she was shaking. I remember being terrified." Years later, Paula seems to have become like her mother: "He loved her. That was why he did it. Fathers were different then. He'd meant it for the best, being cruel to be kind. Carmel hated him. She remembers nothing else" (W, 46–7). Paula's defence of her father is more than it seems and the clue to its psychological complexity is her statement that "Fathers were different then". Her defence of her father expresses her need to have control over her memory of the past — in this case, of her childhood — when the memories she most desperately needs to feel secure about are those of her life with Charlo. Her arguments with Carmel about her father are a sublimation of her arguments with herself about her relationship with Charlo, who ultimately, was no different from her own father. Mr O'Leary's violent reactions to Carmel's sexual maturity recall Charlo's reaction to Nicola in *Family*, and taken along with his inappropriate "horse-play" with his other daughters — one of whom describes herself as "terrified" and her sister as distressed, and the image of his wife, silent, cowed, and "shaking", suggest that he was an abusive parent and husband. Paula "cannot see what she has hidden in her memory and now is hiding in her narrative" (Jeffers, 2002: 58), however, because to admit such a "truth" about her father would shatter the "story" of her childhood which she has told herself. Moreover, the destruction of that memory would raise questions about the truth of her memories about her life with Charlo, during which, until quite recently, she had behaved much like her mother with her father.

The deep source of Paula's conflict with Carmel may be her repressed recognition that her situation at home became a repetition of Carmel's; if Carmel intentionally got pregnant at seventeen in order to get married and escape her father, Paula was not much older when she "fell" for Charlo Spencer, a young man whom she recognised immediately to be some-one her father would not intimidate. She admits that she married because of "Love and my father" (*W*, 129), but while she describes in detail what she means by the first, she does not "unpack" the second, except to describe her marriage as "my great escape" (*W*, 134). The absence of any conscious irony in the latter comment is significant. As with her ingenuous belief that "Fathers were different then", it signifies the psychological work being done by the act of narration as Paula works out her life by addressing the meaning of the past. Charlo *was* her saviour; that he was merely another tormentor disguised as a saviour is something she is not yet prepared to admit. It would destroy her. With Carmel's assaults on her memory of her father and her childhood clearly taking their toll, Paula cannot afford to lose her memory of the early, halcyon days with Charlo. Thinking of her father at the time of her marriage, Paula asks: "What went wrong with Daddy?" (*W*, 54). At the wedding he behaves like an inarticulate, pint-pot Lear, raging in silence at his daughter's betrayal, as she, in a combi-nation of joy and apparently sincere perplexity, literally dances out of his grasp. Except that now, following Charlo's death, he seems to be reaching out — through Carmel — to take her back. This is Paula's predicament: to accept Carmel's version of the past would be to return to her father's kingdom and admit that Charlo had not saved her but had been her father's "double agent" all along; yet to reject Carmel's "truth" and hold to her belief that Charlo always loved her, seems harder and harder the more she looks into the past.

Paula has happy memories of her father during a family holiday at Courtown and on Sunday afternoons when they were young, but Carmel mocks her. When she turns to De-nise for support, Paula is surprised when she agrees:

> Jesus, I felt good. That proved it. . . . I wasn't just
> making it all up. My stomach landed and took off. I
> felt secure. I felt sane. It's a valuable feeling. It's a
> long time since I took it for granted.
>   Denise confirmed it. The man I remembered was
> my father. I wasn't wasting my time or fooling myself.
> Once upon a time my life had been good. My parents
> had loved me. The house was full of laughter. I'd run
> to school every morning. (W, 56)

The poignancy and pathos of "Once upon a time my life had
been good. My parents had loved me" derive from the des-
peration in the voice, not from any sense that Paula has won
possession of solid ground. The consciously anachronistic
"Once upon a time" evokes the world of fairytale and fantasy, and undercuts the hard won victory even as she celebrates that, for a moment, *she* feels "solid":

> I went home happy. I lay in bed happy. . . . I felt
> solid. I felt right. I'd got something right. I could trust
> my memory. My father was my father; my past was
> my past. I could start again. I could believe myself.
> The things that came into my head were true. My fa-
> ther had been a nice man. Charlo had been a loving
> husband. I had been a good-looking woman. It hadn't
> always been like this. I had once been a girl. I used to
> read my stories out in class. I used to drink only at
> the weekends. . . . Men whistled. I had a lovely smile.
> . . . I cooked great Sunday dinners. I made Bisto my
> own. Charlo peeled the spuds and carrots. I lay in
> my cot and the wind lifted the curtains and dropped
> them. All these things were in my head and all of
> them were true. Just a few words from Denise. He
> was nice. Proof. My past was real. I could stand on it
> and it wouldn't collapse under me. It was there.
>   I could start again. (W, 59)

Precisely how Paula's narrative is "about me" is evident here; the inextricable processes of recollection and narration serve a deeper process of self-reconstruction. Paula is trying to put herself back together, beginning with her memories of childhood and adolescence, and ending with Charlo's death. After almost twenty years of a life that has relentlessly erased her, she is trying to make herself "real".

For Doyle, memory is a form of imagination. The above passage shows just how psychologically and emotionally "battered" Paula is at this point, how much she needs experiences that will restore her confidence in her own memory, point of view, and powers of understanding. But what is remarkable about Paula's narration here is the devastatingly honest way that Doyle's construction of the process of her recovery through narrative foregrounds the narrator's delusion while at the same time allowing the narrative's value as contingent, therapeutic "truth". This is only a moment, of course, and Paula's narrative does move into darker territory. What Doyle is developing through Paula's narrative voice at this point in the novel is a replacement for the irony that a third-person narrative voice would have afforded him. While he can make Paula capable of irony, to allow her too much or too deep an irony would undermine her credibility as a character. Thus the irony derives from the reader's recognition of the interplay of contradiction, ingenuousness, pathos, denial, and the realistic limitations of intelligence and imagination in the character. Paula may have a bit of her tongue in her cheek in the passage — "I could start again. Men whistled. Daddy laughed. My husband peeled the spuds" — but her need and desire to "start again" are profoundly sincere nevertheless.

Carmel accuses her of conscious fabrication:

> –I know what you're up to, she said.
> –What?
> . . .

–Rewriting history, she said.

–I don't know what you're talkin' about, I said. –I don't even know what you mean.

–I'm sure you have your reasons, said Carmel.

–Fuck off, Carmel, will yeh.

(I'm not. What Carmel says. Rewriting history. I'm doing the opposite. I want to know the truth, not make it up. She has her reasons too.) (*W*, 56–7)

"She has her reasons too" suggests that on some level of understanding Paula recognises that her desire for the truth will influence the kind of truth she will come up with. The parentheses draw attention to her attempt to quarantine her doubts about her enterprise; conversely, they also draw attention to Doyle's acceptance of the *poetic* nature of identity — "poetic" in the sense of crafted, fabricated, emphasising the "made" in "made up" more than the fictive sense.

Paula's increasing self-consciousness and explicit references to the problem of truth and narrative are a sign of Doyle's growing self-consciousness about the art of fiction. They also obliquely engage the issue — problematic for some — of his appropriation of a female voice. For we can hear Doyle in the dialectical tension between Paula's "I want to be honest" and "I'm messing around here. Making things up; a story. I'm beginning to enjoy it" (*W*, 184). When she goes over what she has written, quoting it, challenging the metaphorical language, recognising "I choose one word and end up telling a different story. I end up making it up instead of just telling it" (*W*, 184–5), Doyle is not using her to affirm a preference for a "plain" style over one rich in metaphor; he is acknowledging both the joy of creativity and the nature of writing as a combination of the willed and the serendipitous.

Doyle's growing self-consciousness, moreover, is reflected in his evolution from the third-person narratives of the Barrytown trilogy to the first-person recollective narratives of *Paddy Clarke Ha Ha Ha*, *The Woman Who Walked into*

Doors and *A Star Called Henry*. Like other important first-person recollective fictions of the period — Robert McLiam Wilson's *Ripley Bogle* (1989), Patrick McCabe's *The Butcher Boy* (1992), Seamus Deane's *Reading in the Dark* (1996) and John Banville's *The Untouchable* (1997), for example — Doyle's novels use the narrator-protagonist's search for truth or self-understanding to foreground not just the ambiguous relations between truth and narrative, but also between memory and identity, and identity and history.

This self-consciousness in Doyle and his contemporaries may reflect the sense developing in the larger culture of the "freeing up" of identity, the sense not just of the fictiveness of identity but the narrativity of history and the freedom of the individual to accept, reject, revise and re-tell the stories of self and society. While having Paula search for herself "through the act of writing" makes *The Woman Who Walked into Doors* "Doyle's most fully realized novel" (Hand, 1996: 14) by this point in his career, Doyle presented the same process of self-discovery through self-representation in *The Commitments*, only there he used music and musical performance and focused on a group rather than an individual. What is significant in Paula's case is her isolation. While the support of her sisters and the love of her children are important to her survival, both come to figure as plot elements in the story she consciously constructs. Paula is alone with her memories and the blank page. In this respect her real progenitor is Paddy Clarke; for both it is the act of narration, poesis, the making of a narrative, that offers the hope of understanding that true catharsis brings. Moreover, the novel does not show Paula finding herself in the sense of an authentic-essential self that was lost because of the conditions of her life with Charlo; on the contrary, it shows that any such archaeological quest is itself a fiction and does not uncover   "solid ground" of un-ambiguous self-understanding. Rath , Doyle shows Paula's narrative activity to itself be the meaiu 1 of a self-invention that might be described as the myth of self-discovery. We need to recognise the ingenuousness in Paula's statement of belief in the accessibility of historical truth and her blindness to the ways self-interest will affect the story she tells.

Paradoxically, it is Paula's ingenuousness and blindness as a narrator that give her narrative the *ironic* truth which is the novel's most important moral and aesthetic achievement. The two most important men in Paula's life remain painful and profoundly disturbing mysteries to her. It is important to recognise the symmetry in her narrative between her preoccupation with her father and the argument with Carmel about his real nature, and the obsession with Charlo and her mystification by the fact that Charlo beat Mrs Fleming for no apparent reason before he shot her. Paula never explicitly connects the two, but her text does — as for example in the "interleafing" of the sections in which Paula remembers her wedding and honeymoon with those in which she imagines what Charlo did to Mrs Fleming. Thinking of the latter, Paula writes:

> Jesus Christ. The hugeness of it; the evil. There were things that had happened in that house that I'd never know about. Because there was no evidence. There were no witnesses. . . .
> –It's okay, love, said Carmel.
> The things we say. Sometimes they make no sense, sometimes they're just packed with lies. I'm grand. Don't mind me. *You fell.* It's okay, love.
> –What did he do, Carmel? I asked. (W, 122)

The first order of reference here is to Charlo and Mrs. Fleming. However, because of the story Paula has been telling, and because of Carmel's remarks about her father, "There were things that had happened in that house that I'd never know about" and Paula's question, "What did he do, Carmel?" echo ominously with earlier sections in the narrative; in particular, with Carmel's insinuation of abuse:

—There's things you never knew about.

I heard Denise gasp when Carmel said that. . . .

—What do you fuckin' mean, Carmel?

Her hints; she'd been making them for years. I didn't want any more of them. They were getting in my way. She made them up as she went along.

. . .

It was the drink. You made things up when you were drinking and you believed them if you were drunk enough. They became absolutely true and real. I knew.

. . .

I knew what Carmel was up to. She'd had a hard time from our father when she was a teenager; they never really recovered from it — they were always at each other . . . and now she was giving herself a good reason for hating him, making it up and believing it. Loving herself for hating herself. I knew well what she was up to.

My father never did anything to her. (W, 84–5)

Paula does not and cannot know this for certain, and her narration, with her admission that she, too, is prone to "making it up and believing it", undercuts her contradiction of Carmel and the authority of her final statement. Elsewhere in her narrative Paula admits her propensity to fantasy. She buses to the scene of Charlo's crime, but when she gets there she walks past the house without looking at it. She imagines Mr Fleming inside, "lonely but fine", with a bank colleague who will soon become his lover: "I was glad now I hadn't seen him. It was better imagining him. It made more sense" (W, 147). "More sense": making sense is always comparative, a choice. Paula thinks she knows "what Carmel was up to", but at this point does not stop to fully consider what she might be "up to" in trying to remember her father her way.

Paula refuses to believe there is any truth in Carmel's version of her father but does not stop to consider why it was "getting in my way". What she writes about Mr Fleming also applies to her father: "It was better imagining him" because otherwise "The hugeness of it; the evil" would be more than she could handle. The enormity of the darkness that looms in regard to her memory of her father cannot be separated from that which threatens her memory of her marriage to Charlo. She imagines scenarios to explain why Charlo hit Mrs Fleming but "It didn't work. I couldn't convince myself. I couldn't deny it or believe it. I hadn't a clue. I kept starting at the beginning and trying to get to an end, an end that wasn't appalling. I wanted an ending that included the facts" (*W*, 157). The answer that Paula cannot bear to consider is that Charlo hit Mrs Fleming for the same reason he hit her — for *no* reason, simply because he *wanted* to and *could*. Why did he hit her, she asks, when she was not his wife: "I wanted none of the answers that started to breathe in me; I smothered them. . . . They mocked my marriage, my love; they mocked my whole life" (*W*, 158). In her battered state, Paula needs to think that there was some *reason* for the abuse she suffered; the possibility that her seventeen-year-long catalogue of injuries (*W*, 175–6) represents merely the *reason-less* whims of a sociopath who did not love her makes no sense to her because it would make her life senseless. Ultimately, the sign of Paula's progress in her effort to make sense of her past in a way that will allow her to move on with her life is her reluctant accommodation of this possible truth in the story she finally tells.

The insertion of self-doubt and uncertainty into the narrative voice only gets Doyle close to a way out of the box his choice of protagonist put him in. What gets him outside is the likewise realistic process of the narrator's acceptance that she will never know the "truth" about her father or ever understand Charlo. She tries to rationalise his life by blaming his behaviour on society and a hidden flaw in his character:

> If he'd been a bit different he would have been great
> at something — he'd have made a different name for
> himself. A businessman or a politician, or even an ac-
> tor. He'd have been a star. If he'd had the education.
> If he'd had other work when all the building around
> Dublin stopped and there was nothing left for him to
> do. He would have put that anger to use. He
> wouldn't have been wasted. . . . (*W*, 191)

But Paula can't sustain this sociological fantasy in good faith:

> But he wasn't unemployed the first time he hit me.
> Beaten by Charlo Spencer. That's a fact that I can't
> mess around with. Robbed by Charlo Spencer. Mur-
> dered by Charlo Spencer. Charlo Spencer lost his
> job and started beating his wife. It's not as simple as
> that. He started robbing. He shot a woman and
> killed her. Because he didn't have a job, was rejected
> by society. It would be nice if it was that easy. . . . I
> could rest if I believed that; I could rest. (*W*, 192)

That Paula does not allow herself to be comforted by the
received wisdom of her times is, as Doyle constructs her,
evidence both of her common sense and of the sincerity of
her desire to be honest with herself. She knows she did not
deserve to be hit; she knows that "You don't hit the people
you love. . . . not the way he did it, again and again" (*W*,
192). Paula knows she was innocent.

In *Paddy Clarke Ha Ha Ha*, Doyle's challenge was to tell a
complex story from the limited perspective of a ten-year-old
boy. This self-imposed restraint, paradoxically, became a
source of expressive power because it allowed him to represent the child's perspective in a naïve, literalistic manner
through the physical and emotional *realia* of his experience.
He could then manipulate the deeper effects of irony and
pathos from the difference between the narrator's and the
reader's capacities for understanding. Paddy's innocence is

his inexperience; Paula's is moral. Doyle makes the point when she recognises her mistake in thinking she was to blame whenever Charlo hit her (*W*, 170) and that the real causes of Charlo's behaviour had nothing to do with her:

> No. No. No! I'm innocent. I'm innocent. I'm innocent. . . .
> It was always coming. Before that night; before we got married; before we met. That was Charlo.
> *Why did you marry him then, Paula?*
> Fuck off and leave me alone.
> He. Hit. Me. (*W*, 171)

This is an important passage. There is a motif in Paula's narrative, her repeated "Ask me. Ask me", when she recalls her experiences with the doctors and nurses who treated her at casualty over the years but who never asked her how she came to be injured. There is an ironic side to this motif, however: one question that many readers might want to put to her is not "Why did you marry him then, Paula?" but why on earth did you stay with the monstrous moron for seventeen years? Doyle has Paula answer this question in her reply to her own (or Doyle's) rhetorical question — which sounds very much like the kind of moralistic question that a certain kind of middle-class reader might put to his character: you married him, you chose him, you stayed with him — for seventeen years; explain that. "He. Hit. Me.": that's the precise moral point. Why she married him; why she stayed with him — all that is irrelevant. The point is: he abused her. *Charlo* was the problem, not Paula. Paula was the victim and there is something deeply sickening — some would say "patriarchal" — about a society that looks to "share" the responsibility for spousal abuse between the abuser and his or her victim.

Doyle's novel *does* explain why Paula married Charlo, however, and why she stayed with him for so long. Her narrative brings the reader to see that in a sense she was *driven* towards Charlo; her character was moulded in such a way and she was put into a situation which made Charlo not only an attractive option, but at a time when she needed one, the only option. In this respect, Doyle's understanding of Paula is based on the fundamental theme of all his fiction: individual self-esteem, particularly working-class self-esteem, in a historical, social and cultural order that makes it difficult.

"Ask me": The Culture that Watches Doors Walk into People

Doyle said he did not research *Family*: "I just allowed my guts to decide what seemed to be right. But I read a lot of case studies as I was writing [*The Woman Who Walked into Doors*] to surround myself with information" (Boland, 1996). In the novel, consequently, Paula and Charlo clearly fit the profiles of the "battered woman" and her abuser in the "battered wife syndrome" (Jeffers, 2002: 52; see Walker, 1984: 203, 11). Recent thinking about this phenomenon, however, does not consider it in terms of "isolated incidents that are peculiar to certain domestic situations. Rather, the syndrome corresponds to something much deeper — the entire political and societal structure" (Jeffers, 2002: 52). Doyle has said that his important insight about Charlo came when he realised that the key to his character was control; that he was the kind of man who used violence to control others (White, 2001: 156). If "the battered woman syndrome exists because at some level, society and culture support this kind of manifestation of power" (Jeffers, 2002: 53), then Doyle has used Paula's story to expose a poisonous substratum of Irish culture and society.

It has become a critical-theoretical commonplace to originate the problems of women in Irish society both in the "deep structure" of Irish myth and in the more recent institutionalisation of that myth in the post-independence history

of the Irish State — particularly in the fall-out from the collu-
sive misogyny of the Catholic Church and nationalist State in
de Valera's 1937 Constitution and its notorious conscription
of women as wives and mothers modelled on the Mother of
God and Mother Ireland. Paula Spencer's question to her
sisters, "What went wrong with Daddy?" is, for the sister-
hood, a rhetorical question: "Daddy" was simply being
"Daddy". In *The Woman Who Walks into Doors*, "Daddy" is
Mr O'Leary, Charlo Spencer, and the patriarchal Irish society
that has spawned them and their unhappy spouses.

Paula is, in all these senses, "Daddy's girl". The way Doyle
shows this is through the constructing and coding of the
young girl as "slut". Significantly, Doyle conveys Paula's "complete entrapment" (Jeffers, 2002: 57) in her class's version of
the patriarchal-heterosexual matrix that organises Irish society through her recollection of the way language "branded"
her as first and foremost a (hetero)sexual object. To begin
with, Doyle shows how Paula was not allowed to grow into
her own body or sexuality but rather was alienated from the
former even as the latter was prescribed for her by the om-
nivorous and omnipresent male gaze of her reptilian teachers:

> it all started happening to me the minute I walked
> into that kip. Waters and his wandering thumb and
> Dillon and his wandering snot made me feel filthy;
> there was something about me that drew them to
> me, that made them touch me. It was my tits that I
> was too young for; I'd no right to them. It was my
> hair. It was my legs and my arms and my neck. There
> were things about me that were wrong and dirty. I
> thought that then. . . . I was a dirty slut in some way
> that I didn't understand and couldn't control; I made
> men and boys do things. (W, 35)

Paula's internalisation of the way others look at and treat her
both reflects her low self-esteem and exacerbates it; it also

sustains the socio-cultural myth that it is "natural" for men to behave this way around young women because it is the female body that makes them behave this way; the young Paula was convinced in herself that "I made men and boys do things" because her society and culture did not offer her — or see the need to offer her — any alternative explanation.

Paula had no choice but to run the gauntlet of adolescent sexuality that her society put before her. Each vulgarising, coarsening, demeaning and delimiting step she took, took her toward Charlo. "Fuck off. –Fuck off, yourself. – Fuck off. Day in, day out. –Get your fuckin' hands off me" (*W*, 35). The only convocation Paula experiences is Martin Kavanagh's equine "Neeaaa!" (*W*, 40) as she "wanks" him during a class in her final year. With this she matriculates to her world's idea of "woman":

> The bell went. Everybody knew.
> I did it to him; he didn't do it to me. I did it.
> My First Wank.
> I was proud. I was a woman. . . .
> I'd survived.
> I was someone. (*W*, 41)

Doyle shows how in this society the invisible female does not become visible "woman", does not feel credited with real presence, does not become "someone", until she enacts her identity by "servicing" the male. Significantly, Paula uses the same language when she describes how Charlo "made me someone" (*W*, 54) when he asked her to dance and walked her home the evening they first met. The girl is not a woman and the woman is not visible until the male "I" — ego, penis and eye — is pleasured or pleased.

The sexual gauntlet is actually a maze and progress through it is entrapment. Paula loses herself in and to the word "slut":

> Where I grew up — and probably everywhere else
> — you were a slut or a tight bitch, one or the other,
> if you were a girl — and usually before you were
> thirteen. You didn't have to do anything to be a slut.
> If you were good-looking; if you grew up fast. If you
> had a sexy walk; if you had clean hair, if you had dirty
> hair. If you wore platform shoes, and if you didn't.
> Anything could get you called a slut. (W, 46–7)

For woman, there is no escaping the patriarchal word, and it is patriarchy that makes the dirty word flesh. "My father called me a slut the first time I put on mascara. . . . –You don't need it, he said" (W, 46). And he is right, of course, as Paula realises; with or without mascara, she will be called a slut. "My brother, Roger, called me a slut because I wouldn't let him feel my up. I was fourteen, he was twelve. . . . –Come on, he said. Jesus, I don't know how many times I heard those words over the next few years":

> Come on. It never stopped. Come on. You were a
> slut if you let fellas put their tongues in your mouth
> and you were a tight bitch if you didn't — but you
> could also be a slut if you didn't. One or the other,
> sometimes both. There was no escape; that was you.
> Before I was a proper teenager, before I knew any-
> thing about sex, before I'd even left primary school
> — I was a slut. My daddy said it, fellas said it, other
> girls said it, men in vans and lorries said it. (W, 47)

In this wordscape, words can mean the opposite of each other, "slut" and "tight bitch", for example, but these appar-ent antonyms can also mean the same. "Everything made you one thing or the other" (W, 48) — or "sometimes both". What is mind-numbing is Paula's recognition that "Everyone. They were all in on it" (W, 49). And so as she says, for her, "There was no escape"; by the time she met Charlo, she was a brainwashed, brain-dead zombie-in-waiting (W, 176).

Paula's descriptions of the physical, verbal, and "scopic" abuse she suffered as a young girl add nuance to her comment about her life with Charlo: "It was one beating; it went on forever" (*W*, 206), a remark that recalls Paddy Clarke's about his parents: "It wasn't lots of little fights. It was one big one, rounds of the same fight" (*PC*, 255–6). It is interesting, too, that in *Paddy Clarke Ha Ha Ha*, language is the means by which the young boy comes to assert his individuality amongst his peers and to his elders, whereas in *The Woman Who Walked into Doors*, language is the instrument of the young girl's stereotyping. Paula's inability to figure out Charlo recalls Paddy's inability to understand his parents, but the injury to Paddy's self-esteem caused by his failure to make sense of his parents' fighting — "I didn't understand. I never would. . . . I was stupid" (*PC*, 255–6) — occurred to Paula's self-esteem long before she met her abusive husband. Paula was made to feel stupid as an adolescent (*W*, 42) and life with Charlo only continued that erosion of her self-confidence. Her narrative in part records the difficult struggle back that she begins once he is gone out of her life. Paula identifies the difference by speaking of herself in the third-person: "She isn't too fond of herself but she isn't too certain that she's stupid anymore" (*W*, 43). *The Woman Who Walked into Doors* is a milestone in contemporary Irish fiction because of its powerful representation of a woman trapped in the "battered-wife syndrome", but what also needs to be recognised is the way Doyle shows the victim being prepared or conditioned for victimhood by her society — specifically, by her experiences in her family and the school system.

Doyle's representation of the education system in *The Woman Who Walked into Doors*, and particularly of the working-class educational experience, extends his satirical treatment of the institution in *Paddy Clarke Ha Ha Ha*. But where the latter novel briefly satirises the unimaginative curriculum, neolithic pedagogy and culture of petty violence, in *The*

Woman Who Walked into Doors, Doyle represents Paula's experience at secondary school to be, even more than her family life, responsible for the relentless acid-drip of abjection that turned her from a bright little girl with hopes and potential into a dull and desperate young woman who would see Charlo Spencer as her redeemer. Paula had done well in primary school and had begun to blossom under the attention and encouragement of a teacher who recognised and praised her skill as a story-teller (W, 25). (Paula's experience here is definitely informed by Doyle's own; see Costello, 2001: 87–8.) But this fragile self-confidence was stripped from her the first morning at secondary school: "I was only in the tech half an hour when I realized that I wasn't good at all"; "It was a fright, finding out that I was stupid. Before I even got in the door" (W, 25, 28).

The extended description of Paula's ordeal at "the tech" is as depressing as anything in her narrative. In the same way that the classroom and playground of Paddy Clarke's school were a seminary for the violence he suffered, perpetrated and witnessed outside of school, so Paula's secondary-school experience is the brutal breeding ground of the life of abuse she enters when she marries Charlo. "That school made me rough. I wasn't like that before I started there" (W, 35), she recognises in retrospect, but what she does not recognise when she says "I ran out of the place" (W, 25), is that she ran into the arms of Charlo Spencer, in part, because of what her school experience had done to her — because of how it had failed her. "It happened to all of us. We went in children and we turned into animals" (W, 36). As in *Paddy Clarke Ha Ha Ha*, Doyle's fictional representation of the profession and professionals he spent so many years with is overwhelmingly negative — repugnant even: "The [teachers] that weren't perverts were either thick or bored or women. That was the only good thing about the women teachers; they didn't mess around with you" (W, 34).

The erosion of Paula's self-esteem at school simply continued in public what was happening at home. Her father's tyrannical behaviour with Carmel and her eventually drove both of them out of the house. As much as she tries to convince herself that she can remember him as "a nice man" (W, 119), she eventually admits that he was really "a bitter little pill and a bully" (W, 120). And when she comes to recognise that her father and Charlo "were very alike" (W, 121), the reader cannot help wonder if Paula's mother, too, was the victim of abuse. "She looked miserable. She looked so sad. . . . She didn't do anything except sit in front of the telly and watch the programmes that he put on and say yes and no when he spoke to her" (W, 120). When Mr O'Leary terrorises Carmel, her mother "agreed" with him; when he disciplines Paula, she "stayed out of it" (W, 46). A victim herself, Paula's mother becomes yet another cipher in the culture of silence and denial, in a pattern that Paula will repeat in her own marriage until she finds the courage and will to break out of it — as she does when she defends Nicola against Charlo.

School, family, neighbourhood conjoin to move Paula O'Leary along the one-way street to becoming Paula Spencer. "Now I had to act rough and think dirty. I had to fight. I had to be hard. Maybe it all happens anyway when you're growing up, no matter where you are; I don't really know" (W, 35). Once she found herself in an abusive marriage, society turned a blind eye to her predicament. Doyle has Paula's narrative corroborate the argument that Irish society at this time chose to see spousal abuse as a "private problem" rather than a socio-cultural issue (O'Connor, 1998: 71–2), as personal "troubles" rather than a socio-cultural pathology. Paula wants the nurses and doctors who treat her in casualty to ask her how she came to be injured; the motif develops a satirical theme of professional and institutional failure — the indifference, apathy or incompetence of those who should know and act better: "What about the burn on my hand? The missing hair? The teeth? I waited to be asked. Ask me. Ask me. Ask me. . . . Ask me about it. Ask" (W, 164; repeated 187, 189–90, 202). "They were all the same; they didn't want to know" (W, 202). Some of the strongest satire in the novel comes when Paula describes how her society makes the abused woman into an "invisible woman":

> The doctor never looked at me. He studied parts of me but he never looked at my eyes. He never looked at me when he spoke. He never saw me. Drink, he said to himself. I could see his nose twitching, taking in the smell, deciding. None of the doctors looked at me.
> . . . I could see all these people but they couldn't see me. . . . My mother looked and saw nothing. My father saw nothing, and he loved what he didn't see. My brothers saw nothing. His mother saw nothing. (W, 186–7).

Of course, Paula should not need to be asked to tell her story and her narrative is a self-interrogation that recognises that she had to make the effort to save herself before anyone else could help her. As a result, Doyle shows that the innermost circle of the culture of silence and denial is, tragically, the victim who refuses to "come out" and around whom, in ever-expanding circles of failure, a familial, institutional, public world revolves in varying degrees of moral indifference, emotional callousness, and institutional incompetence. Significantly, Paula does not mention any assistance from any "social service" following her separation from Charlo; as in *Family*, it is her sisters — ironically, Carmel, in particular (W, 188) — who help her get over that hurdle. But before that, doctors, nurses, priests, friends — no one wants to know. Doyle's scorn for the Catholic Church is evident in Paula's comments about the parish priest (W, 90) and in the reduction of religion to a literally empty symbol

— the dry, cobweb-covered holy water fount (*W*, 221) that is knocked to the floor as Paula pushes the dazed Charlo out the front door.

Paula was attracted to Charlo, ultimately, because he boosted her self-esteem. The reason Paula is such "a sucker for romance" (*W*, 41) is because romance makes her feel good; part of the reason she is so impressed by Charlo at their first meeting is that he made her feel good about herself: "He respected me", she says, twice (*W*, 52, 53). By noticing her, he "made me someone. Not a Queen or a Princess, just someone. It was a start. It filled me" (*W*, 54). The question Doyle's text raises is what had happened to Paula to make her into a "nobody", to make her feel she was an emptiness that needed to be filled? Whether or not Charlo really did love Paula and consciously acted to "fill" her need is irrelevant; even if she deluded herself, the point to consider is what made her so vulnerable to such delusion? The answer is the society and culture that made her think "I stopped being a slut the minute Charlo Spencer started dancing with me. . . . People looked at me and they saw someone different" (*W*, 45). To be perceived as "different": it's what Jimmy Rabbitte Jr promised Outspan and Derek (*C*, 6).

Doyle's characterisation of Paula and the satirical impact of the novel rest primarily on an "environmental" explanation of her predicament: Paula is a product of her family, her class, her failed education and her society. But the text also points to an important psychological experience in Paula's psycho-social development which affects her self-esteem and contributes a more "individual" explanation of her attraction to Charlo. Recalling her early passion for him, Paula remembers that "I'd loved him before I even met him and I never stopped. The minute I saw him, before I saw his face properly, I knew what being in love was" (*W*, 24). What this suggests, paradoxically, is that Paula needed to be in love — to love and be loved — as much as, perhaps more than, she loved Charlo himself. Her narrative records her love for Charlo, but it is significant that immediately before she describes when she "fell" for Charlo, Paula remembers an episode in her relationship with her mother:

> It was after my bath on Saturday night; I was standing on the towel, shaking, pretending I was cold. Mammy was rinsing Denise's hair. I started to dry myself. . . . I saw Mammy looking at me, at my chest. Then at me, my face. I couldn't understand her expression. I thought she was going to lose her temper. She looked away when she saw me looking back at her. Then the part that killed me: she was blushing. . . . She didn't look at me again. . . .
> I'll never forget it, the look on my mammy's face. It left me feeling like I'd done something terrible to her; I'd hurt her badly and I didn't know how, just that I'd done it. (*W*, 15–16)

Although her mother "makes it up to her" a few days later when she takes Paula shopping for a bra and turns it into a special day for her, and even though she prepares Paula for the other changes in her body she should expect — "She was grand when my period came" — Paula still feels "It's one of the only bad things I can remember from my childhood, that expression on my mammy's face in the bathroom, like I'd done something absolutely dreadful, terrible to her" (*W*, 18). She understands how and why her mother felt as she did because she thinks that she felt the same way when Nicola went through the same changes. But what is important is the pattern in which Paula's self-esteem suffers because of the way others look at her. Paula immediately internalises the experience with her mother in terms of guilt over her sexuality. Her mother's problem is Paula's fault. Paula is to blame; her body is to blame. And although Paula seems to move on, she has not forgotten the moment and the same mentality was active when Paula moved out of the home into the street and classroom, the world of the "slut" and "tight bitch". Once again, *she* was to blame; her body was to blame. The moment in the bathroom with her mother was not any "fall" from innocence so much as a sudden opening of distance between them. Significantly, Paula records her mother's "gaze" — not a man's, which feminist theory tells us we should expect — as the agency of her "othering", as what "killed" her. At that moment her "mammy" was replaced by her "mother", the woman who in her own life has been configured by patriarchy, who has run the same gauntlet as her daughter, and who is now, sadly, an agent of patriarchy. Paula's account of this episode in her life casts a different light on her comment that the most pleasure she had from sex with Charlo was when "I fucked him. He had nothing to do with it. It was all me" (W, 101). Her sexual passion seems to express her desire to fill the void created, ironically, when her sexual maturation opened a gap between her and her mother.

Paula's narrative makes clear that "life before Charlo" for her was one long seminar preparing for him. Paula's need made her vulnerable to Charlo. He abused her, but she was already very damaged. She was no accident waiting to happen; they were "made" for each other and Doyle shows the vicious spiral of debasement that Paula's life becomes. As her self-esteem is weakened, she becomes vulnerable to any show of appreciation. When Charlo seems to signal his attraction to her, her esteem begins to recover. But by this point, she has put herself in thrall to him. She becomes dependent on him for her self-image and as he goes to work on her — emotionally and physically — he grinds her down to the abject mess she ultimately becomes:

> He threatened me all the time, reminded me that I
> couldn't cope. I had nothing going for me. I was only

> Paula Spencer because of him. It was the only thing I
> was. People knew me because of him. . . . I was there
> because he looked at me and proved it. (*W*, 211)

Recalling her appearance on her wedding day, Paula thinks:
"I look modern" (*W*, 128). Her phrase recalls Bimbo's remark about Sharon in *The Snapper*: "She's a modern girl" (*S*,
66). Irony attends both usages of "modern". In Paula's case,
as her description of the wedding day continues to that of
the following morning, the details of the traditional social
ritual with all its conventions give way to signs of an equally
conventional future for her.

Ann McClintock has argued that women represent "the
atavistic and authentic 'body' of national tradition (inert,
backward-looking and natural) embodying nationalism's conservative principle of continuity", and men represent "the
progressive agent of national modernity (forward-thrusting,
potent and historic), embodying nationalism's progressive or
revolutionary principle of discontinuity" (McClintock, 1993:
66). If so, then Paula and Charlo are parodies of these en-
gendered identities and Paula's story of abuse may be read
as an allegory of an ambivalent and ambiguous modernity
guiltily taking out its insecurities on the weak and dependent, those who go without in order for those who do not to
have a measure of their success. (The allegorical treatment
of Irish nationalist history and the relations between the
sexes continues in *A Star Called Henry*.) Paula Spencer represents the *new* old face of Ireland, battered by the persistence
within modernisation of traditional patriarchal assumptions in
Irish society that "women should serve the emotional, material, and sexual needs of men" (Jeffers, 2002: 53). The cultural signifiers of Irish modernity that circulate through
Paula's narration — the allusions to films, TV programmes,
songs and musical groups — compose a surface modernity
only, noise and flash wrapped around a hollowed-out soci-

ety. Doyle conveys this hollowness particularly in his representation of the institutions of the family and education. At one point, thinking about how music can spark memory, Paula remarks: "That's one thing about my life; it has a great soundtrack" (*W*, 94); later, however, she notes:

> But I don't know any songs from the 80s; they mean nothing — and the radio was on all the time. What did I do in the 80s? I walked into doors. I got up off the floor. I became an alcoholic. I discovered that I was poor, that I'd no right to the hope I'd started out with. I was going nowhere . . . . Watching my children go there with me; the cruellest thing of the lot. No hope to give them. . . . I was their future. That was what they saw. . . . Do your homework, say your prayers, brush your teeth, say please and thank you — and you'll end up like me. (*W*, 204)

The passage should prick a society that likes to congratulate itself on its love of its children.

In a famous passage in *A Portrait of the Artist as a Young Man*, Joyce's Stephen Dedalus describes how "When the soul of a man is born in this country there are nets flung at it to hold it down from flight" (Joyce, 1992: 220). Stephen's "nets" are "nationality, language, religion", but in Doyle's novel, the nets of Irish society that cripple Paula O'Leary are school, family and class, in particular, and patriarchal society and culture in general. Paula's narrative explicitly connects her sexual development and her development of low self-esteem. Literally on the threshold of her secondary school, actually on the threshold of puberty, and metaphorically on the threshold of what should have been an open future, Paula O'Leary was made to feel "stupid" and "dirty"; she was not seen as an individual with a promising future, but as a class- and gender-stereotype whose future was a forgone conclusion. Tragically, she became the statistic she was more or less doomed to become. The strength and integrity of *The Woman Who Walked into Doors* derive from the combination of the apparently iconoclastic with the apparently stereotypical. Doyle's construction of Paula Spencer is a good example of how "the dividing line between a repressive stereotype and an empowering symbol of cultural identity is often a very narrow one" (Felski, 1980: 37). In Paula, Doyle constructs the credible, singular voice of a fully realised fictive individual whose experiences, however, achieve a representative authority, in terms of gender and class, because of the way the narration shows the slowly integrating image of the narrator-protagonist to emerge from the vivid representation of the familial, institutional, social and cultural environments that have actively thwarted her individuation.

The Way, the Truth, and the Life: "No big Aha"

Self-esteem, personal identity, and their origin in the deeply ambiguous reciprocity of individual and society continue to preoccupy Doyle's creative imagination. For all his research in the "battered woman syndrome" Doyle's representation of Paula's "case" does not reduce it to any pat sociological or feminist orthodoxies. Paula is a vividly imagined individual and it is the combination of her individuality and her environment that results in her acquiescing to her abuse. Echoing Paula in the novel, Doyle ventured that "There's no one reason why women are hit by men and why men hit women. It's a complicated thing and the book is a better book, I think, because it avoids the little sociological pitfalls" (Fay, 1996: 19). Thus, when he has Paula sum up the banal and bloody mystery of her life with Charlo, the passage rings as much with exhaustion as honesty, her bluntness paradoxically encapsulating what seems to be her creator's mature attitude toward his own mystery, the craft of fiction:

Every day. I think about it every minute. Why did he
do it? No real answers come back, no big Aha. He
loved me and he beat me. I loved him and I took it.
It's as simple as that, and as stupid and complicated.
It's terrible. It's like knowing someone you love is
dead but not having the body to prove it. He loved
me. I know it. But if he loved me, why did he hit me?
Why did he hit me so hard and so often? The questions are never answered. They always torment me.
(W, 192)

Metafictively, Charlo comes to represent that "force" without which there can be no story, but which remains *beyond*
the story's capacity to know. In terms of the Orphic parallel,
this passage captures the moment when Paula turns around
to look at what her imagination has hauled out of her memory, the "body" of the past she has dragged toward the light
in order for it to be illumined at last in her mind, only to see
that hope of clarity and understanding recede in the instant,
until she finds herself in a place of silence, staring at a blank
page, and that tormenting emptiness within her which only a
"story" will fill.

The way ahead, for Paula, as for the novelist who envi-
sioned her, is the way of the creative imagination, the way of
the story. To come to terms with her life with Charlo, Paula
has to go back to her childhood, family and school experience. She seems to intuit that the "truth" she is looking for
is in the connections between these, connections the narrative process uncovers and the story "makes". Two years
after throwing him out, one year after his death, there is
part of Paula that still yearns for Charlo (W, 91). She knows
she is vulnerable to delusion still, especially now that Charlo
is not alive to show up and prick the balloon of fantasy. And
so she admonishes herself: "Facts, Paula" (W, 91; repeated
96, 104). She *is* an "unreliable narrator", but it is her struggle
against the weaknesses she recognises as the sources of her

unreliability that makes her narrative so truthful, as when her memory of her wedding suddenly forces her to confront her two "Daddies": "(The man at the wedding has killed the other father I had, the one I had when I was a little girl. I can't get at him any more. I can picture him . . . but he isn't my daddy. He's another man. He's not real. I don't trust him or myself; I'm making him up . . .) (W, 141).

Paula recognises intuitively what any novelist knows, that the "facts" are not "the whole story", that while they may comprise the "truth" they in themselves do not compose it. Only the storyteller or historian can do that, and in this act of composition they are more alike than different. Paula knows Charlo hit Mrs Fleming twice before he killed her, and that there was no sign of sexual assault. But these facts do not "tell" her anything; in fact, they mystify, confuse, and ter- rify her because they do not make sense. And she will not be over Charlo until she can make sense of them, until she can place them in a meaningful relation to the story of her life with Charlo. Paula's story is a combination of history and fiction, fact and fantasy. She comes to recognise as well the difference between fantasy as self-delusion, as when she imagines a "lonely but fine" (W, 147) Mr Fleming, and the sort of heuristic imagination she uses to search for an under- standing of her husband. She comes to recognise that the latter can be a way of seeing the facts more clearly, of under- standing them, because Paula also has come to recognise that there is a difference between *knowing* a fact and *understanding* it. With Paula, Doyle affirms the narrative imagination as a mode of knowing and fiction as a form of knowledge.

The Woman Who Walked into Doors ends with an in- stance of reiteration that is, formally, a fitting end-symbol. Section 31, the last, repeats *almost* word-for-word the clos- ing lines of Section 29:

—What now? said Nicola.

—God knows, I said. —But one thing's for certain. He's not coming back in here again.

She'd heard it before.

—He's not, I said. —I'll bet you a tenner.

—Okay, said Nicola.

It was a great feeling. I'd done something good.

(*W*, 226)

There are two omissions in the later passage. The more important is the phrase "for a while" after "It was a great feeling" (see *W*, 225). The similarity, the *re-iterative*, relation between the passages, reinforces the positive meaning of Paula's action in expelling Charlo. The difference between the passages, however, adds a significant self-referential meaning to the last sentence. "I'd done something good" refers to the narrative that the sentence brings to a close, as well as to the narrative event which in some ways was the catalyst for the narrative. The rewriting connotes the sense of distance travelled from the original moment two years before, when she threw Charlo out but did not know how long the euphoria would last or her will-power hold up. The rewrite is a revision of the first recording in the sense of a re-viewing of the event and the time since and a confirmation that the original hope has become a fact in Paula's new life, a confirmation her narrative itself affirms. This is such a fitting end-symbol because it expresses the open-ended nature of the protagonist's situation and future, as well as the indeterminate nature of her text's viability as a guarantee that her narration *has* been a good thing. In *The Woman Who Walked into Doors* Doyle shows a woman daring to break the unwritten laws of her society that keep her in bondage, courageously acting to protect her daughter and free herself, and further, empowering herself by setting out to understand her life by telling her story.

Chapter Six

A Shocking Substitute:
A Star Called Henry
as Revisionist Fiction

A Star Called Henry stretches Doyle in the manner of *Paddy Clarke Ha Ha Ha* and *The Woman Who Walked into Doors* and in comparison to his previous work, it is by far his most artful. It is certainly his most "researched" novel. In fact, *A Star Called Henry* brings history and fiction together in the manner of what has been called postmodern "historiographical metafiction" (Hutcheon, 1989: 47–61). It is also a novel that should be read in the context of the "new cultural nationalism" that emerged in Ireland during the mid- to late 1990s, as well as the ongoing debate over historical "revisionism" and the more recent discursive-ideological controversy over the application of postcolonial theory to Irish politics, society and culture.

Organised into four parts, the novel begins with the fictitious Henry Smart's account of his parents' meeting and marriage, his own birth on 8 October 1901, and his childhood in the Dublin slums up until the death of his younger brother, Victor, in 1909; Part II begins abruptly seven years later with the fourteen-year-old Henry's military and other actions at the GPO as a member of Connolly's Citizen Army during the 1916 Rising, and concludes with his escape following the surrender; Part III covers the three years following the Rising and recounts Henry's experiences as a stevedore on the Dublin docks, his betrayal of his socialist principles following his recruitment into the Irish Volunteers, then the IRB, and his gradual rise to prominence as an agent-assassin and favourite of Collins, his marriage and campaign activities during the Black and Tan War, and his participation in Collins's elimination of the Cairo Gang on 21 November 1920, after which Henry decides his war is over; Part IV also begins abruptly, with Henry in custody, tortured and interrogated in Kilmainham Jail, his escape and subsequent discovery of his *persona non grata* status with his former comrades-in-arms, and his revenge upon his father's former employer, who turns out to have been his own nemesis as well. The novel concludes with Henry's forced departure from Ireland for Liverpool in 1922.

Publicised as the first instalment of a second trilogy entitled "The Last Roundup", if completed, this turn to historical fiction will bracket Doyle's career as a novelist in many interesting ways. He may very well, of course, publish other works of fiction before completing the trilogy, but if these are set in contemporary Ireland, "The Last Roundup" will provide a historical "vision" to complement his representation of late-twentieth-century and contemporary Irish society.

In *A Star Called Henry*, Dublin is more than the setting; the city rivals the protagonist as a presence in the fiction. But of course it is "historical" rather than contemporary Dublin that is described, the Dublin of Moore and O'Casey, to be sure (Doyle wrote an undergraduate essay on O'Casey (Costello, 2001: 88)), but even more so of James Plunkett's *Strumpet City*, a work Doyle credits in his acknowledgements. Doyle's evident historical imagination thoroughly inhabits the city of "the Famine Queen, Victoria" (*SCH*, 7), and convincingly summons its inhabitants to move between its real and symbolic planes.

Part I, in particular, is a *tour de force* of historical imagination. The descriptions of the Dublin slums, the squalid rooms Henry's parents inhabit, his mother's inevitable downward spiral into alcoholic stupefaction, Dolly Oblong's brothel in Monto, the heart of Henry and Victor's hand-to-mouth existence on the streets, and Victor's death from consumption contain some of the best writing Doyle has done. The themes of working-class poverty and urban deprivation, the relations between husband and wife, mother, father and children, the suffering of women and children and the unbridgeable solitudes which suffering opens within and between people, the failures of religion and institutional education, the violence that poverty does to people and that poverty often drives people to — these are not new themes in Doyle's fiction but what is new is the voice which delivers them (*SCH*, 8). In rhythm, tone, and structure, this voice is unlike anything we've heard in Doyle's fiction before — expansive, metaphorical, musical, rhetorical. The description of the "consumptive city" that kills Victor (*SCH*, 82–3) is a particularly effective example of how a structure of feeling can transform research into a historical seeing. Henry and Victor reprise Paddy and Sinbad, although their relationship is a romantic-sentimental inversion of the earlier Golding-influenced depiction of sibling relations.

Doyle's representation of religion and state education continues to be negative. Henry is irreligious and sarcastic about traditional Irish Catholic beliefs. The Christian God seems more like an Old Testament Baal, greedily devouring Henry's infant siblings, and most importantly, his namesake predecessor whom his mother believes became a star. Henry describes his christening as "mumbo-voodoo" (*SCH*, 29). Religion and education come together at the school where

Henry meets Miss O'Shea. As in *The Woman Who Walked into Doors*, the female primary teacher is a benign figure who nurtures the child's self-esteem (*SCH*, 76), but when the Mother Superior drives Henry and Victor out, Henry remarks:

> "The nun had been the normal one. Mother, she'd wanted to be called. Never. Not even Sister. Fuck her. And religion. I already hated it. *Holy God we praise Thy name*. Fuck Him. And your man on the cross up over the blackboard. Fuck Him too. That was one good thing that came out of all the neglect: we'd no religion. We were free. We were blessed" (*SCH*, 79).

The antireligious sentiment continues in his description of "the rosary drone" (*SCH*, 111) of the Volunteers during the worst of the bombardment of the GPO (*SCH*, 112). From Henry's viewpoint, the Volunteers were doubly damned; not only were they handier with their beads than their rifles, but they showed no respect to the women of Cumann na mBan who risked their lives distributing food during the battle: "I watched a Volunteer turn his back on the tin plate offered to him by one of the . . . women, crouching under the bullets in a nurse's uniform. –Why not? she said. –I won't eat meat on a Friday" (*SCH*, 130).

While hardly new in his work, Doyle's treatment of these themes in *A Star Called Henry* almost makes them new. The return to a straightforward linear narrative after the temporal complexity of *The Woman Who Walked into Doors* is surprising, and the narrative continues to be less dialogue-driven than in the earlier work, but the real stylistic novelties are Henry Smart, the narrator and character, and the use of symbolism — specifically, Henry's father's wooden leg and the underground rivers of Dublin.

Like Paddy Clarke and Paula Spencer, Henry Smart is a retrospective narrator-protagonist looking back on a formative period in his life; but whereas Paddy and Paula tell their stories as a way of trying to understand their lives, the historical subject matter in A Star Called Henry makes the heuristic dimension of Henry's narration quite different. While Henry is indeed trying to understand what happened to him in the first twenty years of his life, his story is just as much about what happened to Ireland. The novel may be read as Doyle's allegorical answer to Paula Spencer's question: "What went wrong with Daddy?" (W, 54), where "Daddy" is Ireland and the Irish State that de Valera, Collins, and the rest built. The novel shows this state to have been born in bloodshed, heroic and sordid, out of idealism and greed, naïveté and cunning, honesty and graft, a state in which the urban poor, women and Jews were no better off — perhaps even worse off — than they were before independence, and in which society and culture were dominated by the conservative ideologies of nationalism and the Church. If Doyle's novels, from the Barrytown trilogy through The Woman Who Walked into Doors, represent Irish society and culture as they work themselves through and out of the ideological legacies of de Valera's Ireland, A Star Called Henry represents a doubling back to the formative years when a newly independent nation crossed the threshold of modernity, only to retreat into the cloakroom of history for its first half-century.

Paradoxically, Doyle's postmodern narrative tells its story in what appears to be a very traditional, linear, transparent manner, but his mimetic mirror is very much the distorting glass of John Barth's Lost in the Funhouse (1969). Henry Smart Jr is as much a "grotesque" as his one-legged, barrel-chested, brothel-bouncer giant of a father — a character who seems to have arrived from the world of Angela Carter's Nights at the Circus (1984). His precocious size, physical strength and sexual aura quickly establish him in the reader's mind as a figure of fable or "tall story", even though Doyle describes him moving through a realistically detailed and historically recognisable time and place. It has been said that all of Doyle's novels tell "the story of a man escaping stereotypes" (O'Toole, 1999: 39), and this is as true for Henry as it is for his creator. In as much as Henry eventually has to escape the "legendary" identity which grows around him but which is about to destroy him, Doyle's representation of the historical events and figures which contribute to Henry's legend — the 1916 Rising, the Black and Tan War, the Civil War, Pearse, Plunkett, Collins and Connolly — subverts the "official histories" and popular myths of these events and figures, making the historical facts into new narrative events that challenge the hegemonic nationalist versions of the birth of the nation which Doyle's generation — like his parents' — was expected to believe and which he had already pilloried as "tea-towel history" in *Paddy Clarke Ha Ha Ha*.

A Shocking Substitute: Henry Smart as Narrator

One of the first things we learn about Henry Smart is that from childhood on, he has thought of himself as "a shocking substitute for the little Henry who'd been too good for this world, the Henry God had wanted for himself" (*SCH*, 1). In her grief, his mother had elevated that other Henry to the stars: "She held me but she looked up at her twinkling boy." Ironically, divine rejection drives him to become a "star" of a different kind — in the American sense of a figure of celebrity and fame. But even though Henry Smart becomes a star of the Irish revolution, a popular legend, a hero, he remains haunted by what he feels was his mother's unspoken judgement: "I was the other Henry. The shadow. The impostor" (*SCH*, 33).

Like Hamlet's father, Henry's ghostly other actually speaks in the text in the anachronistic epigraph Doyle takes from a famous Irving Berlin lyric:

Heaven —
I'm in heaven —
And my heart beats so
That I can hardly
Speak.

Of course, it is because poor dead Henry's heart does not beat that it *does* beat in a way that he can hardly speak but his poor living brother can. Henry's voice itself is thus the pre-eminent mark of his belatedness, his difference and his presence, and what he soon reveals to the reader is that Henry Smart is also "a shocking substitute" (*SCH*, 1) for the conventional, realistic narrative voice we might be expecting from the author of *Paddy Clarke Ha Ha Ha* and *The Woman Who Walked into Doors*. Bearing as he does the name of a dead brother and a missing father, it is no surprise that Henry Smart is haunted by a sense of absence throughout the first twenty years of his life. It also makes it profoundly fitting that towards the end of the novel he should discover, with the aid of his dead father's wooden leg, his talents as a diviner.

In *The Diviners* (1975), the Canadian novelist, Margaret Laurence, used this folk-figure as a symbol for the novelist and divining as a metaphor for the paradoxically conscious-unconscious nature of the novelist's search for the story. Henry Smart's story is a self-divination in what Laurence called the "nuisance grounds" of personal and public history (Laurence, 1988: 45). In Henry's case, this involves the nuisance of narrative indeterminacy and Doyle's playing "nuisance" with history itself. The two are related in that ultimately in *A Star Called Henry*, fiction becomes "a shocking substitute" for historical truth, or what David Lloyd calls "the organizing concerns of official history: the formation of the nation and of the state; the narrative of political institutions and state apparatuses; in short, the modernization of Ireland" (Lloyd, 1999: 37).

On the second page of the novel, after a vivid description of Granny Nash's origins and background, Henry admits
"I don't know any of this . . . I don't know" (*SCH*, 2). He
then continues to describe his mother's childhood, his parents' courtship and his own birth. But it is when he tells his
father's story that his unreliability becomes, paradoxically,
the spine of truth for the rest of the novel. "I know nothing
real about my father; I don't even know if his name was real.
. . . He made his life up as he went along. . . . He invented
himself, and reinvented. . . . Was he just a liar? No, I don't
think so. He was a survivor; his stories kept him going. Stories were the only thing the poor owned. A poor man, he
gave himself a life. He filled the hole with many lives" (*SCH*,
7). Since this is obviously what Henry Jr, who is a more successful "survivor" than his father, does as well, we cannot
know for sure if the account of the father is part of the son's
self-invention. But *A Star Called Henry* is the kind of novel
that renders this particular kind of veridical concern inappropriate. Henry's conceit of his father as "A man created
from his own secrets" (*SCH*, 16) is a sly maggot. Like one of
Granny Nash's clues, it points the way to parable. Henry's
outrageous assumption that the fact of his birth, cosmically
underlined by a shooting star, is commensurate with that of
an earlier saviour-messiah (*SCH*, 22) intimates that his tale
too will be a mixture of myth and history, sacrifice and ran-
cour, death and redemption. Like that other messenger-son,
Henry Smart Jr is an outsider *in* history and his story "slips
and slides all over the page. . . . neither completely believable
nor completely unbelievable" (Jeffers, 2002: 131).

Henry is unlike either of Doyle's previous narrator-
protagonists. Realistic and unrealistic, in the language of *The
Commitments*, he is "superbad". But as a character-type, he is
immediately recognisable: he is an Irish Daniel Boone or
Davy Crockett, a working-class Cuchulainn with a wooden
leg for a *bolga*. He is a "folk-figure" or "urban legend" from

birth: "Only a week in the world and already there were stories spinning up and down the streets and alleys, through the open windows of the slums"; he is "the Glowing Baby", an omen of a "bright future" (*SCH*, 22) who ends up on the streets at three years old, "Infested, hungry and unloved" (*SCH*, 45). Women respond to his sexual aura almost as soon as he can walk (*SCH*, 65). He is a quick study, soon recognising that "information" is "power" (*SCH*, 74), and a wiz at maths, as long as it is not abstract. He picks up Gaelic and a rudimentary literacy in only two days of formal schooling (*SCH*, 72), but learns more from watching and listening than from asking questions (*SCH*, 74). Henry then becomes the "gorgeous warrior": "I was probably the best looking man in the GPO but there was nothing beautiful about me. My eyes were astonishing, blue daggers that warned the world to keep its distance" (*SCH*, 89).

Myth, legend and folklore, the tall tale: these are the underground streams that feed this narrative. While acknowledging that he has "[taken] liberties with reality", Doyle has denied that he was consciously emulating the "magic realism" of South American fiction of the 1980s (Costello, 2001: 90). "I wanted to take liberties and mess around and poke fun. Among these heavy political figures like de Valera and Pearse and Connolly and Collins, there would be the magic of the underground water and the man with the wooden leg. It's to give a cinematic feel to it" (Costello, 2001: 90–1). His intention was to be satirical, parodic, vividly entertaining. Doyle writes more in the manner of a Flann O'Brien than a Marquez or Rushdie. In *A Star Called Henry* he has exaggerated the exaggeration that has always been part of his style.

Entertainment abounds in the descriptions of the brothel madam, Dolly Oblong (*SCH*, 41–3), and of the fighting prowess and physical strength of Henry Smart Sr as he saves his sons from a mob and they escape by jumping through a bush into the Swan river, one of the secret, underground rivers in

Dublin that Henry Sr uses to dispose of his victims' body parts (*SCH*, 55–61). It broadens into farce when Henry and Miss O'Shea have sex in the basement of the GPO while the fighting rages upstairs (*SCH*, 120–1) and later become a husband-and-wife robbery and demolition team, and then becomes grossly satirical in the scene set at Templemore, when Henry is commissioned by Collins to dupe the religious rubes by faking a miracle (*SCH*, 281). But there are moments, too, when this broad narrative mainstream is suddenly fed by the deep underground pools of myth.

While Doyle's narrator-protagonist may seem to perform a work of magic realism, Henry is better approached as the dynamo in a work of historiographical metafiction. Through its subject matter, narrative style, conventions and archetypes, *A Star Called Henry* not only makes the reader aware of "the historical process", it also "interrogates the ways in which the narratives of the past are created" (Donnelly, 2000: 29). Henry admits that he invents facts where he does not know them in order to make sense of the facts he does know, and Doyle constructs him as a representative historical character who is symbolically and literally excluded from the "official history" of the events he was involved in. This is encapsulated in Henry's claim that when de Valera arrived at Richmond Barracks following the surrender at the GPO, "I was beside the great man" when the famous picture was taken ("my elbow was in it, but even that went in later versions" (*SCH*, 138–9)).

To make a metaphor from Doyle's use of the historical photograph, someone has to "develop" the image of the past. What *A Star Called Henry* reminds us of — and it is something Doyle began to explore in *The Woman Who Walked into Doors* — is that for all the facts that distinguish history from fiction, what *joins* the fac s and *makes* them into a narrative is an act of imagination on the part of the historian, an imagination informed and drive by any number of complex forces. Furthermore, the *angle* of narration — Henry's explicit point of view toward the historical events he recounts — is such that it intentionally draws the reader's attention to the *degrees of deviation* between that view and the "official history", "received wisdom", or otherwise dominant version of them. This is what postmodern historiographical metafictions like *The Book of Daniel, Waterland, Midnight's Children* or *Underworld* do; by mixing the orthodoxy of "historical fact" with the heterodoxy of admitted fiction, they destabilise the non-fiction/fiction binary and the hierarchical order that ascribes truth to the one and falsehood to the other. By constructing Henry Smart as he does, as the kind of narrator who, like Paula Spencer, makes us aware of the processes of narration, Doyle writes the kind of postmodern novel that "focus[es] on the process of event becoming fact", that "draw[s] attention to the dubiousness of the positivist, empiricist hierarchy implied in the binary opposing of the real to the fictive . . . by suggesting that the non-fictional is as constructed and as narratively known as is fiction" (Hutcheon, 1989: 76). The past — the facts of 1916, the War of Independence, the Civil War, the motives and characters of Collins and Connolly, Pearse and de Valera — can only be known through some form of textual mediation, be it a tome or a tea-towel. But in whatever form, the representation of the past covers up as much as it reveals. Like Henry Smart Sr, who is original to his son's account of him, history is "created from [its] own secrets".

Doyle's novel brings this serious play of subversive ideas to the foreground, appropriately, at its conclusion, when Henry discovers the plot that he has been an unwitting instrument of throughout his military activity. A "plot" can be a narrative structure or a conspiracy. Postmodern novels often construct elaborate narrative structures only to reveal them as conspiracies of aesthetic form, the point being to raise the reader's consciousness of the ways forms of representation present themselves to us as objects of truth — even when they present themselves as objects of fabrication. The narrative plot in *A Star Called Henry* enacts Doyle's "plot" against the nationalist historiography that has mythologised the 1916–23 period as the heroic struggle for freedom. Through Henry as a protagonist, he parodies the concept of the hero and the myth of a nationalist revolution. Through Henry as a narrator, he demystifies the nationalist icons of Collins, Pearse, Plunkett and de Valera (while bringing Connolly's image out of the archive and polishing it to a new brightness). Henry eventually comes to see the events from 1916 to the Civil War as composing a historical "plot" on the part of Gandon, Dalton, Collins and others — the nefarious cabal of "Catholic and capitalist" (*SCH*, 116) that uses Connolly and the Citizen Army as well as its own Volunteers to bring about a self-serving coup rather than a social revolution.

During the climactic confrontation at Dolly Oblong's brothel, Gandon tells Henry: "You've been working for me for years. Just like your father" (*SCH*, 337). The "messages" — the pieces of paper with the names of his victims — that Henry thought were coming from Collins were coming from Gandon through Collins, just as his father had received his orders from Gandon through Dolly. "A plot, be it seen as a narrative structure or as a conspiracy, is always a totalising representation that integrates multiple and scattered events into one unified story. But the simultaneous desire for and suspicion of such representations are both part of the postmodern contradictory response to emplotment" (Hutcheon, 1989: 68). By ending his novel with Henry's discovery of Gandon's conspiracy, Doyle both concludes and undoes the plot he has constructed as the novel's version of the history it represents, a historical "plot" which is much more than the avarice of Gandon and the lust for power of his minions. It is also the concealment of that plot in the nationalist myth of the revolutionary struggle. As the evil and apparently unstoppable Ivan tells Henry, when it's all over, "It's only my version that'll get talked about" (*SCH*, 216).

Doyle's narrative conspiracy in *A Star Called Henry* is to frame the "heroic period" of the formation of an independent Ireland with the history of the urban poor whose lives, in his opinion, remained materially unchanged by independence. To do this, he has to draw together the "multiple and scattered events" of this complex and extended period into "one unified whole", which he does by having his narrator act in the events he narrates and by having that singular life embody the "revisionist" story of the nation Doyle wants to tell.

A Star Called Henry as Revisionist Fiction

"Revising national history is perilous, especially if cherished legends are debunked or heroes pushed off their pedestals. History is viewed as having the function of inculcation of the young with a sense of their own national past and of recounting a public morality tale legitimising the state, the nation or community" (Boyce and O'Day, 1996: 1). Doyle is not writing history, however, but a postmodern form of historical fiction. He has no new "facts" to contribute to our knowledge of the past, has carried out no original research, includes very little political background, and in a sense, adds "bunk" more than he "debunks" anything — and yet he does want to affect our understanding of the past. He certainly tells a "morality tale" that does *not* "legitimise" state or nation.

A work of historiographical metafiction is a double-edged device for a writer with a revisionist agenda, for while it may substantially subvert the historical orthodoxy it wants to challenge, its destabilising methods also prevent its giving credibility to any rival perspective it may seem to propose. What postmodern fiction and historical revisionism most have in common is the foregrounding of metafictive and metahistorical issues, respectively, and a renewed emphasis on the political and ideological functions of literary and historical discourse.

Boyce and O'Day note that in Germany, historical revisionism regarding the Nazi era has not represented "a genuine challenge to scholarship" but rather "a moral and political discourse . . . conducted through the medium of leading historians, about how far contemporary Germans can cope with this past" (Boyce and O'Day, 1996: 3). Conor McCarthy has observed that Irish revisionism "is the historiographic outrider of the discourse of modernity as it has come to be understood in Ireland"; moreover, it extends beyond the writing of history to contemporary fiction, drama, film and criticism (McCarthy, 2000: 18). If we see Irish revisionism as really "a moral and political discourse" about modernity and modernisation, then in *A Star Called Henry* Doyle is very much a sort of "fellow traveller". O'Mahony and Delanty argue that there is a long tradition of discontent amongst twentieth-century Irish journalists and writers "with their society's institutions — church, educational experience, politics, intellectual life, family" yet which does not "[confront] the reason why these institutions took the form they did": "Neither in revisionist or new nationalist writing, has the central question of the responsibility of Irish nationalism for the subsequent history of the Irish nation-state been directly addressed" (O'Mahony and Delanty, 1998: 14, 13). But from *The Commitments* to *A Star Called Henry*, Doyle has satirised these very institutions through his representations of the economically impoverished, socially disenfranchised and politically weak — the under- and un-employed urban working-class, women, and children. And in *A Star Called Henry* he does offer an explanation of why these institutions evolved the way they did. By showing the nationalist-political revolution to contain and conceal a failed — or repressed — social-economic revolution, Doyle's view of history is that the modern Irish state was born disabled, deformed and retarded.

Doyle's answer to "one of the central questions surrounding the Rising: was it a 'coup d'état' or a 'bloody protest'?" (Boyce, 1996: 165) is that it was the former and that the socialist dimension of "bloody protest" against the deprivations of the working classes and urban poor was buried in the rubble of the GPO. The most important revisionist feature of the novel is its construction of a *social* and *economic* rather than nationalist-political context for the 1916 Rising by telling the story of Henry and Victor's childhood as "street Arabs" in Part I. This also establishes the *moral* and increasingly *ironic* framework for the military and political story told in the rest of the novel. The identity Doyle develops for Henry in Part I is rooted in the same sense of class and place that Jimmy Rabbitte Jr expresses in *The Commitments*. When the five-year-old Henry shouts at King Edward to "Fuck off", it is not because he is anti-English or proto-nationalist, but because he sees the king as a "fat foreigner", a wealthy stranger; Henry sounds very much like Bertie in *The Van* when he says Edward "didn't belong" (*SCH*, 52) there.

Doyle's detailed descriptions of Henry's struggle to survive as a "beggar's assistant", rat-catcher, and cattle-rustler; of Henry's and Victor's hunger, homelessness and rejection by church and school; of Victor's slow death from consumption and Henry's bitter realisation that "the city killed Victor" (*SCH*, 83–4), do not construct an idealistic nationalist but a street-wise socialist. And so, six years later, even though we find him in the GPO in the uniform of the Citizen Army, we should not be surprised by his feelings about the banner he sees at Liberty Hall: "*We Serve Neither King Nor Kaiser* . . . If I'd had my way, *Or Anyone Else* would have been added, instead of *But Ireland*. I didn't give a shite about Ireland" (*SCH*, 91). For Henry does not regard Ireland as his home; rather, "my home and the birthplace of our revolu-

tion" is Liberty Hall, the headquarters of the Irish Transport
and General Workers' Union (*SCH*, 119).

   A Star Called Henry gets a "rise" out of its Irish reader by
deploying a sufficient amount of familiar historical fact to
reinforce the sense of being on known ground, only to affront the reader by inserting a commentary that seems both
counterintuitive and counterfactual. The effect is a form of
the *uncanny*; the historical familiar suddenly becomes unfamiliar history. Doyle leads up to this by having Henry tell us
that he was the bugler who played the "Last Post" at
O'Donovan Rossa's funeral (*SCH*, 90), and, even more mis-
chievously, that he is responsible for some of the language in
the famous Proclamation (*SCH*, 96).

   However, where his revisionist fiction really takes off is
with the pointed juxtaposition of Connolly and the other
leaders, and of the Citizen Army soldiers and the Volunteers. Doyle puts the socialist Connolly at the top of the
pantheon of 1916 martyrs. He and Henry have a special relationship: Connolly taught Henry to read because he knew
the empowering effect literacy would have on the boy and
the self-confidence it would give (*SCH*, 96). "He wasn't just a
man; he was all of us. . . . He'd made us all believe in ourselves" (*SCH*, 127). During the fighting, Connolly directs the
defence and gives the orders. Pearse is presented as a prude,
a mammy's boy (*SCH*, 88), "sweating like a bastard" as he
arrives at Liberty Hall on his bike, with Willie, "his little
brother and faithful hound" (*SCH*, 91) in tow, and chased by
a sister who tells him to come home. Doyle juxtaposes
Pearse reading a speech about "Dublin . . . rising in arms"
and redeeming itself for its failure to support Robert Emmet
in 1803 with a description of the looters outside "welcoming
the new republic" (*SCH*, 113–14). Henry notices that
"[Pearse] was fat and his arms had no more muscle than his
poetry" (*SCH*, 124). The depiction of Joseph Mary Plunkett
also studiously combines historical detail with rhetorical

venom: Plunkett arrives looking "like death congealing" (*SCH*, 93). Useless during the fighting, Doyle reduces him to a theatrical absurdity with his sword and single spur, held up by two men, drawing pointless historical analogies at the high point of the battle, and calling Henry a "cowardly cur" when he is actually showing great courage leading the breakout up Moore Street.

Doyle's derogation of Pearse and Plunkett is actually part of the anti-nationalist, anti-religious "plot" in the novel. His representation of them, along with the depiction of the Volunteers, satirises the orthodox understanding of the heroes and the events:

> Some of the Volunteers had their beads out and were down on their knees, humming the rosary.
> —The revolutionaries, said Felix. —Will you look at them?
> Plunkett was in there with them. He could hardly stand; he spent most of his time on a mattress. The man was dying, a waste of a bullet, but he had the energy to beat his breast and drive his knees into the tiles.
> —The first sorrowful mystery, said Paddy. —How we ever ended up with those gobshites. (*SCH*, 111)

Doyle has Connolly agree: "We're surrounded by gobshites, Henry. . . . Catholic and capitalist. . . . It's an appalling combination" (*SCH*, 115–16). He makes this comment following a confrontation between Henry and his Citizen Army comrades and the rosary-fisted Volunteers, who suddenly do want to take up arms to fire on the Dubliners looting outside rather than British troops. The scene epitomises Doyle's revising of the Rising:

> The Volunteers saw our barrels smiling at them and, before they could respond or do anything at all, the floor between us was awash with generals, comman-

dants and poets, most of the Provisional Government of the Republic. Five seconds that very nearly
shook the world — the revolution, the counter-
revolution and the Civil War were all waiting to
happen in that five-second spell in the GPO, as Dublin outside burned. I put my rifle on Pearse. I didn't
know what was happening upstairs and on the roof
or downstairs with Miss O'Shea — she was still
dancing to my tongue, even as I got ready to shoot
Commandant Pearse — but, where we were, not
one barricade was manned, not even one pair of
eyes faced the street. For the duration of those five,
crawling seconds, Britain stopped being the enemy.
Pearse saw my rifle and saw my eyes and my intentions in them, and he turned slightly, giving me his
profile, hiding his squint; he was ready for an elegant
death. (*SCH*, 114–15)

(Compare John Montague's image of "Pearse's sword-stick
leading to a care- / fully profiled picture" in *The Rough Field*;
Montague, 1995: 62.) It is Connolly, of course, who defuses
the situation. But the scene unfolds the argument that the
rest of the novel will make. During "those five, crawling seconds" when "Britain stopped being the enemy" and Henry
was ready to shoot Pearse, he realises that the Rising is only
the first stage. "We were fighting a class war. We weren't in
the same battle at all as the rest of the rebels. And they'd
find that out soon enough" (*SCH*, 107). Once the British
have been thrown out, the middle-classes and "culchies" will
have to follow. "We looked across and stored away the
faces for another day. I met the hard stares of country boys
and shopkeepers, met and matched them. But, for now, it
was over" (*SCH*, 115). The first shot Henry does fire in anger is not at a British soldier but at his real enemy, "property". He starts shooting out the windows of all the shop-
fronts across the street: "I shot and killed all that I had been

denied, all the commerce and snobbery that had been mock-
ing me and other hundreds of thousands behind glass and
locks, all the injustice, unfairness and shoes — while the lads
took chunks out of the military" (*SCH*, 105). By having
Henry point out the division between Citizen Army and
Volunteers — socialists and nationalists — and their different motives and ideals, the novel challenges the popular
myth of a homogenous group with a single goal.

Doyle "pushes the envelope", of course, when he has
Henry cavorting with Miss O'Shea in the basement of the
GPO while all hell breaks loose above them, and even more
so when he juxtaposes Henry's remembering being in bed
with Piano Annie with his hearing the reports of the executions of the 1916 leaders. Even Connolly's death does not
distract him from Annie, who tells him to "Lie back and
think of Ireland" (*SCH*, 148). But it is the pointedly rhetorical
structure of the juxtaposition (it parodies Neil Jordan's in-
tercutting of the executions with de Valera writing/reciting
his letter at the beginning of *Michael Collins*) that suggests
Doyle is not simply being tasteless or indulging in a kind of
adolescent discursive vandalism. As with the juxtaposition of
Pearse's pep-talk in the GPO and the contradictory behaviour of the Dubliners he was misrepresenting in the speech,
or the unnecessarily demeaning caption Henry puts to the
famous photograph of de Valera at Richmond Barracks —
"He was wearing red socks and he smelt of shite" (*SCH*,
139) — Doyle is constructing a character whose experience,
mentality and outlook set him at odds with the implied
reader's knowledge and attitude toward the events and figures. Henry assaults our expectations.

There is also another effect: Henry's time with Annie in
the period following the Rising, like his actions in the GPO,
show him to be a very young man — in fact, he is still a boy
of 14 — who is motivated both by an ingrained self-interest
as a result of his life of intense poverty and by an idealism he

has taken from Connolly which, while deep enough to make him risk his life, still has less purchase on his character than his basic instinct for survival. It is important to recognise this because it prepares the reader for Henry's "apostasy" in Part III, when he abandons his socialist principles. In Part I, Doyle establishes a social-economic framework for the story of Henry's involvement in the events that the "official history" presents in the framework of nationalist politics. In Part II, Doyle's depiction of the 1916 Rising becomes a form of revisionist fiction when he dramatises a fundamental rift between the narrator-protagonist and the Citizen Army and the Volunteers and the *dramatis personae* of the nationalist myth-history. In Part III, Henry, in one memorable scene, refuses to take Piano Annie's husband's side in a political argument against the nationalist, Archer, and then gradually allows the snake-like Dalton to seduce him into joining the IRB and becoming Collins's deadly messenger-boy. Henry's corruption by his masters reaches its nadir when he murders Annie's husband, but by this point Doyle's other "plot", the exposure of the War of Independence as a "gang war" for control of the country's economy, is about to reach its climax. In Part IV, the feral Ivan Reynolds symbolises the unequivocal failure of the Irish revolution to put an end to the exploitation of the people; for Ivan, Dalton, Gandon and their ilk, independence means the Irish are finally free to exploit the Irish.

If Henry's motives are a combination of self- and class-interest, Doyle's point is that the heroes of the revolution and their silent partners had similar motives. Henry does not see Dalton's duplicity until too late, and by then he has lost the integrity that earlier would have led him to act against it. When Dalton recruits him for the IRB in 1917, Henry realises that Dalton's goal is an Ireland that will be "a very small place" — purged of Protestants, Jews, and even buildings built from Wicklow stone, but his desire to belong to something after years of isolation and the trauma of the defeat at the GPO makes him "Ready to fall dead for a version of Ireland that had little or nothing to do with the Ireland I'd gone out to die for the last time" (*SCH*, 171). Dalton soon reveals himself to be anti-socialist (*SCH*, 172) as well as anti-semitic — "we want no more strangers in our house" (*SCH*, 325) — but although Henry says he is fighting for the right of people to eat well (*SCH*, 219), he listens when Dalton justifies withholding food from those who need it by arguing "We don't want to interfere with internal trade . . . We have to show the factory owners and the rest of them that these things will go on without the English. And that they'll go on even better without them" (*SCH*, 178). Henry passively watches Dinnie Archer berate and insult the Volunteers who were in the British Army during the War, and attack union men and even Jim Larkin because he was "an Englishman" (*SCH*, 182). Although Henry realises that Archer is insulting everything he believes and has fought for, he does nothing because of his trust in Dalton, who assures him that there are "wheels within wheels. . . . Cells inside cells" (*SCH*, 183) and that Henry must trust his betters.

But by 1918, Henry recognises that the Volunteers are being used by the IRB — "the secret society at the centre of the centre of all things" (*SCH*, 184) — and that "the election was being controlled by men who did not believe in it" (*SCH*, 208). "The vote meant choice, but there was no choice. There was only the one right way. Some of us knew the way and it was up to us to lead, not to ask permission of a voting majority . . . To inspire, provoke and terrify" (*SCH*, 209). Henry becomes an assassin for Collins in the same way that his father was a killer for Gandon; he even uses his father's wooden leg on his first assignment, the killing of a policeman (*SCH*, 185). Henry is deluded by Dalton in same way his father was by Dolly Oblong. Collins calls his Squad "My Black and Tans" (*SCH*, 287); his strategy is to co-opt the enemy's: "They did exactly what we'd expected and wanted them to do. . . . We pulled the trigger and they went off" (*SCH*, 263). Later, Henry realises he was always patronised and never accepted by those he worked and fought for — "it took me years to realize what was going on" (*SCH*, 240) — and he is helped by one of his own recruits.

Ivan Reynolds is one of the "Frankenstein's monsters" of the Irish revolution who go on to become its leading citizens. When Henry returns to the west and reunites with his former recruit, he realises that "Power had gone to Ivan's soul" (*SCH*, 235) and he had become a dangerous IRA gangster. Ivan threatens Henry's wife because she is complicating his business deals with the British army; "There had to be a reason for the killing . . . It's about control of the island, that's what the soldiering's all about, not the harps and martyrs and the freedom to swing a hurley" (*SCH*, 314). Henry soon learns that although the psychopathic Ivan has become a kind of Mafia godfather in his region — he controls the Tans and Auxiliaries as well as the IRA, and the "war" has become a business for him — he has the full support of Dublin (*SCH*, 315). He tells Henry about the peace talks and the civil war that will follow and his plans: "I'll be ready to lead my people into the new Ireland," to which Henry replies: "And it'll be very much like the old one" (*SCH*, 315). Whatever Henry thought he was once fighting for, and however those ideals were lost or destroyed by the parties that won, Ivan is smugly confident that no one will ever know: "It's only my version that'll get talked about" (*SCH*, 316).

It is Ivan who warns Henry that Dublin wants him out of the way. The student has become the teacher; Henry realises he has been "a complete and utter fool", fighting all along "for Ivan and the other Ivans, the boys whose time had come. That was Irish freedom, since Connolly had been shot — and if the British hadn't shot him one of the Ivans would have" (*SCH*, 317–18). Ivan's hero, Alfie Gandon, ironically runs the country from his jail cell, where he belongs as a murderer and fraud, but where he sits transforming himself into the nationalist hero, O'Gandúin. Back in Dublin, Dalton tells Henry that he supports Ivan and his kind — "they're our own, aren't they" (*SCH*, 326) — and tells Henry he has become a liability, a man with "no stake in the country . . . Never had, never will" (*SCH*, 327). Doyle uses Henry's meetings with Ivan and Dalton in Part IV to thoroughly trash the nationalist myth: the war was over power, control of wealth.

A Star Called Henry, *Michael Collins* and the New Cultural Nationalism

If "nationalist historiography was itself the first great revisionist school in Ireland", rewriting "the official imperial narratives of native history" (Eagleton, 1998: 320), then it should not surprise that recent revisionist history should attempt to rewrite the official *nationalist* narrative of native history, nor also that contemporary cultural nationalism can at times be informed by revisionist historical attitudes. The new cultural nationalism would seem to be at odds with the old political-cultural nationalism in important respects.

Such would seem to be the case with Neil Jordan's *Michael Collins* which, while taking a revisionist pro-Collins, anti-de Valera view of the events, is not anti-nationalist so much as an expression of the new cultural nationalism. Jordan's film appeared while Doyle was writing *A Star Called Henry*, and the overlap in subject matter must have struck Doyle forcefully, as would have Jordan's "heroic" approach to Collins's story. At times, Doyle's novel seems to be engaged in a critical dialogue with the film; images and scenes read like silent allusions to it. When Henry says Collins "slept in the beds of men who'd just been arrested. . . . The safest bed in town, he said (*SCH*, 191), it's the same language Collins uses with Harry Boland in the film (Jordan, 1996: 87). The wrestling match between Collins and Henry (*SCH*, 198–9) apes the horseplay between Collins and Boland in the film. When Henry murders Piano Annie's husband up in the Dublin mountains, the description (*SCH*, 256–7) matches the scene in the film when Liam Tobin (Brendan Gleeson) shoots a kneeling man in the back of the head. Archer and Henry shoot a man in bed with a prostitute (*SCH*, 285–7) in a reprise of another scene in the film (Jordan, 1996: 123–4). A telling intertextual connection is the fact that Jordan's much-noted anachronism of the car-bomb (Jordan, 1996: 112) reappears in the novel (*SCH*, 233) — either as a coincidence or because Jordan's film image stayed with Doyle. These and other connections establish that Jordan's film was in Doyle's "sights" as he wrote his novel.

What is important is to see how *A Star Called Henry* engages the new cultural nationalism of the 1990s by means of an implicit critique of Jordan's representation of Collins and the events of 1916–22. Doyle's novel appeared three years after Jordan's film and it can be argued that the novel aggressively challenges Jordan's self-consciously "heroic" project. Doyle's farce clashed with the afterglow of the film's popular and critical success. Moreover, the novel's representation of the discourse of history as self-interested fiction made the film's status as "official" historical truth, following the quasistate imprimatur of a government minister, seem yet another example of the kind of nationalist myth-making that the "new Ireland" was so confidently telling itself was "old hat". That is, *A Star Called Henry* in a sense called the "new Ireland's" bluff. Just how "new" was it if it still revelled in such atavistic, black-and-white concoctions (in vivid colour, of course)?

Doyle shows Collins as a figure of physical strength and courage at the GPO (*SCH*, 102) but also pointedly includes him among the anti-Dublin "culchies": "The poets and the farm boys, the fuckin' shopkeepers. They detested the slummers — the accents and the dirt, the Dublinness of them. When was the last time Collins had been hungry? I knew the answer just by looking at the well-fed puss on him" (*SCH*, 103). The representation of the fighting at the GPO in Jordan's film is brief and heroic, whereas Doyle devotes over a quarter of the novel to it, using heroic and anti-heroic imagery, as well as considerable sarcasm, anti-religious commentary, and the theme of class division.

Jordan's film totally lacks the social and economic perspective of Doyle's novel; there is no suggestion, for example, that some of the participants were fighting for a "workers' state" (*SCH*, 98). Jordan's story follows the traditional nationalist-political line except to invert the de Valera/Collins hierarchy. Where Jordan's Black and Tans are the stereotypes of Dalton's propaganda — "The sweepings of England's jails, he'd called them . . ." — Doyle has Henry observe "What they actually were was veterans who'd been unable to get work in England and Scotland after the War and who'd now been promised good money, ten shillings a day, to sort out Ireland. They were soldiers of a kind, not the peelers we'd been fighting up to now" (*SCH*, 258). Doyle's Collins is a womaniser (*SCH*, 103), whereas Jordan leaves that out. But like Jordan's Collins, Doyle's is clearly the brains behind the military campaign. When Henry becomes an assassin for Collins, Doyle's construction of the Gandon–Dalton–Collins triangle becomes the dirty secret at the heart of his revisionism. Jordan's Coppola-influenced gangster-style freedom-fighters become simply Doyle's gangsters.

O'Mahony and Delanty identify "two perceived major problem complexes" that the new "code of 'Irishness'" in the new cultural nationalism attempts to address — personal identity and "a new nation code". Doyle's fiction has always addressed the former; *A Star Called Henry* addresses both and it is this novel in particular which exposes Doyle's ambivalent relationship to the "new Ireland". While not a historian, he nevertheless engages in what to some is the "unnecessary and iconoclastic demythologization" (O'Mahony and Delanty, 1998: 10) of nationalist heroes like Pearse, Collins and de Valera. If revisionism expresses the values of "enlightenment rationalism and liberal pluralism", and the former underlies the revisionists' "distrust for what is perceived as a certain primordialism and irresponsibility in Irish nationalism associated with its culture of romantic will that . . . is always in danger of falling into unnecessary and illegitimate episodes of violence" (O'Mahony and Delanty, 1998: 10), then Doyle's invention of Henry Smart expresses revisionist leanings. Henry clearly champions democratic politics, openness to cultural pluralism, and (by the end of the novel) the rejection of the politics of violence.

Doyle and his generation straddle the second and third phases in the evolution of the Irish nation-state in the twentieth century, the first phase being the revolutionary era to the 1930s and 1940s. Doyle was born and grew up at the end of the second phase, which saw "a gradual shedding of the more extreme versions of anti-modernism . . . with a slow acceptance of growing secularization, state welfare provision, sexual liberation, [and] more pronounced liberalism", and his adult life has taken him into the third phase, which has been characterised by a "return to the nation" (O'Mahony and Delanty, 1998: 5–6). The latter has been described as composed of "two strands": one, "backward looking . . . seeking a return to the certainties of traditional Catholic Ireland", the other "forward looking, accommodating itself if somewhat uneasily to social change while seeking to create a new cultural nation-code extending beyond existing institutional frameworks" (O'Mahony and Delanty, 1998: 6). Doyle's body of work suggests a sensibility that would revolt against any attempt to "return to the certainties of traditional Catholic Ireland" — he contemplated emigration if the second divorce referendum had been defeated — as well as one that is attempting to accommodate itself to

the social and cultural changes that Ireland's economic fortune in the late twentieth century have brought. However,
until his recent engagement with the issues of racism and
immigration in his writing for *Metro Éireann*, Doyle was not
interested in contributing to the creation of "a new cultural
nation-code". In *A Star Called Henry*, the myth of the Irish
nation is a con-job from which the narrator-protagonist
barely escapes with his life.

Doyle's career suggests that he would be highly suspi-
cious of the cultural nationalism described by David Lloyd,
whose theoretical justification for the "recovery of kitsch"
(Lloyd, 1999: 89) could substitute for a lucid abstract of cultural policy in Germany under National Socialism. Lloyd argues that "independence founded in cultural integrity" will
be achieved by "deploying artefacts that are the symbols of
national culture, parts which represent a whole that is often
yet to be constituted: ballads or *corridas*, myths, tales, poetry, music and costumes, murals. Around these, the sentiment of national culture is to be forged in each and every
individual" (Lloyd, 1999: 89). Miss Watkins's tea-towel in
Paddy Clarke Ha Ha Ha has already suggested Doyle's attitude to nationalist kitsch and *A Star Called Henry* is a con-
certed "opening out" of the symbols of nationalist culture to
reveal their hollowness.

Whether Neil Jordan's *Michael Collins* (1996) represents
a form of neo-nationalist kitsch is debatable, but *A Star Called
Henry* critiques the film's heroic view of history as the story
of how "great men" achieve their "destiny". By constructing
Henry as an *unbelievably heroic* character, Doyle parodies the
very notion of the "great man". (Doyle probably would also
reject Jordan's tragic-apocalyptic view of history that sees
the birth of a free Ireland to require the sacrificial death of a
Christ-like scapegoat.)

Doyle subscribes to a materialist view of history which
sees murder, mayhem and massacre where others see

"blood sacrifice", and so he places at the centre of his outrageous account of the birth of his nation a hero who refuses not only the "mumbo-voodoo" of martyrdom — "It needed blood to survive and it wasn't getting mine" (*SCH*, 342) — but eventually citizenship in an Ireland that was becoming a vampire preying on the poor and deluded. The novel is in this sense a parodic inversion of the Lloydite project in cultural nationalism. Its story "retrieves an authentic tradition" (Lloyd, 1999: 89) only to reconstitute it in oppositional terms. It reveals that tradition of cultural and racial difference to be based on sexist and racist xenophobia (Ivan's misogyny, Dalton's anti-Semitism). It suggests that the moment of national "origin" was not marked by the emancipation of the class which had suffered most from dependence and inferiority, but simply its subordination to a new set of "masters" (*SCH*, 326).

Doyle's revisionist fiction critiques contemporary Irish cultural nationalism as much as it "winds-up" traditional nationalist sensibilities. When Henry comes to recognise that the "new Ireland" — i.e. independent Ireland — will be very much like the old one, Doyle is making a comment on *his* generation's "new Ireland" — the Ireland of the Celtic Tiger — which, as his previous novels showed, is hardly new for the Paula Spencers and Jimmy Rabbitte Srs. The "new Ireland" of the Free State was the game-board of the Gandons and Daltons; that of the Celtic Tiger is the playground of the "Beemer" brigade, the "Merc" mercenaries who have plundered the country while it slept or dithered in the neonationalist twilight.

Ruined Beyond Repair: Poor Mother/Eire and the Others

A feature of all of Doyle's fiction which becomes a "revisionist" feature in a narrative with this subject matter is its inclu-

siveness towards those who have been called Ireland's "internal Others" (Cullingford, 2001: 6–7) — women, abused
children and the working class — and to which *A Star Called
Henry* adds, Jews, prostitutes, and the Irish who fought in the
British army during World War I. Doyle told Paschel that he
found Michael Collins's view of the "real Ireland" — essentially Achill Island — "quite frightening" (Paschel, 1998: 148)
and he has Henry recognise that the Gaelic League and Sinn
Féin — "the party of money and faith" (*SCH*, 207) — had
created the sense that "Ireland was everywhere west of
Dublin" (*SCH*, 212). By having his hero come from the inner-
city slums and ultimately be betrayed by the "real Ireland"
that used him, Doyle tells the story of the making of modern
Ireland from the point of view of the urban poor whom the
"real Ireland" pushed into the margins of the national(ist)
narrative. The two Jewish figures in the novel, the fair and
decent scrap-dealer, Lipman, and the Latvian refugee, David
Climanis, both represent qualities the native Irish in the
novel are shown to lack; in Lipman's case, respect and com-
passion for the urban poor, and in Climanis's, openness to
the racially and culturally "other".

It has been argued that "the violence of the state operates
through its institutions continuously, producing the material
effects of poverty, unemployment, sickness, depopulation and
emigration" but that these effects go unrecognised because
"the violence of the state [also] lies in its capacity to control
representation, both political and cultural, thus regulating to
a remarkable extent the 'common sense' . . . of any given
society" (Lloyd, 1999: 4). *A Star Called Henry* challenges the
state-sanctioned view of the past, the Irish state's myth of
origin; this makes Doyle's novel radical in the sense of
"uprooting". Doyle's representation of the 1916–23 period
establishes a continuity between the "poverty, unemployment, sickness, depopulation and emigration" suffered by the

Rabbittes and Spencers of his earlier novels and the Nashes
and Smarts of his most recent.

Melody Nash, Henry's "Poor Mother", soon seems a figure for Mother Ireland. Joyce's Stephen described the latter
as "the old sow that eats her farrow" (Joyce, 1992: 220), and
she will be so for Doyle, as well, by the end of the novel, but
at this point Melody-Mother Ireland is the mother who cannot feed her young. As with Paula Spencer, Doyle risks creating a character that collapses into a stereotype. A prolific
breeder, she is fertile with death. As many of her offspring
die as survive. "Poor Mother. She wasn't much more than
twenty . . . but she was already old, already decomposing,
ruined beyond repair, good for some more babies, then finished" (*SCH*, 1). Like Paula Spencer, Melody is also a figure of
wasted potential, but one who is worn down not by an abusive husband but by the poverty that victimises them both.

A Star Called Henry advances Doyle's concern with feminist issues considerably. The novel contains more female
characters than all Doyle's other novels combined and each
one is vividly presented and intrinsic to the novel's fictive
world. Four in particular — Melody, Granny Nash, Dolly
Oblong and Miss O'Shea — carry significant thematic bur-
dens. Although the last eventually becomes "Missus Smart",
she remains "Miss O'Shea" to Henry. Doyle's characterisation of this figure is as much agenda-driven as determined by
plot requirements; while her feminist values are not anachronistic, she is more allegorical than realistic, though no less
enjoyable for that.

When they are reunited at the GPO, Miss O'Shea,
"mesmerised" by the figure of Henry in britches, "makes a
man of him", more than once (*SCH*, 120–1), in the basement
while the fighting rages above them. The episode — in which
Henry becomes a composite of Tom Jones and Flashman —
is an adolescent fantasy realised in the midst of adult horror.
But that seems to be Doyle's intention, setting the erotic cat

of fiction amidst the solemn pigeons of nationalist history. Also, it allows Miss O'Shea to explain her presence at the GPO by telling Henry that she is fighting for her freedom "to do what I want" (*SCH*, 122) — to which the already worldly wise Henry replies: "But they'll never let you" (*SCH*, 123) (see Tallon, 1996: 112).

When they marry, three years later, she becomes "Our Lady of the Machine Gun" (*SCH*, 273). During a raid on a police barracks, although shot more than once herself, she manages to carry the more seriously wounded Henry to safety (*SCH*, 265) — a combination of Irish Amazon and female Rambo. Following the Treaty, she fights against the Free State forces, gives birth to their daughter, arranges for Henry's escape from Kilmainham, and is there herself at the end of the novel when Henry leaves for Liverpool. Miss O'Shea is more "action-figure" than character, a two-dimensional cartoon-character whose function is to stir Doyle's revisionist pot in a counter-patriarchal direction in a novel which is itself a paradoxical hybrid of historical realism and comic-book fantasy.

Granny Nash, the "leathery old witch" (*SCH*, 1) who is Melody's mother, is likewise a feminist agent and larger-than-life character. It is through Granny Nash that Doyle introduces the metafictive theme in the novel; she elicits Henry's first act of narrative invention and the revelation that he is a *reliably* unreliable narrator. However, Granny Nash is more a seer-sybil. Whenever she appears, she is reading or carrying books — Shakespeare, Dickens and Tolstoy, to begin with, but then a steady stream of women-authored texts that Henry provides for her in exchange for information, which she gives in a suitably cryptic manner. The motif of women's books is part of another *uncanny* aura in the novel in that through these titles Doyle inserts into the masculinist tale of the fight for Irish independence allusions to the unfamiliar alternative histories of women's oppression, survival and triumph in a patriarchal world that includes Irish nationalism. One point *A Star Called Henry* makes quite strongly is that women's freedom was not part of the revolution planned by men.

Doyle might have borrowed Dolly Oblong from his be-loved Dickens, but she is cut from the same imaginative cloth as Angela Carter's Fevvers in *Nights at the Circus*. A mystery woman and *femme fatale*, if she does not embody an epistemological mystery at the core of the novel, like Fevvers, her brothel, like Fevvers' circus, is the metafictive funhouse and epistemological maze, the city in microcosm, in which both Henrys ultimately go to search for the truth. In *Nights at the Circus*, Carter parodies a traditional patriar-chal form of the search for identity — the separation of truth from appearance through the discovery of the "truth" about (a) "woman". The representation of woman as mys-tery is a convention of patriarchal pathology; it paradoxically anaesthetises as it "eroticises" male anxiety about the world and the self. In the figure of the *femme fatale*, the male gaze fantasises woman as both question and answer, a phantasm of desire and fear.

When Henry Sr gazes upon Dolly, however, rather than possessing her and the knowledge he seeks, he is trans-formed into a watchdog who curls up and goes to sleep be-neath her stairs; an unlucky Odysseus, his phallic wooden leg is no sacred moly. When his son confronts her in her lair, however, he ends up liberating her from the pimp-turned-government minister who had imprisoned her literally and symbolically within the patriarchal institution of prostitution.

Gandon's relationship with Dolly Oblong is emblematic of the sexual hypocrisy that the novel places alongside the ideological deception at the centre of the revolution. But when Dolly asks Henry to kill Gandon before Gandon kills her, Henry obliges for his own reasons. Gandon makes the transition from pimp to politician, from an informal and "ille-gal" institution to a formal and political institution, as easily as he transforms himself from Gandon into O'Gandúin, because all he is doing is deploying the same patriarchal power in a different form — the patronising patriotism that propagandists like Dalton concoct to conceal the "business as usual" nature of the middle-class coup that presents itself as a revolution.

The parody of the archetypal narrative forms of the quest — the detective story and the male search for the truth about woman — are not as extreme or as sophisticated in *A Star Called Henry* as in *Nights at the Circus*, but the Oedipal triangle formed — ironically, to be sure — by Dolly Oblong and the two Henry Smarts, neither of whom is very smart and the younger of which only grows into his name at the last moment, is a metafictive minefield within the novel.

The Last Roundup, or *Little Big Man* on the Liffey

Revisionist fictions and films like *A Star Called Henry, The Whereabouts of Aeneas McNulty* (Sebastian Barry, 1998), *Sunrise with Sea Monster* and *Michael Collins* belong to the "struggle over representation" (Lloyd, 1999: 4) of the past between the state and its ideologues, and those with other ideological outlooks. The struggle matters because it is really about the present and future more than the past. Doyle's images of Connolly, Pearse, Collins, de Valera and others, the image of the period the novel as a whole projects through the character, voice and perspective of Henry Smart, "brush history against the grain" (Benjamin, 1969: 682). Be it the specific issues of the occlusion of Connolly, the sanctification of de Valera, the rehabilitation of Collins, or the general "thesis" that the achievement of independence made no difference in the class relations within Ireland, Doyle has written a historical fiction that enters into a "negative dialectic" with both "official history" and "elite nationalist historiography" (Lloyd, 1999: 37, 43–4).

Authentic revisionist fiction engages the history and the history of representation of the past. Ersatz revisionist fiction only does the latter, and as such can end up being simply "nationalist kitsch". In *A Star Called Henry*, Doyle successfully constructs a *seamless* join between fiction and history, invention and research: Henry inhabits the history he is constructed to illuminate; whereas Jamie O'Neill, for example, in *At Swim, Two Boys* (2001), does not achieve the same organic linking of the novel's plot and the novelist's "conspiracy". O'Neill's story of gay love could have been set in any place or period in Irish history and setting it when he does does not lead the reader to see either gay love or the history of the Rising differently because of their conjunction. *At Swim, Two Boys* uses the period of the 1916 Rising the way classical Hollywood films used history, as a "set" to impress those who were not interested in history at all. While O'Neill's novel successfully challenges the genre of the historical novel in a way that it needs to be challenged, it does not challenge the history of the representation of the 1916 Rising. Doyle's novel challenges both, and more successfully.

Writing before *A Star Called Henry*, Joseph O'Connor remarked that Doyle's work and his humour have always been "deeply iconoclastic" and "passionately moral" (O'Connor, 1995: 143). The hostility to nationalist mystification that Doyle expresses in *A Star Called Henry* belongs to his earliest fictional impulse, the unpublished *Your Granny Is a Hunger Striker*, which he worked on between 1981 and 1985. There are also patterns of plot and characterisation that repeat those in the first trilogy. Writing about Jimmy Rabbitte Sr and Jr, O'Toole says "Their quixotic adventures are actually attempts to fit in with the ideology of the times and to do what the great and good tell them they should be doing" (O'Toole, 1999: 39). The same might be said about Henry Smart Sr and Jr. The father's life of crime as the henchman of a "respectable businessman" represents the most he can aspire to in his world and his son's "success" is likewise defined and dictated by his "betters". Neither Henry is very smart, of course, in that both are played for suckers. The son, at least, "wises up" — after many deaths, which is progress of a sort.

The relations between fathers and sons, and father-figures and sons are prominent in all of Doyle's novels (see O'Toole, 1999: 39). For Doyle, as for Fanon, "the family is a miniature of the nation" and "As the child emerges from the shadow of his parents, he finds himself once more among the same laws, the same principles, the same values. A normal child that has grown up in a normal family will be a normal man" (Fanon, 1952: 142). A great paradoxical strength of Doyle's fiction is the way it represents the "normal" while at the same time questioning the normative. In five of Doyle's six novels, the family-nation is shown going through some form of crisis, surviving in *The Snapper* and *The Van*, equivocally so in *Paddy Clarke Ha Ha Ha* and *The Woman Who Walked into Doors*, and failing abjectly in *A Star Called Henry*. In March 1996, Doyle told White that he was dividing his time between a screenplay of O'Flaherty's *Famine* and a new novel that he hoped would be "funny" (White, 2001: 158). He seems to have started *A Star Called Henry* with the idea of a very old man telling his life story (White, 2001: 161) — perhaps in the manner of Robert Altman's *Little Big Man*, another orphan who survives the storm of history. The original idea was not to write a trilogy, "but the story was getting so big it became one": "The character is walking through this huge history and I couldn't take short-cuts . . ." (Costello, 2001: 90). This "huge history" is the history of modern Ireland, including, if the ending is any indication, the modern diaspora. One can only wonder if Doyle's "take" on that phenomenon will be as "revisionist" as his version of the birth of the modern Republic.

Conclusion

"We are on our own, but we are together. We sustain ourselves"

Individually and collectively, Roddy Doyle's novels cohere around a single focal concern: the defence of the individual's struggle to live with dignity and decency in the face of all those forces, concrete and abstract, human and institutional, local and distant, direct and indirect, which in the forms of history, ideology, religion, class, patriarchy or poverty, attempt to coerce the individual to accept the way things are or have been as "natural" or the way they have to be. Doyle's parody of *Bildungsroman* and historical romance in *A Star Called Henry* culminates neither in "the cultivation and social reconciliation of the individual subject" nor in "the recuperation of a national subject or community" (McCarthy, 2000: 125); rather, it ends with the protagonist going into exile, fleeing for his life and rejecting both the new national community and the ambiguous identity of hero-murderer to which that community has subjected him. Like Stephen at the end of *A Portrait of the Artist as a Young Man*, Henry is running away from both a national and a personal history. He has become his father, an assassin on the run who must abandon his wife and child. He seeks to escape the cycle of history even as he repeats it in his forced emigration to Liverpool and then America.

If Henry Smart's "biggest problem is belatedness" (Jeffers, 2002: 121), then his allegorical significance as both a figure for modern Ireland and for his creator is profoundly suggestive. For it is a striking coincidence that Doyle's second trilogy should begin by circling back on his first by having another father-son set of characters. In *A Star Called Henry*, the beloved father ultimately symbolises the dead hand of the past reaching out to determine the present and future, to rob the new generation of its right to self-determination and self-invention. In *The Commitments*, *The Snapper* and *The Van*, the son is shown "breaking" with the father in the sense of going his own way, reinventing himself, and generally being open to change in ways his father is not. In *Paddy Clarke Ha Ha Ha*, a distant and emotionally enigmatic father eventually becomes an absent father; in *Family* and *The Woman Who Walked into Doors*, the father is a tyrant-monster.

The recurring problematic of fathers and sons in Doyle's fiction is an expression of the continuing fallout of what Conor McCarthy describes as the "crisis of authority" (McCarthy, 2000: 11) that occurred in Irish society during the 1960s and 1970s, and which was most evident in the collapse of the meta-narrative of nationalism. In *The Commitments*, Doyle provided an image of the "constructed" nature of the Irish persona; in *A Star Called Henry*, he shows the dissolution of the self based on the masks of nationalism, Catholicism and relation to rural landscape.

The absence of explicit reference to matters of Irishness and Irish identity in Doyle's fiction until the explicitly *anti*-nationalistic *A Star Called Henry* situates Doyle's writing in the context of the "crisis of narratives" (McCarthy, 2000: 33) that has made Irish social, cultural, literary and political discourse over the past twenty years so lively. Along with writers like Dermot Bolger, Joseph O'Connor, and Fintan

O'Toole, Doyle broke the quiet, stirred the pot, set in motion the dialogue in fiction and criticism about contemporary
Ireland, bursting the balloon, in a sense, of the hucksters and
flunkies of "Ireland's ersatz modernity" (McCarthy, 2000: 18).
Doyle's characters represent a class that feels no connection
to the nationalist or colonialist versions of Ireland, Irish history, and Irish identity through which it is expected to see
itself and understand its position in Irish society. If *The Commitments* (1987) did not begin the wave of new Irish writing
in the late 1980s and early 1990s, a wave that was "characterised by an intense re-examination of what it might mean
to be Irish in the late twentieth century" (Smyth, 1997: 66), it
was part of the beginning and Doyle's novels and films since
The Commitments have both reflected and contributed to the
complex processes of socio-cultural introspection which
have distinguished Irish writing and film in recent decades.

Joseph O'Connor offers an eloquent defence of Doyle's
fiction (and implicitly of his own) when he asserts that
"Naming the world . . . describing it with faith and precision
and affection . . . and in that process changing the world.
Surely this is the real purpose of art, to change the world.
But if you want to change the world, the first thing you do is
change the way people see it. We really do need to do that
in Ireland . . ." (O'Connor, 1995: 141). This is what Gordan
recognises when she begins her review of *The Woman Who
Walked into Doors* by describing Doyle as the contemporary
Irish novelist who has contributed "a new set of images for
the Ireland of the late 20th century" (Gordan, 1996: 7).
Doyle himself, however, seems uncomfortable discussing the
political dimensions of his writing:

> I . . . see myself as being socially committed and po-
> litically engaged — I always have done. At the same
> time, I would not inflict it on a writer. To me, one of
> the greatest enemies of writing is political correct-

ness and it's only going to get worse, I suspect. It's
the refusal to acknowledge satire. It's important to
upset and outrage people. (Costello, 2001: 91)

"I do what I want to do. My novels come from within me"
(Gerrard, 2001): thus Jimmy Rabbitte Jr and The Commitments may be a version of Paul Mercier or John Sutton and
Passion Machine, but Jimmy is also a mask for Roddy Doyle.
His rejection of "Fianna fuckin' Fáil" (*C*, 8) reflects Doyle's
disenchantment with traditional Irish politics. Doyle belongs
to a generation of writers that emerged from adolescence
with an irreverent, sceptical, ironic attitude towards authority, institutions, traditions and conventions. The real critical
issue is how Doyle relates to the new self-consciousness and
self-interrogation of contemporary Ireland. A healthy de-
mocracy needs writers who question and satirise, but it also
needs them to contribute constructive images of a renewed
civil society to replace those that have been debunked and
rejected. Does Doyle's fiction make a *positive* contribution
to contemporary Ireland? If it helps to free it from the drag
of the past, does it also help to move it forward?

O'Connor has summarised Irish critical response to
Doyle's fiction as "snobbish, elitist and class-obsessed gar-
bage":

> They say his work is clichéd and full of stereotypes.
> They says it's childish, moronic, sentimental, too full
> of dialogue, that it's mawkish and leans too heavily
> on a certain outmoded "gas" approach to Dublin life.
> They say — with some force — that if it had been
> written by an English writer, Doyle's work would be
> accused of being racist. (O'Connor, 1995: 139)

But for O'Connor, the point is that "it isn't written by an
English writer. And surely Roddy Doyle is as entitled as any
other Irish novelist to expose what he sees as the country's

shortcomings in his own way, and on his own terms" (O'Connor, 1995: 139). Doyle's great value to his culture is the awkwardness and embarrassment he represents to those Irish who would rather appear to themselves and to the world in a different light altogether, and his writing does make a positive contribution to a new imagining of "Ireland" if, rather than focusing on Doyle's rejection of a traditional Irish nationalism and the narrow range of identity it validated (O'Mahony and Delanty, 1998: 181), we recognise his representation of the diversity of contemporary Irish society, not only in his representation of urban, working-class men and women but, most recently, of contemporary urban Ireland's changing racial composition.

Doyle describes the script for his recent film, the romantic comedy *When Brendan Met Trudy* (2000), as "portray[ing] the new multi-racial society we're living in"; likewise, in his recent children's books and short stories, "I bring black and white people together or Irish and Romanian. I get people to meet in the fictional sense and to come away knowing but not necessarily liking each other" (Costello, 2001: 92). This is a repetition in racial terms of what Doyle set out to achieve with his first five novels in class terms. Where his early career set out to bring into literary visibility the world and culture of the urban working-class, now he writes to acknowledge "the existence of these people and to make sure that visually they are included and that eventually you can reach a point where you can like or dislike a person but the colour of the person won't matter" (Costello, 2001: 93); "Now I am writing about Nigerians and I am forcing Irish people to come up to Nigerians and to shake hands with them, their first black hand" (Costello, 2001: 97).

This new theme in Doyle's writing goes along with his active support of *Metro Éireann*, a Dublin-based multi-cultural newspaper started by two Nigerian journalists, Abel Ugba and Chinedu Onyejelem, in April 2000. Since May of that year Doyle has written three short stories for the paper: "Guess Who's Coming for the Dinner?", "The Deportees" and "57% Irish", all dealing with issues of race, ethnicity and identity. He has also served as patron and judge for its annual Media and Multiculturalism Awards. "Guess Who's Coming for the Dinner?" was also published as "The Dinner", in *The New Yorker*, and turned into a play which premiered at the Andrews Lane Theatre in Dublin in October 2001.

Thanks to frequent circuits of the Artane roundabout, Larry, the protagonist of "Guess Who's Coming for the Dinner?" (Jimmy Rabbitte Sr is re-named this in the film version of *The Van*), has gotten used to feeling "modern, successful, Irish" (Doyle, May 2000: 7). But Doyle is less interested in the continuing economic boom of the new century than in confronting those who have risen with the economic tide with what the tide has brought in with it. Doyle's "new Ireland" has become the Ireland of Nigerian refugees and immigrants from eastern Europe. After centuries of leaving home for better opportunities abroad (and more to the point, of being welcomed in America, Canada and Australia to the extent that they were given the opportunity to flourish there), the Irish themselves are now faced with the fact that for many *Ireland* is now a land of opportunity — or more basically, of peace and freedom from persecution. Is Doyle saying it is "payback time"? This could be quite a challenge to a people whose identity has for so long been informed by a deep sense of being the victim but who now are confronted with many who are today's victims of famine, political oppression, economic deprivation, violence or sheer hopelessness. The challenge, of course, is not to Irish generosity — another staple of the national self-image — but to the genuineness of that generosity. The Irish have an admirable history of generous giving to Africa; but it is one thing to send aid to the heart of darkness, and another to welcome Africans into white Ireland. Doyle could not allegorise these issues better than he does in this story that presents the conflict evoked in Larry when he is told that his daughter has invited a Nigerian refugee to share a meal with her family and he concludes that they might be thinking of getting married.

Larry is at first "surprised, and angry, and hurt, and confused", and Doyle does a fine job of conveying a clash of instinct and reason in his automatic reaction to the idea of his daughter's relationship with Ben. Larry honestly cannot understand why, but his whole sense of a "safe" world is suddenly disoriented and destabilised. After "squirming" for a week under the pressure of the "rough questions" his feelings have forced him to ask himself, he comes to recognise that what he feels is fear — fear of difference. Ben comes from a world that "was too different; that was it. Too unknowable, and too frightening for his daughter" (Doyle, August 2000: 7). Of course, "it" is not frightening for Stephanie, not because she has no intention of marrying Ben, but because apparently there is no "it" to be frightened of. Doyle is cutting deep into the issue here, which is not that the Other is "too unknowable" but that, to some, the effort of knowing another threatens the stability of what is known and "safe". By the end of the meal, "[Larry] was happy enough. He wasn't a racist. There was a black man sitting across from him and he wanted to be his father-in-law. He wasn't sure why, but that didn't matter. Larry was happy with himself" (Doyle, January 2001: 7). But Larry's "conversion" is not as straightforward as it seems; by the end he knows there's no likelihood of Stephanie marrying Ben, and he only warms to Ben after he tells the history of his family's suffering in Africa and Larry can pity him. But he will never *not* be able to see the colour of Ben's skin before he sees Ben. "Guess Who's Coming for the Dinner?" shows both the need to open to the racial Other as well as the need to be open for the right reasons and in the right way.

Like "Guess Who's Coming for the Dinner?" but even
more so, "The Deportees" and "57% Irish" are fiction as social intervention. The Deportees are nine Dublin musicians
and singers whom Jimmy Rabbitte Jr, ten years after the collapse of The Commitments, has formed into a band. They are
African, Russian, Spanish, American, Romanian — as well as a
couple of Dublin-born natives; one is a sixty-year-old trav-
eler, another a single mother. When Jimmy asks the latter if
she's "Northside or southside?", her reply — "–Ah, grow up,
would yeh" — announces how far Doyle has come since the
Barrytown trilogy, with its focus on class and locale. Then the
challenge was to find a base in self-esteem for the construction of a personal and collective identity. But as the narrator
of the new story says, "That was then and this is fuckin' now"
(Doyle, April 2002: 7). With "The Deportees", Doyle is looking outward to a new Irish society with an increasingly multi-
racial and multi-cultural presence and the issue of identity is
now cast in terms of race, ethnicity, and sexual orientation:
the focus is on inclusion, not employment. The story is both
vibrantly celebratory and disturbingly ominous. At one point,
the juxtaposition of two sentences, "Christianity had left the
tent" and "They were happy, sexy; they were cooking and
Irish" (Doyle, March 2002: 7), recalls the Doyle of the trilogy
while at the same time recognising that a new confidence has
indeed emerged in Ireland since the late 1980s. The story
ends optimistically as the band mesmerises the crowd with a
performance of "Somewhere" (Doyle, April 2002: 7). And
yet earlier, when Doyle has Jimmy Jr's elation at the birth of
his fourth child interrupted by an anonymous phone call from
someone who's been harassing him as a "nigger lover", he
makes clear that "That evil out there" (Doyle, September
2001: 7) — the fear of difference and the demonisation of
the other — is as real and persistent in the "new Ireland" as
it was in the old. But when one compares how Doyle used
"nigger" in *The Commitments* with the way it functions in this

story, it is clear that a new world of difference has indeed entered Doyle's fiction.

It is possible to approach Doyle's protagonists in relation to what Pat O'Connor, borrowing from R.W. Connell, describes as the "crisis tendencies" at the structural level of identity that are a consequence of the various institutional crises that have beset Irish society and culture over the past two decades, specifically within and between the institutions of church, state and patriarchy (O'Connor, 1998: 24–5). Doyle's poignant imagining of the predicament of Paddy Clarke and his complex elaboration of the character of Veronica Rabbitte through Briget Finnegan in *War* to Paula Spencer in *Family* and then *The Woman Who Walked into Doors* express the "increasing awareness of the extent to which the concept of 'family' has been and can be used to exploit and/or nullify the needs of women and children" (O'Connor, 1998: 4).

Also, rather than responding to the signs of a creeping postmodernism in Irish culture with cultural-nationalist paranoia (see Herr, 1994: 221), Doyle's comfort and confidence in a "macaronic" (Cosgrove, 1996: 236) Irish culture has been evident ever since *The Commitments* and is particularly prominent in *When Brendan Met Trudy* (2000) and the recent short fiction. From its title and opening-shot allusion to *Sunset Boulevard*, the film is a highly self-conscious, indeed meta-filmic, representation of a different "Dublin" than the one Doyle made his name representing in his early novels. Allusions to films function in this film the way the song lyrics function in *The Commitments*. Doyle recognises that a healthy culture is one that adapts and assimilates more than it resists, one that makes the "foreign" native. In "The Deportees" Jimmy Jr admires the musicians because "They'll play anything and make it theirs"; music remains Doyle's spiritual medium, concentrating the personal even as it transcends it, expressing the individual in a way that opens the self to oth-

ers. From the invasive but instrumentally liberating American
"pop" music in *The Commitments* to Henry's Huck-like light-
ing-out for the American west at the end of *A Star Called
Henry*, Doyle depicts a contemporary Irish culture that is a
complex processor of exogenous (largely American) influences and indigenous tastes and needs. The obverse of letting go of an identity based on the traditional signifiers is
taking up the task of an identity based on other "constructive" elements — class, local place and culture, generation
and, what seems most important to Doyle now, an inclusive
acceptance of difference.

Doyle seems liberated more than threatened by the possibilities of a postmodern, post-national "Ireland" and the
basis of his security, like that of his aesthetic — and of his
own personal identity — seems to be what the American
poet, William Carlos Williams, called "a local pride" (Williams, 1963: 2) or what the Irish poet, Patrick Kavanagh,
called "parochialism" (see Kavanagh, 1988: 204–6). Gerry
Smyth understands the latter as "Kavanagh's solution to the
aesthetic and personal dilemma caused by modern Ireland",
and as what Kavanagh himself described as the need "to find
some substitute for the national loyalty, some system to
take the place of the enslaving State" (Smyth, 1998: 107).
Doyle's Dublin-centred oeuvre represents his aesthetic and
personal negotiation with late-twentieth-century Ireland, not
only in the sense that it expresses *his* need to fill the vacuum
caused by a discredited nationalism and disrespected State,
but in the sense that it is a response to the crisis in urban
identity caused by the blurring of urban-suburban distinc-
tions with the growth of Dublin since the 1950s. Kevin
Whelan has theorised an identity-crisis at the "townland"
level in Ireland as a consequence of the challenge to regional
"economic and social solidarity" that has ensued since EC
membership: "The townland level is the 'neighborhood level'
or the practical farmland community size, which in the past

shared farm work, tools, and equipment" (Jeffers, 2002: 14; see Whelan, 1993: 7–12). Perhaps Doyle's fiction — and that of others — should be read less in terms of the rural/ urban, traditional/modern binaries in Irish discourse than in terms of an increasingly fractured urban identity which sub- sumes "old" and "new" within its own sense of a local his- tory more central to its identity than the national story.

In 1962, Sean O'Faolain argued that "The lesson of our time is that Irish writers cannot any longer go on writing about Ireland, or for Ireland, within the narrow confines of the traditional Irish life-concept; it is too slack, too cosy, too evasive, too untense. They must, or perish as regionalists, take as writers everywhere do, the local (since they know its detail most intimately) and universalise it, as Joyce did" (O'Faolain, 1962: 746). Doyle's "local pride" or "parochial- ism", like Kavanagh's, is "a capacity to hold the local and the universal in fructifying tension" (Smyth, 1998: 108), but his aesthetic is perhaps better theorised as a literary form of what Kenneth Frampton, discussing postmodern architec- ture, has called "Critical Regionalism": "The fundamental strategy of Critical Regionalism is to mediate the impact of universal civilization with elements derived *indirectly* from the peculiarities of a particular place. . . . Critical Regionalism depends upon maintaining a high level of critical self- consciousness" (Frampton, 1983: 21). Doyle practises a form of literary critical regionalism in his co-option of American "soul" in *The Commitments*.

But more generally, his hallmark reliance on "Dub" dia- lect in his fiction is the keystone of a critical regionalism that mediates not only between "local" Irish and non-Irish cul- tural signifiers, but *within* the Irish national discourse, be- tween his "local" north Dublin sense of place-identity and the Irish version of "standard" English that ghosts all Irish literary discourse. Furthermore, in this latter sense, it is im- portant to recognise that the "mediation" that Doyle's use of dialect practises is itself "critical" of the homogenising, identity-subjecting drag not only of "standard" Irish English but also of the middle-class literary culture that regards such dialect as "infra dig".

Doyle has asserted that "I have no manifesto or agenda myself" (Paschel, 1998: 153) and has said he is "wary" of Ferdia MacAnna's notion of a "Dublin Renaissance" because the writers MacAnna discusses "don't have much in common" (Paschel, 1998: 149; see also Sbrockey, 1999). Doyle has suggested that the 1990s saw "the beginning of something new" rather than a "renaissance" (Paschel, 1998: 149) and the critical regionalism that his work — as well as that of the Raven Arts writers and Passion Machine — represents, is perhaps better understood in terms of what Frampton theorises as an "*arrière-garde* position" rather than as the delusions of a *faux* or failed oppositional avant-garde (McCarthy, 2000: 135–64). Speaking in architectural terms, Frampton describes an "*arrière-garde* position" as

> one which distances itself equally from the Enlightenment myth of progress and from a reactionary, unrealistic impulse to return to the architectonic forms of the preindustrial past. A critical *arrière-garde* has to remove itself from both the optimization of advanced technology and the ever-present tendency to regress into nostalgic historicism or the glibly decorative. . . . Only an arrière-garde has the capacity to cultivate a resistant, identity-giving culture while at the same time having discreet recourse to universal technique. (Frampton, 1983: 20)

Doyle's novels and films of contemporary Ireland *do* "cultivate a resistant, identity-giving culture while at the same time having discreet recourse to universal technique" by giving expression to a distinctive and recognisably "Irish" experience, while also acknowledging that an important contributor to that experience is Ireland's participation in a postmodern global economy. Whether it is James Brown, Man. U, Hollywood films or African refugees, Doyle writes toward a "new Ireland" that will be a society and culture increasingly open to alterity, but more importantly, less and less threatened or made insecure by difference.

Doyle's openness reflects the security that his "local pride" instils in him. When asked if contemporary Ireland possesses a "soul", he replied: "my patch does. Having said that, I don't know what it is. When I walk around my patch, in north-east Finglas, I feel it. I hope it's not too bubble-like. I hope it's open to change and not a closed sealed community. . . . We are opening ourselves to different cultures. The possibilities are fantastic and I would like to think that these possibilities aren't just cultural but social too" (Costello, 2001: 98).

Doyle is, of course, in the middle of his career and any discussion of his work in relation to contemporary Ireland should end interrogatively, not conclusively. Will the rest of Doyle's career be as critically reflective of Ireland in the coming years as it has been of the Ireland of the past twenty years? Will "The Last Roundup" — the work-in-progress — achieve the coherence and scope of a major work of fiction? Will Doyle's recent turn to issues of race affect Henry's journey through America? In *A Star Called Henry*, by re-siting his signature themes of class and family in the sacred matter of nationalist Ireland, Doyle seems to posit that the roots of the contemporary malaises his earlier fiction explored are to be found in the birth of the "first" modern Ireland. The current pressures and strains on Irish society and culture are as much the continuing consequences of history as the supervention of completely novel issues. How the rest of the trilogy unfolds is crucial here because, depending on the upward or downward direction of the spiral form which the remaining novels will complete, an overall comic or tragic vision may emerge.

Dominic Head claims that in the second half of the twentieth century, the English social novel became "the privileged form of moral discourse in a secular world" (Head, 2002: 251). My reading of Doyle's work has been framed by the view that, by the end of the twentieth century in Ireland, the novel and film had become the most important forms of popular moral discourse in an increasingly secular Irish society and that Doyle played a major role in that development during the 1990s. For all their humour, Doyle's novels — like Graham Greene's, a writer he much admires — are seriously *moral* entertainments. At their deepest level of inspiration, they emerge from the passionate and optimistic commitment to human community that is Doyle's response to his profound sense that "we are on our own, but we are together. We sustain ourselves" (Costello, 2001: 99). If "The novel, with its imaginative range, and its freedom from 'factual' codes . . . [is] . . . an important focus for the society's alternative, redemptive, and connective thought" (Head, 2002: 251), one must hope that Roddy Doyle will continue to write novels that will focus, in such affective and provocative ways, the effects on individuals of the competing visions of an "Ireland" that can only ever be "new" to those who, like Doyle, are passionately committed to its moral and social well-being.

Bibliography

Works by Roddy Doyle

Novels

The Commitments (1988), London: Heinemann (originally, Dublin: King Farouk, 1987).

The Snapper (1990), London: Secker and Warburg.

The Van (1991), London: Secker and Warburg.

Paddy Clarke Ha Ha Ha (1993), London: Secker and Warburg.

The Woman Who Walked into Doors (1996), London: Jonathan Cape.

A Star Called Henry (1999), London: Jonathan Cape.

Not Just for Christmas (1999), Open Door Series for Adult Literacy, Dublin: New Island Books.

Plays

War (1989), Dublin: Passion Machine.

Brownbread (1992), London: Secker and Warburg.

Guess Who's Coming for the Dinner (2001).

The Woman Who Walked into Doors (2003).

Scripts for Film and Television

The Commitments (1991), UK: Beacon Communications/First Film Company/Dirty Hands Productions (credited with Dick Clement and Ian La Frenais).

The Snapper (1993), UK: BBC Films/Screen 2 (screenplay).

Family (1994), UK: BBC (teleplay).

The Van (1996), Ireland: Deadly Films/BBC Films/Fox Searchlight (screenplay).

Hell for Leather (1998), Ireland: RTE (screenplay).

When Brendan Met Trudy (2001), Ireland: Deadly Films (screenplay).

Children's Books

The Giggler Treatment (2000), London: Scholastic.

Rover Saves Christmas (2001), London: Scholastic.

Short Stories and Book Chapters

"Room . . .[?]" (1997), *Finbar's Hotel*, ed. Dermot Bolger. Dublin: New Island Books.

"Guess Who's Coming for the Dinner?" (May 2000 – January 2001), *Metro Éireann*, 7.

"The Dinner" (2001), *The New Yorker*, 5 February, 72–81.

"Chapter One" (2001), *Yeats Is Dead! A Mystery by Fifteen Irish Writers*, ed. Joseph O'Connor, London: Jonathan Cape, pp. 3–20.

"The Deportees" (March 2001 – May 2002), *Metro Éireann*, 7.

"57% Irish" (August 2002 – April 2003), *Metro Éireann*, 7.

Non-Fiction

"Introduction" (1992), *Brownbread and War*, London: Secker and Warburg, pp. 1–2.

"Introduction" (1996), *The Stranger and Other Stories*, ed. Clement Cairns. Durrus, Bantry, Co. Cork: Fish Publishing, pp. *iii–viii*.

"Dead Bones and Chickens" (1988), *Invisible Cities: The New Dubliners: A Journey through Unofficial Dublin*, ed. Dermot Bolger. Dublin: Raven Arts Press, pp. 27–9.

Rory & Ita (2002), London: Jonathan Cape.

Interviews with Roddy Doyle

Boland, John (1996), Interview with Roddy Doyle, *The Irish Times*, 2 March.

Costello, Stephen J. (2001), "Roddy Doyle: Writer", in *The Irish Soul: In Dialogue*, Dublin: The Liffey Press, pp. 85–99.

Fay, Liam (1996), "What's the Story", Interview with Roddy Doyle, *Hot Press*, 3 April, pp. 18–20.

Gerrard, Nicci (2001), "What keeps Roddy rooted", *The Observer*, Sunday, 15 April. www.books.guardian.co.uk/departments/generalfiction/story/0,6000,473369,00.html

Paschel, Ulrike (1998), "Interview with Roddy Doyle, Dublin 5 May 1997", in *No Mean City? The Image of Dublin in the Novels of Dermot Bolger, Roddy Doyle and Val Mulkerns*, Aachen British and American Studies, Vol. 10, Frankfurt am Main: Peter Lang, pp. 147–60.

Sbrockey, Karen (1999), "Something of a Hero: An Interview with Roddy Doyle", in *Literary Review* (Summer 1999). www.findarticles.com/cf_0/m2078/4_42/56184292/print.jhtml

Taylor, Charles (1999), "The Salon Interview: Roddy Doyle", www.salon.com/books/feature/999/10/28/doyle/index2.html

White, Caramine (2001), "An Interview with Roddy Doyle," in Caramine White, *Reading Roddy Doyle*, Syracuse: Syracuse University Press, pp. 149–83.

Works about Roddy Doyle: Books, Chapters, Essays, Reviews

Appelo, Tim (1992), "Down the Rabbitte Hole", review of *The Van*, *New York Times Book Review*, 20 September, pp. 3, 15.

Battersby, Eileen (1993), "Not Bord Failte's Ireland", *Irish Times*, 20 May, p. 10.

Bernstein, Richard (1999), "Enslaved, With Abandon, to Independence", review of *A Star Called Henry*, *The New York Times*, 10 September, p. E44.

Booker, M. Keith (1997), "Late Capitalism Comes to Dublin: 'American' Popular Culture in the Novels of Roddy Doyle", *ARIEL: A Review of International English Literature*, Vol. 28, No. 3, pp. 27–45.

Bradshaw, Nick (1994), "Doyle's Dubliners", *Details*, February, pp. 128–30.

Cosgrove, Brian (1996), "Roddy Doyle's Backward Look: Tradition and Modernity in *Paddy Clarke Ha Ha Ha*", *Studies*, Vol. 85, No. 339, pp. 231–42.

Donnelly, Brian (2000), "Roddy Doyle: From Barrytown to the GPO", *Irish University Review*, Vol. 30, No. 1, pp. 17–31.

Donoghue, Denis (1994), "Another Country", *New York Review of Books*, 3 February, pp. 3–6.

Eder, Richard (1999), "Unrest Was General All Over Ireland", review of *A Star Called Henry*, *The New York Times Book Review*, 12 September, p. 7.

Edwards, Ruth Dudley (1999), "Though Rich and Famous He Still Cares", review of *A Star Called Henry*, *Literary Review*, September, pp. 47–8.

Fitzgerald, Penelope (1991), "Fried Nappy", review of *The Van, London Review of Books*, 12 September, p. 16.

Foran, Charles (1996), "The Troubles of Roddy Doyle", *Saturday Night*, Vol. 111, No. 3 (April), pp. 58–64.

Gordan, Mary (1996), "The Good Mother", review of *The Woman Who Walked into Doors*, *The New York Times Book Review*, 28 April, p. 7.

Hand, Derek (1996), review of *The Woman Who Walked into Doors*, *Irish Literary Supplement*, Vol. 15 (Fall), p. 14.

Hopkin, James (1999), "Mired in History", review of *A Star Called Henry*, *The New Statesman*, 6 September. www.findarticles.com/cf_0/m0FQP/4452_128/56749535/print.jhtml

Jeffers, Jennifer M. (2002), *The Irish Novel at the End of the Twentieth Century: Gender, Bodies, and Power*, New York: Palgrave.

Keen, Suzanne (1996), "Irish Troubles", review of *The Woman Who Walked into Doors*, *Commonweal*, Vol. 123, No. 17 (11 October), pp. 21–3.

Lane, Anthony (1994), "Dubliners", review of *Paddy Clarke Ha Ha Ha*, *The New Yorker*, 24 January, pp. 91–4.

Lehmann-Haupt, Christopher (1993), "Window Into the Mind of a 10-Year Old Irish Boy", review of *Paddy Clarke Ha Ha Ha*, *The New York Times*, 13 December, p. C18.

Mac Anna, Ferdia (1991), "The Dublin Renaissance: An Essay on Modern Dublin and Dublin Writers", *Irish Review*, No. 10, Spring, pp. 14–30.

Mahony, Christina Hunt (1998), *Contemporary Irish Literature: Transforming Tradition*, New York: St Martin's Press.

O'Connor, Joseph (1995), "The Write Stuff: Irish Writers and Writing" in *The Secret World of the Irish Male*, London: Mandarin, pp. 134–62.

Onkey, Lauren (1993), "Celtic Soul Brothers", *Éire-Ireland*, Vol. 28, No. 3 (Fall), pp. 147–58.

O'Toole, Fintan (1999), "Working-Class Dublin on Screen: The Roddy Doyle Films", *Cinéaste*, Vol. XXIV, No. 2–3, pp. 36–9.

Paschel, Ulrike (1998), *No Mean City? The Image of Dublin in the Novels of Dermot Bolger, Roddy Doyle and Val Mulkerns*, Aachen British and American Studies, Vol. 10, Frankfurt am Main: Peter Lang.

Riding, Alan (1999), "Chipping Away the Blarney", review of *A Star Called Henry*, *The New York Times*, 22 September, pp. E1–2.

Rockwell, John (1993), "Is It Autobiography or Fiction? But Then Does it Really Matter?" *The New York Times*, 20 December, C11, p. 15.

Smyth, Gerry (1997), *The Novel and the Nation: Studies in the New Irish Fiction*, London: Pluto Press, pp. 66–71.

Strongman, Luke (1997), "Toward an Irish Literary Postmodernism: Roddy Doyle's *Paddy Clarke Ha Ha Ha*", *Canadian Journal of Irish Studies*, Vol. 23, No. 1, pp. 31–40.

Turbide, Diane (1993), "Dublin Soul", *Maclean's*, 30 August, p. 50.

White, Caramine (2001), *Reading Roddy Doyle*, Syracuse: Syracuse University Press.

Other Works Cited

Adorno, Theodor (1988), *Prisms*, trans. Samuel and Sherry Weber, Cambridge, Mass.: MIT Press.

Allen, Kieran (2000), *The Celtic Tiger: The Myth of Social Partnership in Ireland*, Manchester: Manchester University Press.

Anderson, Benedict (1991), *Imagined Communities: Reflections on the Origins and Spread of Nationalism* (second edition), London: Verso.

Bakhtin, Mikhail (1981), *The Dialogic Imagination: Four Essays*, ed. Michael Holquist, trans. Caryl Emerson and Michael Holquist, Austin: University of Texas Press.

Barry, Dan (1997), "From Poets to Pubs, Irish Imports Are in Demand", *The New York Times*, 17 March, A1, B4.

Barthes, Roland (1972), *Mythologies*, trans. Annette Lavers, London: Jonathan Cape.

Benjamin, Walter (1969), "Theses on the Philosophy of History" in *Critical Theory Since 1965*, eds. Hazard Adams and Leroy Searle, Tallahassee: Florida State University Press, 1986, pp. 680–5.

Bolger, Dermot (1988a), "Introduction" in *Invisible Cities: The New Dubliners: A Journey through Unofficial Dublin*, ed. Dermot Bolger, Dublin: Raven Arts Press, pp. 7–12.

Bolger, Dermot (1988b), "Introduction" in *16 on 16: Irish Writers on The Easter Rising*, ed. Dermot Bolger, Dublin: Raven Arts, pp. 7–8.

Bolger, Dermot (1991), "Introduction" in *Letters from the New Island*, ed. Dermot Bolger, Dublin: Raven Arts, pp. 7–14.

Bolger, Dermot (1998), "Realist or Fetishist: Dermot Bolger talks with Neil Sammells" in *Reviewing Ireland: Essays and Interviews from "Irish Studies Review"*, eds. Sarah Briggs, Paul Hyland, Neil Sammells, Bath: Sulis Press, pp. 287–90.

Boyce, D. George and O'Day, Alan (1996), "Introduction: 'Revisionism' and the 'revisionist' controversy" in *The Making of Modern Irish History: Revisionism and the Revisionist Controversy*, eds. D. George Boyce and Alan O'Day, London: Routledge, pp. 1–14.

Boyce, D. George (1996), "1916, Interpreting the Revising" in *The Making of Modern Irish History: Revisionism and the Revisionist Controversy*, eds. D. George Boyce and Alan O'Day, London: Routledge, pp. 163–87.

Bradshaw, Brendan (1994), "Nationalism and Historical Scholarship in Modern Ireland" in *Interpreting Irish History: The Debate on Irish Historical Revisionism*, ed. Ciaran Brady, Dublin: Irish Academic Press, pp. 191–216.

Brady, Ciaran, ed. (1994), *Interpreting Irish History: The Debate on Irish Historical Revisionism*, Dublin: Irish Academic Press.

Brannigan, John (2002), *Brendan Behan: Cultural Nationalism and the Revisionist Writer*, Dublin: Four Courts.

Brown, Terence (1985), *Ireland: A Social and Cultural History 1922–1985*, London: HarperCollins.

Cleary, Joe (2000), "Modernization and Aesthetic Ideology in Contemporary Irish Culture" in *Writing in the Irish Republic: Literature, Culture, Politics 1949-1999*, ed. Ray Ryan, pp. 105–29.

Clinch, Peter et al. (2002), *After the Celtic Tiger*, Dublin: O'Brien.

Connor, Steven (1996), *The English Novel in History 1950-1995*, London: Routledge.

Considine, June (1988), "Buried Memories" in *Invisible Cities: The New Dublins. A Journey Through Unofficial Dublin*, Dublin: Raven Arts, pp. 37–45.

Corcoran, Neil (1997), *After Yeats and Joyce: Reading Modern Irish Literature*, Oxford: Oxford University Press.

Cullingford, Elizabeth Butler (2001), *Ireland's Others: Gender and Ethnicity in Irish Literature and Popular Culture*, Critical Conditions: Field Day Essays, No. 10, Cork: Cork University Press.

Dunne, T. (1992), "New Histories: Beyond 'Revisionism'", *Irish Review*, No. 12, pp. 1–12.

Eagleton, Terry (1998), *Crazy John and the Bishop and Other Essays on Irish Culture*, Critical Conditions: Field Day Essays, No. 5, Cork: Cork University Press.

Fanon, Frantz (1952), *Black Skin, White Masks*, trans. Charles Lam Markmann, New York: Grove Press, 1967.

Felski, Rita (1989), *Beyond Feminist Aesthetics: Feminist Literature and Social Change*, Cambridge, MA: Harvard University Press.

Foster, Roy (1989), *Modern Ireland: 1600–1972*, Harmondsworth: Penguin.

Frampton, Kenneth (1983), "Towards a Critical Regionalism: Six Points for an Architecture of Resistance" in *The Anti-Aesthetic: Essays on Postmodern Culture*, ed. Hal Foster, Port Townshend, Washington: Bay Press, pp. 16–30.

Graham, Colin (2001), *Deconstructing Ireland: Identity, Theory, Culture*, Edinburgh: Edinburgh University Press.

Gray, Tony (1996), *Ireland This Century*, London: Warner Books.

Harte, Liam (1997), "A Kind of Scab: Irish Identity in the Writings of Dermot Bolger and Joseph O'Connor", *Irish Studies Review*, No. 20 (Autumn), pp. 17–22.

Head, Dominic (2002), *The Cambridge Introduction to Modern British Fiction, 1950–2000*, Cambridge: Cambridge University Press.

Herr, Cheryl (1994), "A State o' Chassis: Mobile Capital, Ireland, and the Question of Postmodernity" in *Irishness and (Post)Modernism*, ed. John S. Rickard, Lewisburg: Bucknell University Press, pp. 195–229.

Honderich, Ted. ed. (1995), *The Oxford Companion to Philosophy*, Oxford: Oxford University Press.

Hutcheon, Linda (1989), *The Politics of Postmodernism*, London: Routledge.

Jordan, Neil (1996), *Michael Collins: Screenplay and Film Diary*, London: Vintage.

Joyce, James (1992), *A Portrait of the Artist as a Young Man*, Harmondsworth: Penguin Books.

Joyce, James (1976), *Dubliners*, Harmondsworth: Penguin Books.

Kavanagh, Patrick (1988), "The Parish and the Universe" in *Poetry and Ireland Since 1800: A Source Book*, ed. Mark Storey, London: Routledge, pp. 204–6.

Kelly, Shirley (2002), "Which Way Will the Celtic Cat Jump?" review of Peter Clinch, Frank Convery, Brendan Walsh, *After the Celtic Tiger*, *Books Ireland*, April, 77.

Kenner, Hugh (1978), *Joyce's Voices*, Berkeley: University of California Press.

Kiberd, Declan (1996), *Inventing Ireland: the Literature of the Modern Nation*, Cambridge: Harvard University Press.

Kirby, Peadar (2002a), *The Celtic Tiger in Distress: Growth with Inequality in Ireland*. Basingstoke: Palgrave.

Kirby, Peadar (2002b), *Reinventing Ireland: Culture, Society and the Global Economy*, London: Pluto Press.

Laurence, Margaret (1988), *The Diviners*, Toronto: McLelland and Stewart.

Lloyd, David (1999), *Ireland After History*, Critical Conditions: Field Day Essays, No. 9, Cork: Cork University Press.

Lyons, F.S.L. (1985), *Ireland Since the Famine*. London: Fontana.

Macherey, Pierre (1978), *A Theory of Literary Production* (1966), trans. Geoffrey Wall, London: Routledge & Kegan Paul.

McCarthy, Conor (2001), *Modernisation: Crisis and Culture in Ireland 1969–1992*, Dublin, Four Courts Press.

McClintock, Anne (1993), "Family Feuds: Gender, Nationalism and the Family", *Feminist Review*, Vol. 44, pp. 66–81.

Montague, John (1995), *Collected Poems*, Winston-Salem, NC: Wake Forest University Press.

Moretti, Franco (1987), *The Way of the World: The Bildungsroman in European Culture*, London: Verso.

O'Brien, Eugene (2002), *Seamus Heaney: Creating Irelands of the Mind*, Dublin: The Liffey Press.

O'Connor, Joseph (2000), *Inishowen*, London: Secker & Warburg.

O'Connor, Pat (1998), *Emerging Voices: Women in Contemporary Irish Society*, Dublin: Institute of Public Administration.

O'Faolain, Sean (1962), "Fifty Years of Irish Writing", reprinted in *Irish Writing in the Twentieth Century: A Reader*, ed. David Pierce, Cork: Cork University Press, 2000, pp. 740–7.

O'Hearn, Denis (1998), *Inside the Celtic Tiger: The Irish Economy and the Asian Model*, London: Pluto.

O'Loughlin, Michael (1988), "Michael O'Loughlin" in *16 on 16: Irish Writers on The Easter Rising*, ed. Dermot Bolger, Dublin: Raven Arts, pp. 43–4.

O'Mahony, Patrick and Delanty, Gerard (1998), *Rethinking Irish History: Nationalism, Identity and Ideology*, London: Macmillan.

O'Neill, Jamie (2001), *At Swim, Two Boys*, London: Scribner.

O'Toole, Fintan (1988), "1916: The Failure of Failure" in *16 on 16: Irish Writers on The Easter Rising*, ed. Dermot Bolger, Dublin: Raven Arts, pp. 41–2.

O'Toole, Fintan (1991), "The Southern Question" in *Letters from the New Island*, ed. Dermot Bolger, Dublin: Raven Arts, pp. 15–43.

O'Toole, Fintan (1992), "Introduction", *A Dublin Quartet*, ed. Dermot Bolger, Harmondsworth: Penguin.

O'Toole, Fintan (1997a), *The Ex-Isle of Erin: Images of a Global Ireland*, Dublin: New Island Books.

O'Toole, Fintan (1997b), "Perpetual Motion" in *Arguing at the Crossroads: Essays on a Changing Ireland*, eds. Paul Brennan and Catherine De St Phalle, Dublin: New Island Books, pp. 77–97.

Shade, William G. (1979), "Strains of Modernization: The Republic of Ireland Under Lemass and Lynch", *Éire-Ireland*, Vol. 14, pp. 26–46.

Smith, Dinitia (1996), "The Irish Are Ascendant Again", *The New York Times*, 3 October, C15, p. 20.

Smyth, Gerry (1998), *Decolonisation and Criticism: The Construction of Irish Literature*, London: Pluto Press.

Sutton, John (1989), "The Passion Machine Plays Series", in *Home*, by Paul Mercier, Dublin: Passion Machine Ltd., p. i.

Tallon, Ruth (1996), *When History Was Made . . . The Women of 1916*, Belfast: Beyond the Pale Publications.

Traynor, Desmond (2002), "Fictionising Ireland", *Irish Studies Review*, Vol. 10, No. 2 (August), pp. 125–32.

Walker, Lenore E. (1984), *The Battered Woman Syndrome*, New York: Springer Publishing.

Welch, Robert, ed. (1996), *The Oxford Companion to Irish Literature*, Oxford: Clarendon Press.

White, Timothy J. (1997), "The Changing Social Bases of Political Identity in Ireland", in *Representing Ireland: Gender, Class, Nationality*, ed. Susan Shaw Sailer, Gainesville: University Press of Florida, pp. 113–29.

Whelan, Kevin (1993), "The Bases of Regionalism" in *Regions: Identity and Power*, ed. Proinsias O Drisceoil, Belfast: Institute of Irish Studies, Queen's University.

Williams, William Carlos (1963), *Paterson*, New York: New Directions.

Yeats, W.B. (1983), *W.B. Yeats: The Poems: A New Edition*, ed. Richard J. Finneran, New York: Macmillan.

Index

["